THE
COLONIAL SOCIETY
OF PENNSYLVANIA

✵

Charter   Constitution
By-Laws   Officers
Members etc.

CLEARFIELD

SOCIAL MEETINGS

The Society has adopted March 15, the Anniversary of the Granting of the Charter to William Penn, and November 8, the Anniversary of his Landing in Pennsylvania, as occasions for holding social gatherings.

Originally published
Pennsylvania, 1950

Reprinted for Clearfield Company by
Genealogical Publishing Company
Baltimore, Maryland
1999, 2013

ISBN 978-0-8063-4859-9

Made in the United States of America

CONTENTS

Officers Councillors and Committees

OFFICERS* 1947-1948

PRESIDENT

SAMUEL BUNTING LEWIS

FIRST VICE-PRESIDENT

ORMOND RAMBO, JR.

SECOND VICE-PRESIDENT

JAMES TRUMAN SWING

SECRETARY

MALCOLM SIDNEY HUEY

TREASURER

LEWIS MAPES EVANS

COUNSELLOR

GUSTAVE PLANTOU MIDDLETON

REGISTRAR

CLARENCE CRESSON BRINTON

CHAPLAIN

REVEREND CROSSWELL McBEE

*Officers when Register was authorized.

OFFICERS 1950-1951

PRESIDENT

EVAN RANDOLPH

FIRST VICE-PRESIDENT

FRANK WORTHINGTON MELVIN

SECOND VICE-PRESIDENT

SYMINGTON PHILLIPS LANDRETH, JR.

SECRETARY

MALCOLM SIDNEY HUEY

TREASURER

LEWIS MAPES EVANS

COUNSELLOR

GUSTAVE PLANTOU MIDDLETON

REGISTRAR

CASPAR WISTAR HAINES

CHAPLAIN

REVEREND CROSSWELL McBEE

7

COUNCILLORS 1950

HENRY INGERSOLL BROWN

DAVID BURPEE

THOMAS HART

BENJAMIN ROSE HOFFMAN

MORTON JENKS

ROBERT CHARLES LIGGETT

LOUIS IUNGERICH MATTHEWS

EWING LAWRENCE MILLER, JR.

ALFRED DURAND NORRIS

WINTHROP SARGENT, JR.

SAMUEL BOOTH STURGIS, M.D.

JAMES TRUMAN SWING

COMMITTEES 1950-1951

9

OFFICERS AND COUNCILLORS, 1895-1950

PRESIDENTS

November 12, 1895. . John Woolf Jordan . . . . November 9, 1896
November 9, 1896. . . Peter Penn-Gaskill Hall . . . . February 1, 1905
March 8, 1905 . . . . . . Charles Henry Jones . . . . December 2, 1911
January 10, 1912 . . . . Samuel Davis Page . . . . October 11, 1921
November 8, 1921 . . . Josiah Granville Leach . . . . May 27, 1922
November 8, 1922 . . . Norris Stanley Barratt . . . . April 25, 1924
November 8, 1924 . . . George Fales Baker, M.D . . . . November 8, 1926
November 8, 1926 . . . Caleb Jones Milne, Jr . . . . November 9, 1931
November 9, 1931 . . . *Effingham Buckley Morris . . . . . December 16, 1931
December 16, 1931 . . . Caleb Jones Milne, Jr . . . . November 9, 1936
November 9, 1936 . . . John Edgar Burnett
                                    Buckenham, M.D., November 19, 1941
November 19, 1941 . . Henry Paul Busch . . . . April 22, 1942
May 12, 1942 . . . . . . William Innes Forbes . . . . November 8, 1944
November 8, 1944 . . . William Caner Wiederseim . . . . . . November 8, 1945
November 8, 1945 . . . Edwin Owen Lewis . . . . November 8, 1946
November 8, 1946 . . . Samuel Bunting Lewis . . . . November 8, 1948
November 8, 1948 . . . Ormond Rambo, Jr . . . . September 16, 1949
October 11, 1949 . . . . . Evan Randolph . . . .
*Resigned.

FIRST VICE-PRESIDENTS

November 12, 1895 . . Samuel Whitaker Pennypacker . . . November 8, 1907
November 8, 1907 . . . Samuel Davis Page . . . . January 10, 1912
January 10, 1912 . . . . Abraham Lewis Smith . . . . July 19, 1914
October 14, 1914 . . . . . Josiah Granville, Leach . . . . November 8, 1921
November 8, 1921 . . . Gregory Bernard Keen . . . . November 8, 1926
November 8, 1926 . . . Henry Douglas Hughes . . . . December 5, 1927
December 5, 1927 . . . . Henry Paul Busch . . . . November 19, 1941
November 19, 1941 . . William Innes Forbes . . . . November 9, 1942
November 9, 1942 . . . Thomas Ridgway . . . . December 6, 1943
February 8, 1944 . . . . William Caner Wiederseim . . . . . . November 8, 1944
November 8, 1944 . . . Edwin Owen Lewis . . . . November 8, 1945
November 8, 1945 . . . Samuel Bunting Lewis . . . . November 8, 1946
November 8, 1946 . . . Ormond Rambo, Jr . . . . November 8, 1948
November 8, 1948 . . . Evan Randolph . . . . October 11, 1949
November 10, 1949 . . Frank Worthington Melvin . . . . .

SECOND VICE-PRESIDENTS

November 12, 1895. . Joseph Eddy Gillingham . . . . November 9, 1896
November 9, 1896. . . John Woolf Jordan . . . . November 8, 1907
November 8, 1907. . . Abraham Lewis Smith . . . . January 10, 1912
January 10, 1912. . . . Josiah Granville Leach . . . . October 14, 1914
October 14, 1914. . . . . Gregory Bernard Keen. . . . . November 8, 1921
November 8, 1921. . . Norris Stanley Barratt. . . . . November 8, 1922
November 8, 1922. . . George Fales Baker. . . . . November 8, 1924
November 8, 1924. . . Earl Bill Putnam. . . . . November 8, 1926
November 8, 1926. . . Henry Paul Busch . . . . December 5, 1927
December 5, 1927. . . . Harrold Edgar Gillingham. . . . . . . November 8, 1936
November 9, 1936. . . Meredith Biddle Leach. . . . . November 8, 1940
November 8, 1940. . . William Innes Forbes. . . . . November 19, 1941
November 19, 1941. . Charles Francis Clement. . . . . November 9, 1942
November 9, 1942. . . William Caner Wiederseim. . . . . . . February 8, 1944
February 8, 1944. . . . Edwin Owen Lewis. . . . . November 8, 1944
November 8, 1944. . . Samuel Bunting Lewis. . . . . November 8, 1945
November 8, 1945. . . Ormond Rambo, Jr. . . . . November 8, 1946
November 8, 1946. . . James Truman Swing. . . . . November 8, 1948
November 8, 1948. . . Lawrence Johnson Morris. . . . . . . November 8, 1949
December 13, 1949. . . Symington Phillips Landreth, Jr. .

SECRETARIES

November 12, 1895. . Henry Douglas Hughes. . . . . April 14, 1897
April 14, 1897 . . . . . . Edwin Jaquett Sellers . . . . November 8, 1898
November 8, 1898. . . Frank Earle Schermerhorn. . . . . April 12, 1905
April 12, 1905 . . . . . . Henry Heston Belknap. . . . . June 23, 1924
November 8, 1924. . . Hazleton Mirkil, Jr. . . . . November 8, 1926
November 8, 1926. . . John Edgar Burnett
Buckenham, M.D., November 9, 1936
November 9, 1936. . . Samuel Bunting Lewis. . . . . November 9, 1942
November 9, 1942. . . Symington Phillips Landreth, Jr. November 8, 1944
November 8, 1944. . . Malcolm Sydney Huey. . . . .

ASSISTANT SECRETARIES

November 12, 1895. . Frank Earle Schermerhorn. . . . . . . November 8, 1898
November 8, 1898. . . Herbert Hart Boyd. . . . . November 8, 1904
November 8, 1904. . . Henry Heston Belknap. . . . . April 12, 1905
June 14, 1905 . . . . . . Aubrey Herbert Weightman. . . . . November 8, 1913
November 8, 1913. . . Theodore Glentworth, 3rd. . . . . . . November 8, 1919
November 8, 1919. . . Hazleton Mirkil, Jr. . . . . November 8, 1924
November 8, 1924. . . Ernest Spofford. . . . . December 10, 1924
November 10, 1938. . Francis Mark Brooke. . . . . November 9, 1942
November 9, 1942. . . Edmund Carter Taylor . . . . September 19, 1945
*The office of Assistant Secretary was abolished by changing the By-Laws
on November 8, 1945.

11

12

November 9, 1896...Craige Lippincott..............November 8, 1902
November 9, 1896...Eugene Zieber.....................June 6, 1897
November 9, 1896...Morton McMichael..............March 28, 1904
November 9, 1896...William Henry Jenks..........November 8, 1902
November 8, 1897...Robert Winder Johnson.......December 14, 1898
November 8, 1897...Joseph Leidy, M.D............November 8, 1910
November 8, 1897...Joseph Eddy Gillingham.......November 8, 1900
November 8, 1898...George Howard Earle..........November 8, 1900
November 8, 1898...Edwin Jaquett Sellers...........February 8, 1905
November 8, 1898...Thomas Allen Glenn...........December 14, 1898
November 8, 1898...Gregory Bernard Keen.........November 8, 1901
January 11, 1899....Henry LaBarre Jayne..........November 8, 1900
November 8, 1899...Henry Howard Ellison...........January 10, 1900
November 8, 1899...Thomas Allen Glenn.............March 12, 1902
November 8, 1899...Thomas George Morton, M.D....January 14, 1903
November 8, 1899...William Brooke Rawle........November 30, 1915
May 9, 1900.......Louis Henry Carpenter,
                       Brigadier General, U.S.A., November 8, 1910
November 8, 1900...Caleb Jones Milne...................July 1, 1912
November 8, 1900...Charles William Potts...............May 22, 1904
November 8, 1900...Earl Bill Putnam...............November 8, 1924
November 8, 1901...Charles Smith Turnbull, M.D....November 9, 1914
November 8, 1902...Henry Pemberton, Jr...........November 8, 1913
November 8, 1902...Stevenson Hockley Walsh......November 8, 1910
November 8, 1902...Jay Bucknell Lippincott........November 7, 1903
November 8, 1902...Abraham Lewis Smith.........November 8, 1907
November 7, 1903...Walter Lippincott..............December 9, 1903
November 7, 1903...Harman Yerkes................November 9, 1914
June 8, 1904.......Charles Barnsley McMichael ...November 16, 1926
June 8, 1904.......Horace Magee.................November 8, 1910
April 12, 1905......Ogden Dungan Wilkinson......November 16, 1926
November 8, 1905...Frank Earle Schermerhorn.......November 9, 1908
November 8, 1907...John Woolf Jordan.............November 8, 1919
November 8, 1907...Ellicott Fisher................December 19, 1908
November 8, 1907...Hon. Norris Stanley Barratt.....November 8, 1921
November 8, 1908...William Penn-Gaskell Hall......November 8, 1915
June 9, 1909.......William Supplee Lloyd...............May 4, 1920
November 8, 1910...Clarence Sweet Bement........November 8, 1917
November 8, 1910...Alfred Percival Smith..........November 8, 1911
November 8, 1910...Charles Davis Clark..........November 16, 1926
November 8, 1910...Charles Sydney Bradford.........October 11, 1911
November 8, 1911...Louis Henry Carpenter, Brigadier,
                       General U. S. A. (retired), November 9, 1914
November 8, 1911...Stevenson Hockley Walsh.......December 29, 1923
June 12, 1912......James Emlen..................November 8, 1913
October 9, 1912.....Henry Graham Ashmead........November 8, 1920
November 8, 1913...Harrold Edgar Gillingham.......November 8, 1924

13

November 8, 1913...Caleb Jones Milne, Jr..........November 8, 1921
November 9, 1914...John Henry Sinex.............November 8, 1921
November 9, 1914...Howard Barclay French.........October 16, 1924
November 9, 1914...George Fales Baker, M. D......November 8, 1922
May 12, 1915......Henry Howard Ellison.........November 8, 1915
November 8, 1915...Arthur Peterson, U. S. N.......November 8, 1916
January 12, 1916....James Tyson, M.D............December 12, 1917
November 8, 1916...John Morin Scott.............December 13, 1916
April 12, 1917......Wilbur Paddock Klapp, M.D....November 8, 1926
November 8, 1917...Edward Horne Bonsall.........November 8, 1926
November 8, 1918...Francis Mark Brooke..........November 8, 1926
November 8, 1919...Charles Francis Jenkins........December 18, 1929
June 9, 1920.......Charles Francis Gummey......December 21, 1923
November 8, 1920...Aubrey Herbert Weightman....November 16, 1926
November 8, 1921...Joseph Brooks Bloodgood Parker, November 16, 1926
November 8, 1921...Miers Busch.................November 10, 1938
November 8, 1921...Ralph Beaver Strassburger.....November 16, 1926
November 8, 1922...Lindsay Coates Herkness.......November 16, 1926
February 13, 1924...Thomas Lynch Montgomery.......October 1, 1929
November 8, 1924...William Wonderly Fitler.......November 16, 1926
November 8, 1924...Meredith Hanna...............December 5, 1927
November 8, 1924...John Morin Scott.............November 8, 1928
November 8, 1924...Henry Paul Busch.............November 8, 1926
November 8, 1924...Wilmon Whilldin Leach, M.D., September 26, 1926
November 16, 1926..George Fales Baker, M.D............June 3, 1929
November 8, 1926...Meredith Biddle Leach.........November 9, 1936
November 16, 1926..Frank Battles................December 18, 1929
November 16, 1929..William Marriott Canby, Jr......November 9, 1931
November 16, 1926..Francis Chapman...............November 8, 1934
November 16, 1926..Lemuel Howell Davis..........November 8, 1928
November 16, 1926..Harrold Edgar Gillingham.......December 5, 1927
November 16, 1926..George Henderson.............December 5, 1927
November 16, 1926..Gregory Bernard Keen..............April 30, 1930
November 16, 1926..Samuel Bunting Lewis.........November 9, 1934
November 16, 1926..Hazleton Mirkil, Jr...........November 16, 1926
November 16, 1926..George Clifford Thomas, Jr. .....December 5, 1927
November 16, 1926..Clarence Cresson Brinton.......December 5, 1927
November 16, 1926..Earl Bill Putnam..............December 5, 1927
December 5, 1927....Herman Wells Coxe...........November 8, 1937
December 5, 1927....Donald dePuy Crawford........December 18, 1929
December 5, 1927....Benjamin Rose Hoffman........November 8, 1948
December 5, 1927....Effingham Buckley Morris..........April 17, 1929
November 8, 1928...John Browning Clement........December 18, 1929
November 8, 1928...Joseph Green Lester.............April 28, 1938
November 8, 1928...Lawrence Johnson Morris.......November 8, 1948
December 18, 1929...Francis Mark Brooke..........November 8, 1937
December 18, 1929...Thomas Munroe Dobbins.......November 9, 1942

14

December 18, 1929...Joseph Knox Fornance.........November 8, 1940
December 18, 1929...Clarence Foster Hand.........November 10, 1938
December 18, 1929...Frank Worthington Melvin.....November 19, 1941
December 18, 1929...Ernest Spofford...............November 19, 1941
November 8, 1930...John Browning Clement........November 9, 1936
November 8, 1930...Henry Howard Ellison.........December 17, 1930
November 9, 1931...Jay Gates....................November 9, 1932
November 9, 1931...Howard Cooper Johnson........November 8, 1934
November 7, 1932...Washington Atlee Burpee.......December 20, 1939
November 8, 1934...Tristram Coffin Colket, 2nd......November 8, 1937
November 9, 1936...Howard Longstreth.............November 9, 1942
November 9, 1936...Caleb Jones Milne, Jr..............May 23, 1941
November 9, 1936...Joseph Gravenstein
                   Rittenhouse, Jr., November 9, 1939
November 9, 1936...Paul Judd Sartain, M.D........November 19, 1941
November 8, 1937...Meredith Hanna..............November 19, 1941
November 8, 1937...Alan Corson.................November 19, 1941
November 8, 1937...Isaac Anderson Pennypacker....November 19, 1941
November 10, 1938..Leander Chapin Claflin.........November 8, 1945
November 10, 1938..Thomas Haines Griest.........February 10, 1947
November 10, 1938..Alexander Reed McIntire.......November 9, 1939
November 10, 1938..William Caner Wiederseim......November 9, 1942
November 9, 1939...William Innes Forbes..........November 8, 1940
November 8, 1940...Nathan Myers Fitler...........November 8, 1948
November 8, 1940...Bertram Graeme Frazier.......November 19, 1941
November 8, 1940...Meredith Biddle Leach........November 19, 1941
November 8, 1940...Edmund Carter Taylor.........November 9, 1942
November 19, 1941..Edwin Owen Lewis............November 8, 1944
November 19, 1941..Thomas Ridgway..............December 6, 1943
November 19, 1941..Edward Carey Gardiner........November 9, 1942
November 19, 1941..James Truman Swing..........November 8, 1946
November 19, 1941..Malcolm Sidney Huey.........November 8, 1944
November 19, 1941..Clifford Lewis, Jr.............November 8, 1944
November 19, 1941..John Edgar Burnett
                   Buckenham, M.D., November 8, 1944
November 9, 1942...Isaac Hallowell Clothier, Jr......November 8, 1944
November 9, 1942...William Augustus Muhlenberg
                   Fuller, November 8, 1944
November 9, 1942...Thomas Sovereign Gates........November 8, 1945
November 9, 1942...Diedrich Jansen Haines....................1943
November 9, 1942...Samuel Bunting Lewis.........November 8, 1944
November 9, 1942...Evan Randolph...............November 8, 1944
November 8, 1943...Clarence Cresson Brinton........November 8, 1945
November 8, 1943...Sydney Emlen Hutchinson......November 8, 1944
November 8, 1943...Gustave Plantou Middleton.....November 8, 1945
November 8, 1944...Symington Phillips Landreth, Jr., November 8, 1944
November 8, 1944...Philipp Ernest Lueders.........November 8, 1947

November 8, 1944...Alfred Durand Norris...........November 8, 1947
November 8, 1944...John Stogdell Stokes...........September 26, 1947
November 8, 1944...Theodore Edward Wiederseim....November 8, 1945
November 8, 1945...Nathan Myers Fitler...........November 8, 1947
November 8, 1945...Symington Phillips Landreth, Jr., November 8, 1946
November 8, 1945...Randall Groves Hay............November 8, 1946
November 8, 1945...Arthur March Kennedy.........November 8, 1946
November 8, 1945...Robert Charles Ligget..........November 8, 1946
November 8, 1946...Robert McCay Green, 3rd......November 10, 1949
November 8, 1946...Frank Worthington Melvin.....November 10, 1949
November 8, 1946...Lewis Harlow Van Dusen.......December 10, 1948
November 8, 1946...Joseph Moore Watkins........November 10, 1949
November 8, 1947...Clifford Lewis, Jr..............November 8, 1950
November 8, 1947...Evan Randolph................November 8, 1949
November 8, 1947...Thomas Leaming Smith.........November 8, 1950
November 8, 1947...Meredith Hanna..............November 8, 1948
November 8, 1947...Henry Kendall Seal...........November 8, 1950
November 8, 1948...Samuel Booth Sturgis, M.D.....
November 8, 1948...Symington Phillips Landreth, Jr., December 13, 1949
November 8, 1948...Morton Jenks................
November 8, 1948...Robert Charles Ligget.........
November 10, 1949..James Truman Swing..........
November 10, 1949..Winthrop Sargent, Jr..........
November 10, 1949..Henry Ingersoll Brown........
November 10, 1949..David Burpee................
February 14, 1950 :..Thomas Hart................
November 8, 1950...Benjamin Rose Hoffman.......
November 8, 1950...Louis Iungerich Matthews......
November 8, 1950...Alfred Durand Norris.........
November 8, 1950...Ewing Lawrence Miller, Jr......

CHARTER AND CERTIFICATE OF
INCORPORATION

OF THE

Colonial Society of Pennsylvania

*To the Honorable the Judges of the Court of Common Pleas
No. 2 for the County of Philadelphia:*

In compliance with the requirements of an Act of the General
Assembly of the Commonwealth of Pennsylvania, entitled
"An Act to provide for the Incorporation and Regulation of
Certain Corporations," approved the 29th day of April,
A. D. 1874, and the supplements thereto, the undersigned, all
of whom are citizens of Pennsylvania, having associated
themselves together for the purposes hereinafter specified, and
desiring that they may be incorporated according to law, do
hereby

CERTIFY

First. The name, style, and title of the proposed Corporation is "The Colonial Society of Pennsylvania."

Second. Said Corporation is formed for the purpose of
celebrating anniversaries of events connected with the settlement of Pennsylvania prior to 1700; of collecting, preserving,
and publishing records and documents, printed or in manuscript, relating to the early history of that Colony, and to
perpetuate the memory of the early settlers of the American
Colonies.

Third. This Society is seated and located in the City of
Philadelphia, State of Pennsylvania.

Fourth. This Society shall have power to adopt a constitution and by-laws for its government, to carry out the

17

objects above set forth, and such similar objects as are not antagonistic to the laws of this State or of the United States of America.

Fifth. The said Corporation is to exist perpetually.

Sixth. The officers of the Society for the ensuing year are as follows:

President—John Woolf Jordan.
Vice-President—Samuel W. Pennypacker.
Second Vice-President—Joseph E. Gillingham.
Secretary—Henry Douglas Hughes.
Assistant Secretary—Frank Earle Schermerhorn.
Registrar—Francis M. Brooke.
Treasurer—Joseph T. Bailey.
Councillors—William Spohn Baker, Thomas A. Glenn, Henry T. Coates, Henry A. du Pont, Pemberton S. Hutchinson, Effingham B. Morris, Edward Shippen, Charles Henry Jones, J. Granville Leach, George M. Conarroe, Charles R. Hildeburn, Craige Lippincott, Charlemagne Tower, Jr., Eugene Zieber, Howard W. Lloyd, Edward S. Sayres, Charles Williams.

Witness our hands and seals this twenty-fifth day of April, Anno Domini one thousand eight hundred and ninety-six (1896).

JOHN WOOLF JORDAN [Seal]
SAMUEL W. PENNYPACKER [Seal]
HENRY DOUGLAS HUGHES [Seal]
JOSEPH TROWBRIDGE BAILEY [Seal]
THOMAS ALLEN GLENN [Seal]
PEMBERTON S. HUTCHINSON [Seal]
HOWARD W. LLOYD [Seal]
EUGENE ZIEBER [Seal]
J. GRANVILLE LEACH [Seal]
WILLIAM SPOHN BAKER [Seal]
HENRY T. COATES [Seal]
CHARLES R. HILDEBURN [Seal]
FRANK EARLE SCHERMERHORN [Seal]
EDWARD SHIPPEN [Seal]
CHARLES WILLIAMS [Seal]
CHARLES HENRY JONES [Seal]
CRAIGE LIPPINCOTT [Seal]

CONSTITUTION

OF THE

Colonial Society of Pennsylvania

ARTICLE I

NAME AND OBJECT

SECTION 1. This Society shall be known by the name of The Colonial Society of Pennsylvania.

SECTION 2. The object of the Society shall be to celebrate anniversaries of events connected with the settlement of Pennsylvania which occurred prior to 1700; to collect, preserve, and publish records and documents, printed or in manuscript, relating to the early history of that Colony, and to perpetuate the memory of the early settlers of the American Colonies.

ARTICLE II

SEAL, INSIGNIA, COLORS, AND ROSETTE

SECTION 1. The *Seal* of the Society shall be the obverse of the great seal of Pennsylvania (1699) surrounded by a double circle, in which is the inscription: The Colonial Society of Pennsylvania.

SECTION 2. The *Insignia* of the Society shall consist of: obverse, a cross formée gules, in the centre thereof the shield of Penn proper; reverse, a circular disk for the name and number; and shall be suspended by a gold ring from a watered silk ribbon one and five eighths inches wide, white with red border edged with white.

SECTION 3. The *Standard* of the Society shall be: upon a field argent the obverse of the badge proper.

SECTION 4. The *Rosette* of the Society shall be: a red field with a white centre and the same red upon the rim.

ARTICLE III

MEMBERSHIP

SECTION 1. Any male person over twenty-one years of age, of good character, who is lineally descended from a male or female actually settled prior to the year 1700 in any Colony of America (now the United States), shall be eligible to membership. But whenever and as long as there shall be three hundred members, no one shall be elected.

SECTION 2. All members shall be elected by the Council.

SECTION 3. The Council shall have the power to expel any member who may conduct himself in a manner unbecoming a member of the Society.

SECTION 4. No resignation shall be accepted unless presented in writing and approved by the Council.

ARTICLE IV

OFFICERS

SECTION 1. The Annual Meeting of the Society shall be held on the 8th day of November, the anniversary of the landing of William Penn in Pennsylvania, at which meeting the Election of Officers of the Society shall be held. In case that day shall fall upon a Sunday, the Annual Meeting shall be held on the day following.

SECTION 2. The Officers of the Society shall consist of a President, two Vice-Presidents, a Secretary, a Counsellor, a Treasurer, a Registrar and a Chaplain, who shall hold their office for one year and until their successors shall be duly qualified. All elections shall be by ballot.

SECTION 3. The Council of the Society shall consist of the Officers, all Past Presidents, *ex-officio*, and twelve members divided into three groups of four members each, to be elected as follows:

(a) the first group for a term of one year,

(b) the second group for a term of two years,

(c) the third group for a term of three years,

(d) at the expiration of the term of office of said groups, their successors shall be elected for terms of three years each, and in each instance the members shall serve for the term in each case specified and until their successors have been elected and qualified. No councillor having served three consecutive years shall be eligible for immediate re-election. All elections shall be by ballot.

SECTION 4. The Council shall have the entire management of the affairs of the Society and shall make by-laws; and to every Annual Meeting of the Society they shall make a general report.

SECTION 5. In case a vacancy shall occur by death or resignation of any of the Officers or Councillors of the Society, such vacancy shall be filled by the Council.

ARTICLE V
QUORUM

Fifteen members of the Society shall constitute a quorum for the transaction of business at all meetings of the Society.

ARTICLE VI
PERMANENT FUND

All money derived from Life and Hereditary Memberships shall constitute a permanent fund of the Society, and the income only thereof shall be used.

ARTICLE VII
AMENDMENTS

No amendments to this Constitution shall be made except at an Annual Meeting and unless such amendments shall have been proposed in writing, signed by ten members. Thirty days' notice thereof, with the printed information of the proposed amendments, shall be given to each member of the Society by mail. A three quarters vote of the members present shall be required to adopt such amendments.

BY-LAWS

ARTICLE I

MEMBERSHIP

SECTION 1. Applicants for admission to membership in this Society must be proposed by two members in good standing to whom the applicant is personally well known.

SECTION 2. The proposer shall give the full name, occupation, and residence of the candidate, and recommendations as to his worthiness for membership in the Society. This information shall be given on a Preliminary Application Blank and sent to the Secretary, who shall submit the same to the Council. If approved by them, the Secretary shall then furnish Final Application Blanks, which must be filled out in accordance with the instructions accompanying the same and be forwarded to the Secretary, who shall submit them to the Committee on Membership, and upon their approval the Council shall have power to elect the applicant to membership.

SECTION 3. Applications shall contain, or be accompanied by, proof of eligibility, and such applications and proofs shall be submitted to the Council, who shall have full power to determine the qualifications of the applicant. Upon favorable action by said Council, and payment of the dues, he shall thereupon become a member of the Society.

SECTION 4. No member of the Society shall be allowed to continue in membership if his proofs of eligibility shall be found to be defective.

SECTION 5. Any former member of the Society, who shall have resigned in good standing, may be restored to membership upon his application. If approved by the Membership Committee, he may be elected by the Council to the next vacancy, retaining his former membership number.

ARTICLE II

DUES

SECTION 1. Each member within thirty days after notification of election shall pay to the Treasurer his Annual Dues, which shall be Five Dollars; otherwise his name shall be reported to the Council for its action.

SECTION 2. Any member who neglects or refuses to pay his Annual Dues within sixty days after receiving notice from the Treasurer shall be reported to the Council for its action.

ARTICLE III

LIFE AND HEREDITARY MEMBERSHIP

The payment of One Hundred Dollars at any one time shall constitute a Life Membership. The payment of One Hundred Dollars at any one time shall constitute an Hereditary Membership, which shall descend to his eldest male descendant, subject to the approval of the Council. Life and Hereditary Memberships shall be exempt from all dues.

ARTICLE IV

DUTIES OF OFFICERS

SECTION 1. The *President*, or in his absence a *Vice-President*, or in their absence a Chairman *pro tempore*, shall preside at all meetings of the Society, and at all meetings of the Council.

SECTION 2. The *Secretary* shall be the keeper of the Seal of the Society; he shall conduct the general correspondence and keep full records of the meetings of the Society and the Council. He shall be the custodian of the Insignia and keep a record of each one which he shall issue under such rules as may be formulated by the Council.

SECTION 3. The *Treasurer* shall collect all dues and keep the funds and securities of the Society, and deposit and invest them in the name of the Society, subject to the direction of the Council. He shall keep full accounts of all receipts and disbursements ordered by the Council or the Society, and be prepared to report thereon at each meeting of the Council. He shall make an Annual Report to the Society. For the

23

faithful performance of his duty he shall give such security as the Council may deem proper.

SECTION 4. The *Treasurer* shall keep the securities of the Society in a safe deposit box in a bank or trust company and only the Treasurer and the President or the Treasurer and the Secretary shall have authority to open such box or examine said securities.

SECTION 5. The *Registrar* shall preserve all proofs of membership. By virtue of his office he shall be a member of the Committee on Membership.

SECTION 6. The *Chaplain* shall be an officer of the Society and shall perform customary chaplaincy services, and such other duties as ordinarily appertain to such office. He shall be excused from the payment of any dues.

SECTION 7. A *Committee on Genealogy and Heraldry* shall be appointed by the President for the purpose of collecting information relating to the genealogy of the early settlers of Pennsylvania and their descendants.

SECTION 8. The President shall appoint a *Committee on Membership*, to consist of the Registrar and two other members of the Council, whose duty it shall be to examine all applications for membership and report the same to the Council. The President also shall appoint a Finance Committee, an Entertainment Committee, and such other committees as the Council may authorize.

ARTICLE V

ORDER OF BUSINESS

The order of business for all meetings of the Society and Council shall be:

1. Reading of the Minutes.
2. Reports of Officers.
3. Reports of Committees.
4. Reading of Communications.
5. Election of Members.
6. Election of Officers.
7. Unfinished Business.
8. New Business.

ARTICLE VI

SECTION 1. The meetings of the Council shall be held on the second Tuesday of the months of October, December, February, April and June, and five members shall constitute a quorum.

SECTION 2. A Special Meeting of the Council for the purpose of electing Officers and Councillors to vacancies caused by death or resignation shall be called upon notice of ten days by the Secretary, or in case of his absence or illness, by any other officer, when such meeting is requested by five of the Officers and Councillors.

SECTION 3. A Special Meeting of the Council for other objects shall be called upon notice of ten days by the Secretary when such meeting is requested by five of the Officers and Councillors.

SECTION 4. The Council shall order a Special Meeting of the Society whenever twenty members of the Society make such request in writing, and also may order a Special Meeting to be held for such purposes and at such a time as the Council may deem proper. Notice of a Special Meeting shall state the proposed business to be transacted and only such business shall be considered.

SECTION 5. The Council shall appoint annually three of its members to act as a *Committee on Publications*. The Committee shall select the subjects of all publications and submit the same, together with an estimate of the cost, to the Council, whose action in the matter shall be final. The Committee shall have power to fix the price of all publications as well as the number to be printed. Every member of the Society shall be entitled, for a time to be limited by the Committee, to subscribe for one copy of each of the Society's publications at the price fixed by the Committee. All the copies unsubscribed for at the expiration of the time limited shall be sold by the Committee to any persons or institutions desiring them, provided the price obtained be not less than double that paid by the members of the Society: *Provided however,* that the Council may at its discretion distribute free one copy of any publication to each member of the Society at the time of publication.

SECTION 6. No publications by the Society shall be made without the approval of the Council expressed by a resolution passed at a regular meeting.

SECTION 7. Any person serving out an unexpired term of less than one year on the Council will be eligible for re-election for a full term on the Council at the next Annual Meeting of the Society.

ARTICLE VII
MANNER OF WEARING INSIGNIA

Members of the Society shall wear the Insignia fastened to the coat upon the left breast. Officers and Councillors may wear the Insignia suspended from a ribbon passing around the collar.

ARTICLE VIII
ADDITIONAL MEETING

In addition to the Annual Meeting, a meeting may be held on the evening of March 15, the Anniversary of the Granting of the Charter for Pennsylvania to William Penn, at which meeting business may be transacted at the discretion of the Council.

ARTICLE IX
AMENDMENTS OF BY-LAWS

These By-Laws may be amended, altered, or repealed by a majority vote at any meeting of the Council, the proposition for such a change having been made at a previous meeting, and due notice thereof having been given to the members of the Council.

Members

Acton

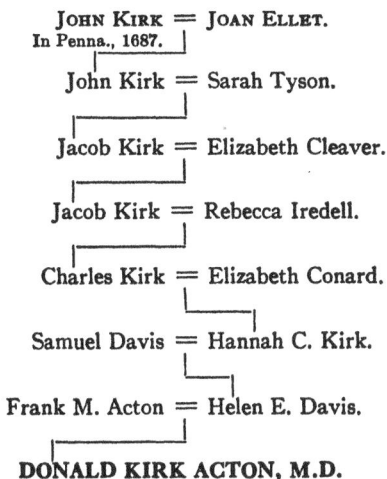

JOHN KIRK = JOAN ELLET.
In Penna., 1687.

John Kirk = Sarah Tyson.

Jacob Kirk = Elizabeth Cleaver.

Jacob Kirk = Rebecca Iredell.

Charles Kirk = Elizabeth Conard.

Samuel Davis = Hannah C. Kirk.

Frank M. Acton = Helen E. Davis.

DONALD KIRK ACTON, M.D.

Adams

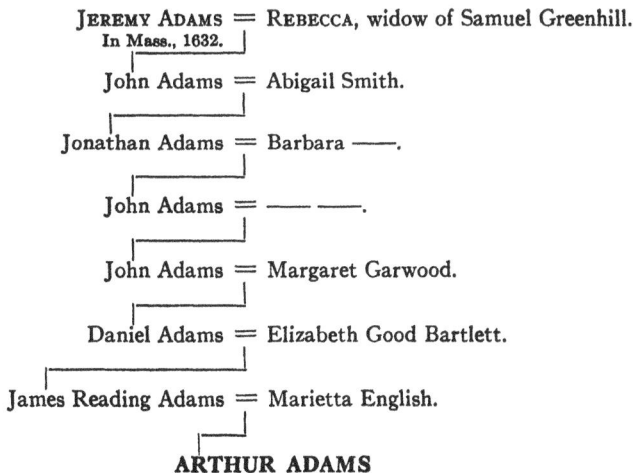

JEREMY ADAMS = REBECCA, widow of Samuel Greenhill.
In Mass., 1632.

John Adams = Abigail Smith.

Jonathan Adams = Barbara ——.

John Adams = —— ——.

John Adams = Margaret Garwood.

Daniel Adams = Elizabeth Good Bartlett.

James Reading Adams = Marietta English.

ARTHUR ADAMS

𝕬𝖑𝖊𝖝𝖆𝖓𝖉𝖊𝖗

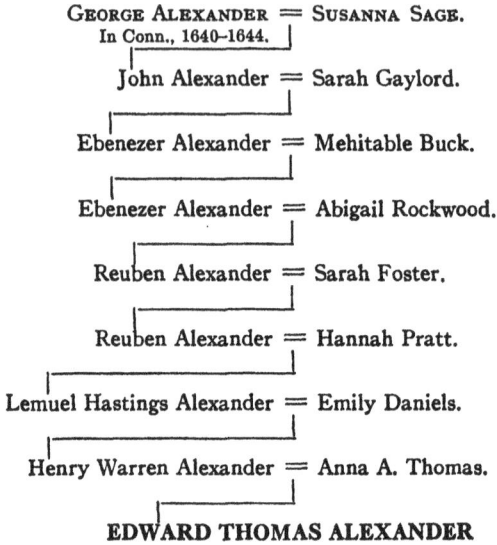

GEORGE ALEXANDER = SUSANNA SAGE.
In Conn., 1640–1644.

John Alexander = Sarah Gaylord.

Ebenezer Alexander = Mehitable Buck.

Ebenezer Alexander = Abigail Rockwood.

Reuben Alexander = Sarah Foster.

Reuben Alexander = Hannah Pratt.

Lemuel Hastings Alexander = Emily Daniels.

Henry Warren Alexander = Anna A. Thomas.

EDWARD THOMAS ALEXANDER

Aller

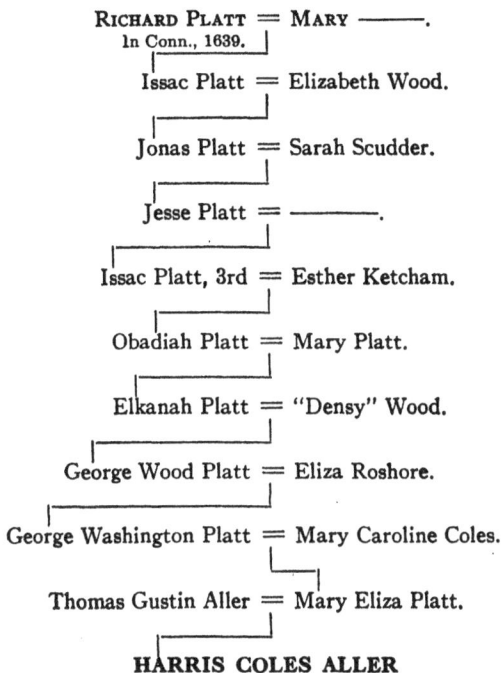

RICHARD PLATT = MARY ———.
In Conn., 1639.

Issac Platt = Elizabeth Wood.

Jonas Platt = Sarah Scudder.

Jesse Platt = ———.

Issac Platt, 3rd = Esther Ketcham.

Obadiah Platt = Mary Platt.

Elkanah Platt = "Densy" Wood.

George Wood Platt = Eliza Roshore.

George Washington Platt = Mary Caroline Coles.

Thomas Gustin Aller = Mary Eliza Platt.

HARRIS COLES ALLER

Ambler

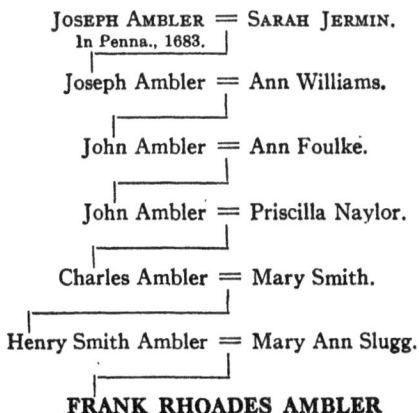

JOSEPH AMBLER = SARAH JERMIN.
In Penna., 1683.

Joseph Ambler = Ann Williams.

John Ambler = Ann Foulke.

John Ambler = Priscilla Naylor.

Charles Ambler = Mary Smith.

Henry Smith Ambler = Mary Ann Slugg.

FRANK RHOADES AMBLER

Ambler

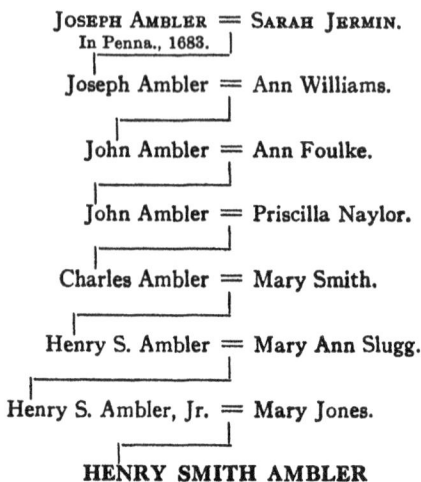

JOSEPH AMBLER = SARAH JERMIN.
In Penna., 1683.

Joseph Ambler = Ann Williams.

John Ambler = Ann Foulke.

John Ambler = Priscilla Naylor.

Charles Ambler = Mary Smith.

Henry S. Ambler = Mary Ann Slugg.

Henry S. Ambler, Jr. = Mary Jones.

HENRY SMITH AMBLER

Anderson

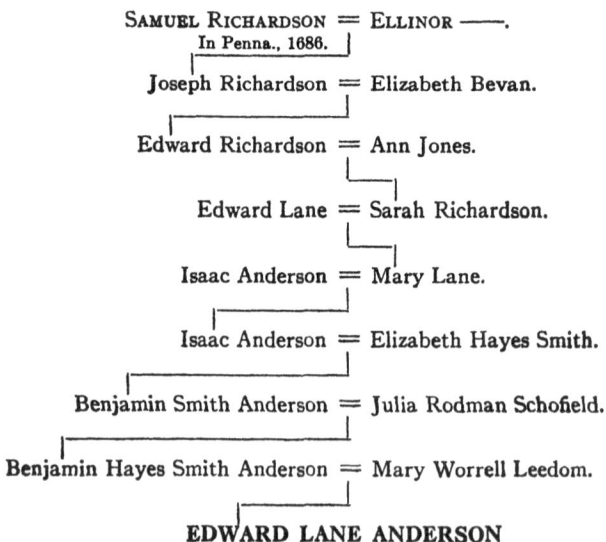

SAMUEL RICHARDSON = ELLINOR ——.
In Penna., 1686.

Joseph Richardson = Elizabeth Bevan.

Edward Richardson = Ann Jones.

Edward Lane = Sarah Richardson.

Isaac Anderson = Mary Lane.

Isaac Anderson = Elizabeth Hayes Smith.

Benjamin Smith Anderson = Julia Rodman Schofield.

Benjamin Hayes Smith Anderson = Mary Worrell Leedom.

EDWARD LANE ANDERSON

𝔄𝔯𝔤𝔬

WILLIAM BRADFORD = ALICE CARPENTER.
In Plymouth Colony, 1620.

William Bradford = Alice Richards.

John Bradford = Mercy Warren.

Edward Mitchell = Alice Bradford.

Edward Mitchell = Elizabeth D. Cushing.

William Mitchell = Elizabeth Ward.

Roswell Hubbard = Sarah Mitchell.

Fordyce Mitchell Hubbard, D.D. = Martha Henshaw Bates.

Thomas Monroe Argo = Martha Henshaw Hubbard.

FORDYCE HUBBARD ARGO, D.D.

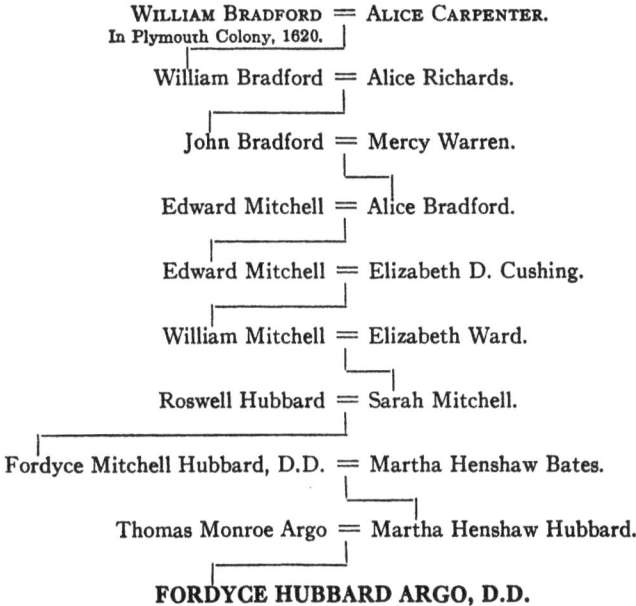

SUPPLEMENTALS

Ninth in descent from James Bate, in Mass., 1635.
Ninth in descent from John Hopkins, in Conn., 1634.
Ninth in descent from William Ward, in Mass., 1639.
Ninth in descent from Richard Warren, in Plymouth Colony, 1620.
Eighth in descent from Francis Cooke, in Plymouth Colony, 1620.
Eighth in descent from George Hubbard, in Conn., 1636.
Seventh in descent from Joshua Henshaw, in Mass., 1670.
Seventh in descent from Experience Mitchell, in Mass., 1623.

𝔄𝔰𝔥𝔟𝔯𝔦𝔡𝔤𝔢

GEORGE ASHBRIDGE = MARY MALIN.
In Penna., 1698.

George Ashbridge = Jane Hoopes.

George Ashbridge = Rebekah Garrett.

George Garrett Ashbridge = Rachel Valentine Sharples.

Abram Sharples Ashbridge = Elizabeth Downing Sharpless.

Abram Sharples Ashbridge, Jr. = Emma St. Clair Whitney.

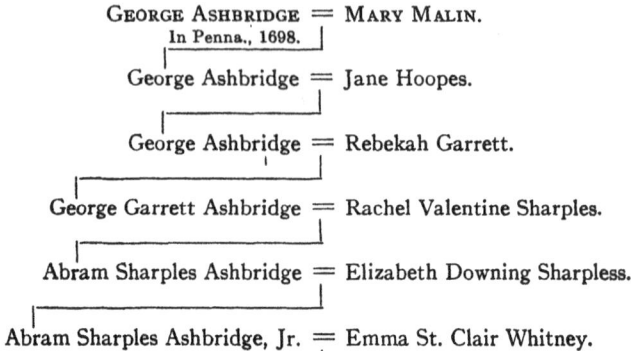

WHITNEY ASHBRIDGE

SUPPLEMENTALS

Ninth in descent from Humphrey Atherton, in Mass., 1635.
Ninth in descent from Peter Larssen Cock, in Penna., 1641.
Eighth in descent from James Trowbridge, in Mass., 1638.
Eighth in descent from John Whitney, in Mass., 1635.
Seventh in descent from Grimstone Boude, in East Jersey, 1699.
Seventh in descent from John Sharples, in Penna., 1682.

𝔅ainbridge

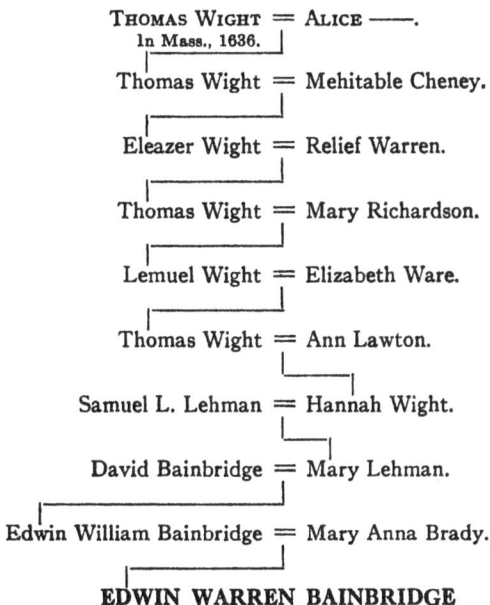

THOMAS WIGHT = ALICE ——.
In Mass., 1636.

Thomas Wight = Mehitable Cheney.

Eleazer Wight = Relief Warren.

Thomas Wight = Mary Richardson.

Lemuel Wight = Elizabeth Ware.

Thomas Wight = Ann Lawton.

Samuel L. Lehman = Hannah Wight.

David Bainbridge = Mary Lehman.

Edwin William Bainbridge = Mary Anna Brady.

EDWIN WARREN BAINBRIDGE

𝔅arnes

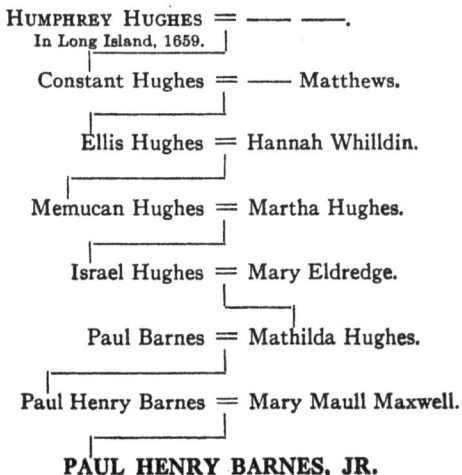

HUMPHREY HUGHES = —— ——.
In Long Island, 1659.

Constant Hughes = —— Matthews.

Ellis Hughes = Hannah Whilldin.

Memucan Hughes = Martha Hughes.

Israel Hughes = Mary Eldredge.

Paul Barnes = Mathilda Hughes.

Paul Henry Barnes = Mary Maull Maxwell.

PAUL HENRY BARNES, JR.

𝔅arnsley

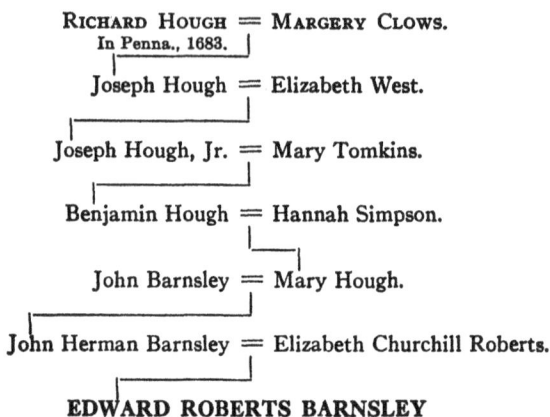

RICHARD HOUGH = MARGERY CLOWS.
In Penna., 1683.

Joseph Hough = Elizabeth West.

Joseph Hough, Jr. = Mary Tomkins.

Benjamin Hough = Hannah Simpson.

John Barnsley = Mary Hough.

John Herman Barnsley = Elizabeth Churchill Roberts.

EDWARD ROBERTS BARNSLEY

𝔅artow

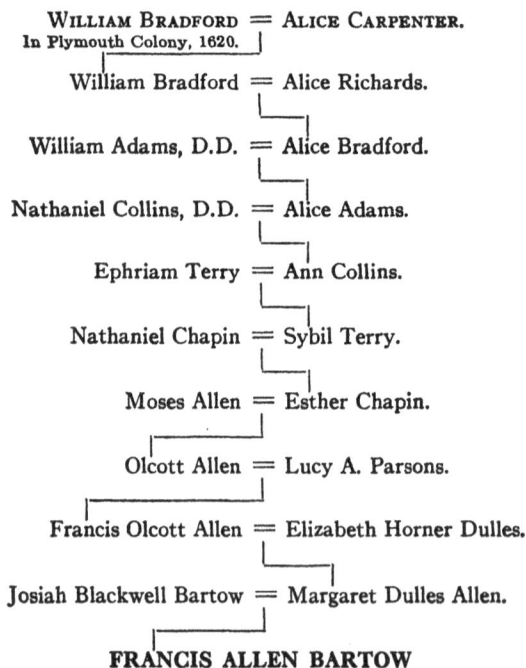

WILLIAM BRADFORD = ALICE CARPENTER.
In Plymouth Colony, 1620.

William Bradford = Alice Richards.

William Adams, D.D. = Alice Bradford.

Nathaniel Collins, D.D. = Alice Adams.

Ephriam Terry = Ann Collins.

Nathaniel Chapin = Sybil Terry.

Moses Allen = Esther Chapin.

Olcott Allen = Lucy A. Parsons.

Francis Olcott Allen = Elizabeth Horner Dulles.

Josiah Blackwell Bartow = Margaret Dulles Allen.

FRANCIS ALLEN BARTOW

John Fisher = Margaret (Hindle?).
In Penna., 1682.

Thomas Fisher = Margery Maud.

James Miers = Margery Fisher.

John Clarke = Mary Miers.

Miers Clarke = Aletta Clowes.

Robert Morris Hudson = Elizabeth Clarke.

Nathaniel Bayne = Elizabeth Clarke Hudson.

HERBERT NATHANIEL BAYNE

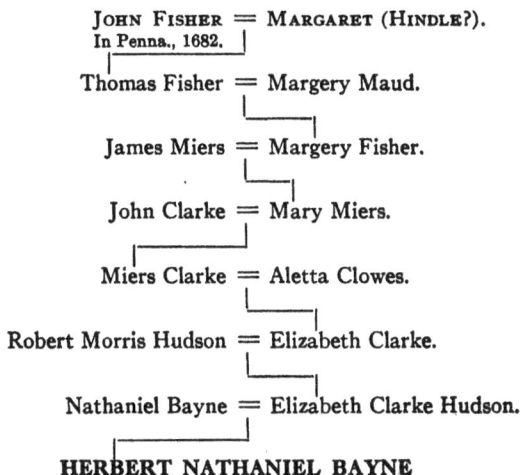

SUPPLEMENTALS

Eighth in descent from John Avery, in Maryland, 1665.
Eighth in descent from John Kipshaven, on the Delaware, 1671.
Seventh in descent from Garrett Dow, in New York, 1689.
Seventh in descent from Alexander Draper, in Maryland, 1660.
Sixth in descent from Samuel Clowes, in Long Island, 1687.
Sixth in descent from Margery Maud, in Penna., 1682.
Sixth in descent from John Miers, in Penna., 1682.

𝔅𝔢𝔠𝔨

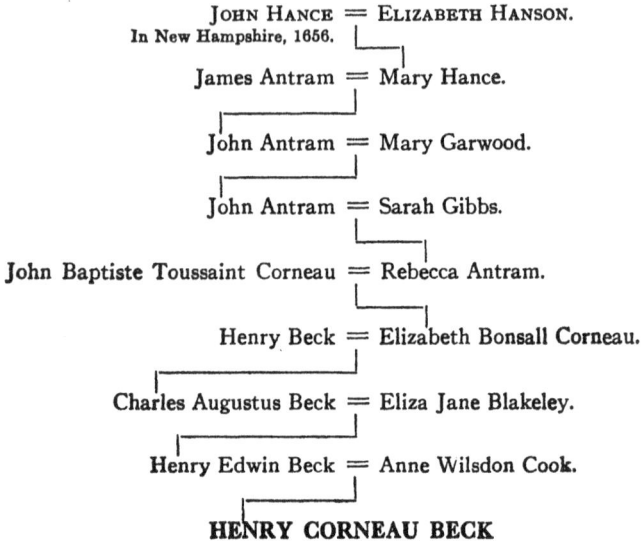

JOHN HANCE = ELIZABETH HANSON.
In New Hampshire, 1656.

James Antram = Mary Hance.

John Antram = Mary Garwood.

John Antram = Sarah Gibbs.

John Baptiste Toussaint Corneau = Rebecca Antram.

Henry Beck = Elizabeth Bonsall Corneau.

Charles Augustus Beck = Eliza Jane Blakeley.

Henry Edwin Beck = Anne Wilsdon Cook.

HENRY CORNEAU BECK

JOHN HANCE = ELIZABETH HANSON.
In New Hampshire, 1656.

James Antram = Mary Hance.

John Antram = Mary Garwood.

John Antram = Sarah Gibbs.

John Baptiste Toussaint Corneau = Rebecca Antram.

Henry Beck = Elizabeth Bonsall Corneau.

Charles Augustus Beck = Eliza Jane Blakeley.

HENRY EDWIN BECK

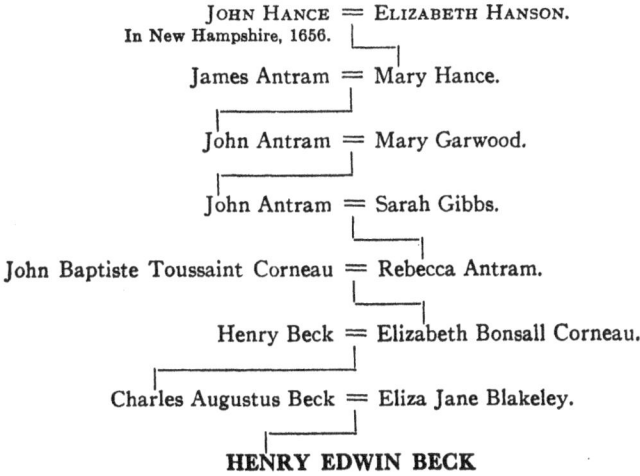

SUPPLEMENTALS

Eighth in descent from Thomas Hanson, in New Hampshire, 1657.
Eighth in descent from Thomas White, in East Jersey, 1670.
Sixth in descent from James Antram, in West Jersey, 1685.
Sixth in descent from Thomas Garwood, in West Jersey, 1685.

𝕭elcher

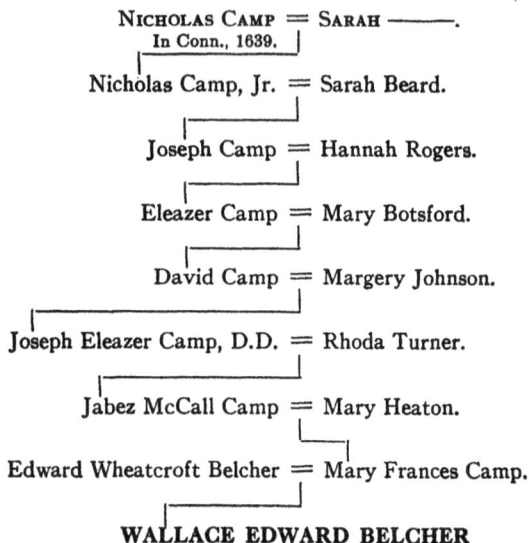

NICHOLAS CAMP = SARAH ———.
In Conn., 1639.

Nicholas Camp, Jr. = Sarah Beard.

Joseph Camp = Hannah Rogers.

Eleazer Camp = Mary Botsford.

David Camp = Margery Johnson.

Joseph Eleazer Camp, D.D. = Rhoda Turner.

Jabez McCall Camp = Mary Heaton.

Edward Wheatcroft Belcher = Mary Frances Camp.

WALLACE EDWARD BELCHER

𝕭ell

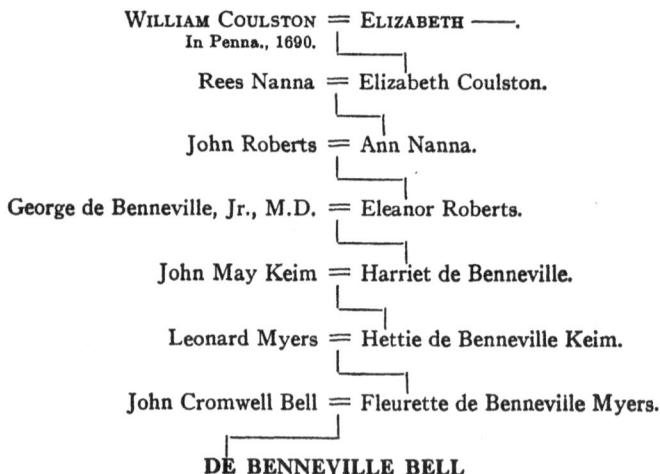

WILLIAM COULSTON = ELIZABETH ———.
In Penna., 1690.

Rees Nanna = Elizabeth Coulston.

John Roberts = Ann Nanna.

George de Benneville, Jr., M.D. = Eleanor Roberts.

John May Keim = Harriet de Benneville.

Leonard Myers = Hettie de Benneville Keim.

John Cromwell Bell = Fleurette de Benneville Myers.

DE BENNEVILLE BELL

SUPPLEMENTAL
Seventh in descent from John Brooke, in West Jersey, 1699.

WILLIAM COULSTON = ELIZABETH ——.
In Penna., 1690.

Rees Nanna = Elizabeth Coulston.

John Roberts = Ann Nanna.

George de Benneville, Jr., M.D. = Eleanor Roberts.

John May Keim = Harriet de Benneville.

Leonard Myers = Hettie de Benneville Keim.

John Cromwell Bell = Fleurette de Benneville Myers.

JOHN CROMWELL BELL, JR.

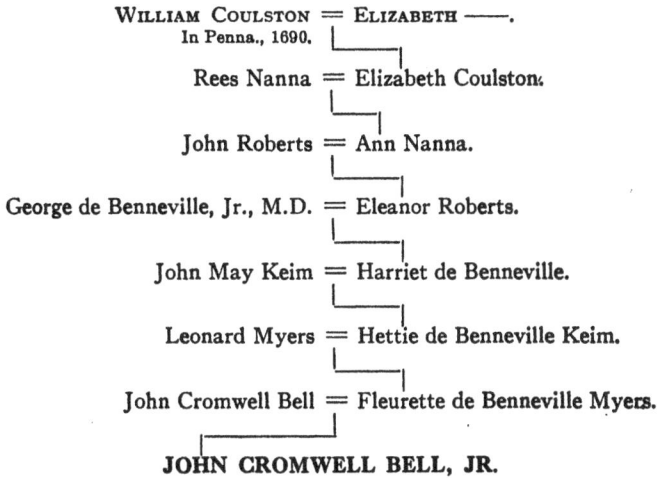

SUPPLEMENTAL

Seventh in descent from John Brooke, in West Jersey, 1699.

WILLIAM PRESTON = ANN TAYLOR.
In Penna., 1683.

Paul Preston = Elizabeth (Oldman) Gilbert.

William Preston = Sarah Carlisle.

William Preston = Barbara Heisler.

William Preston = Catherine Black.

John Markley = Mary Preston.

John Fonderlet Belsterling = Catherine Markley.

William Franklin Belsterling = Ida Julia Sutterle.

CHARLES STARNE BELSTERLING

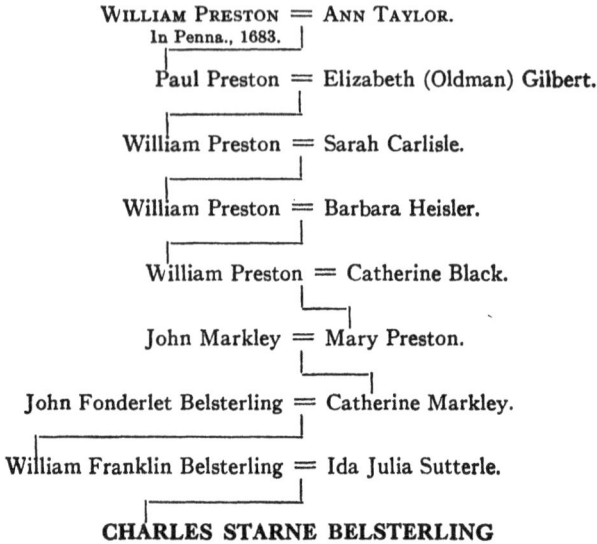

SUPPLEMENTALS

Ninth in descent from James Sykes, in Penna., 1687.
Eighth in descent from Thomas Gladwin, in West Jersey, 1684.
Eighth in descent from Thomas Oldman, in Penna., 1683.
Seventh in descent from John Carlisle in West Jersey, before 1700.

42

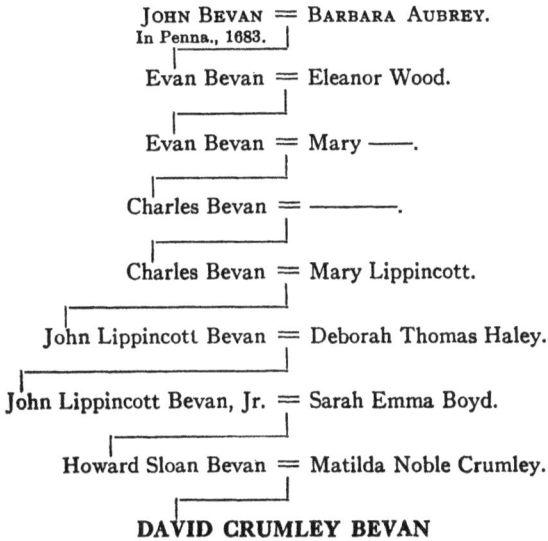

JOHN BEVAN = BARBARA AUBREY.
In Penna., 1683.

Evan Bevan = Eleanor Wood.

Evan Bevan = Mary ——.

Charles Bevan = ————.

Charles Bevan = Mary Lippincott.

John Lippincott Bevan = Deborah Thomas Haley.

John Lippincott Bevan, Jr. = Sarah Emma Boyd.

Howard Sloan Bevan = Matilda Noble Crumley.

DAVID CRUMLEY BEVAN

𝕭igelow

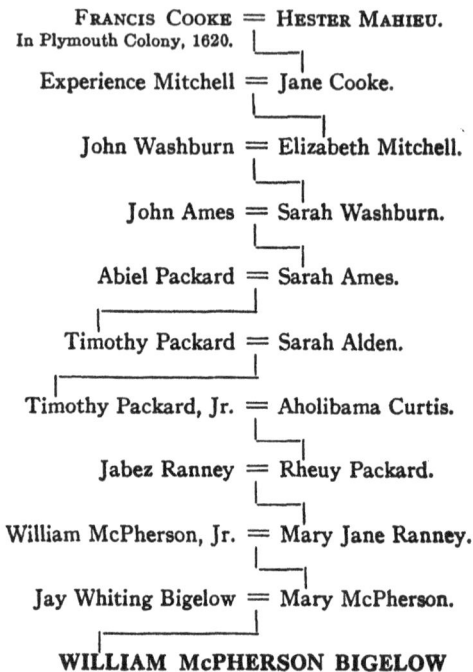

FRANCIS COOKE = HESTER MAHIEU.
In Plymouth Colony, 1620.

Experience Mitchell = Jane Cooke.

John Washburn = Elizabeth Mitchell.

John Ames = Sarah Washburn.

Abiel Packard = Sarah Ames.

Timothy Packard = Sarah Alden.

Timothy Packard, Jr. = Aholibama Curtis.

Jabez Ranney = Rheuy Packard.

William McPherson, Jr. = Mary Jane Ranney.

Jay Whiting Bigelow = Mary McPherson.

WILLIAM McPHERSON BIGELOW

Black

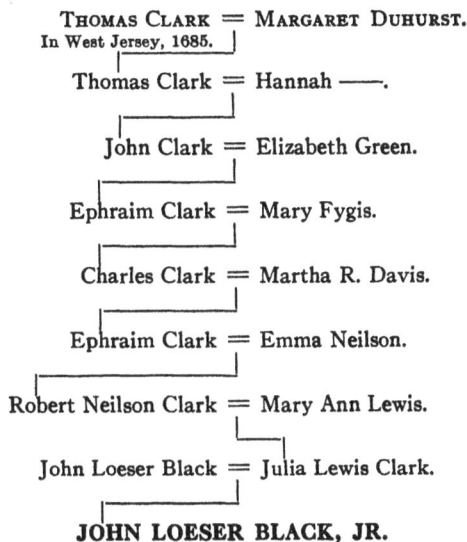

THOMAS CLARK = MARGARET DUHURST.
In West Jersey, 1685.

Thomas Clark = Hannah ——.

John Clark = Elizabeth Green.

Ephraim Clark = Mary Fygis.

Charles Clark = Martha R. Davis.

Ephraim Clark = Emma Neilson.

Robert Neilson Clark = Mary Ann Lewis.

John Loeser Black = Julia Lewis Clark.

JOHN LOESER BLACK, JR.

Bland

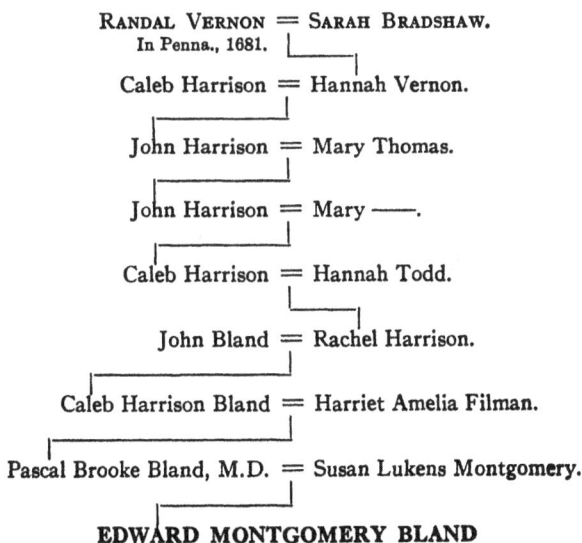

RANDAL VERNON = SARAH BRADSHAW.
In Penna., 1681.

Caleb Harrison = Hannah Vernon.

John Harrison = Mary Thomas.

John Harrison = Mary ——.

Caleb Harrison = Hannah Todd.

John Bland = Rachel Harrison.

Caleb Harrison Bland = Harriet Amelia Filman.

Pascal Brooke Bland, M.D. = Susan Lukens Montgomery.

EDWARD MONTGOMERY BLAND

𝕭𝖑𝖎𝖓𝖓

PETER BLIN = ⸺.
In Conn., 1675.

James Blin = Margaret Denison.

William Blin = Elizabeth Stillman.

James Blin = Jane Gilmore.

James Blin = Abigail Delano.

Joshua Blinn = Julia Hilton.

Silas Payson Blinn = Harriet Augusta Blagden.

Charles Payson Blinn = Ida Ware Chadbourn.

CHARLES PAYSON BLINN, JR.

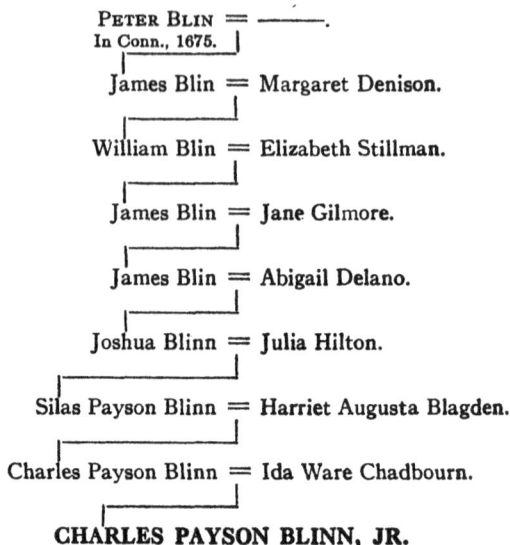

SUPPLEMENTALS

Eleventh in descent from William Mullins, in Plymouth Colony, 1620.
Eleventh in descent from Roger Pritchard (Prichard), in Conn., 1640.
Tenth in descent from John Alden, in Plymouth Colony, 1620.
Tenth in descent from John Moss, in Conn., 1639.
Tenth in descent from John Pabodie, in Plymouth Colony, 1636–7.
Tenth in descent from Christopher Todd, in Conn., 1639.
Ninth in descent from Edward Clarke, in Mass., 1639.
Ninth in descent from Philip Delano (Philippe de la Noye), in Plymouth Colony, 1621.
Ninth in descent from Abraham Doolittle, in Mass., 1640.
Ninth in descent from Zachariah Field, in Mass., 1629.
Ninth in descent from Moses Simmons, in Plymouth Colony, 1621.
Ninth in descent from Samuel Smith, in Mass., 1634.
Ninth in descent from George Soule, in Plymouth Colony, 1620.
Ninth in descent from James Treworgy, in Maine, 1636.
Ninth in descent from Christopher Wadsworth, in Mass., 1632.
Ninth in descent from Jacob Waterhouse (Watrous), in Conn., 1639.
Eighth in descent from Humphrey Chadbourne, in New Hampshire, 1631.
Eighth in descent from Edward Johnson, in Maine, 1621.
Eighth in descent from Thomas Riggs, in Mass., before 1658.
Eighth in descent from William Sargent, Sr., in Mass., 1649.
Eighth in descent from Job Tyler, in Mass., 1640.

𝕭𝖔𝖌𝖊𝖗

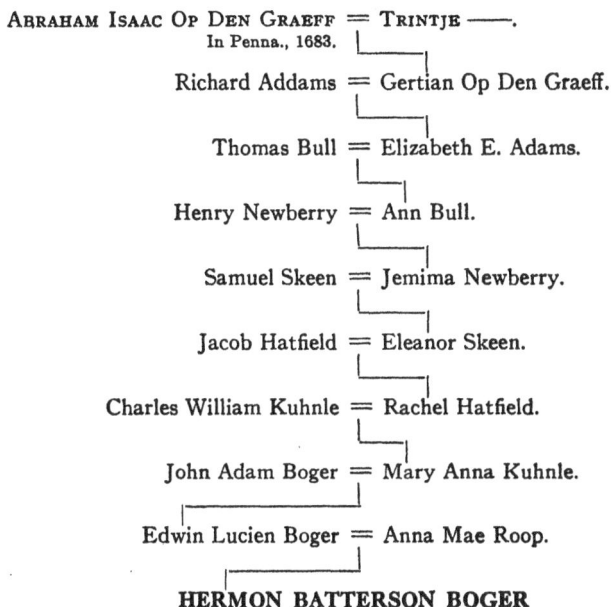

Abraham Isaac Op Den Graeff = Trintje ——.
In Penna., 1683.

Richard Addams = Gertian Op Den Graeff.

Thomas Bull = Elizabeth E. Adams.

Henry Newberry = Ann Bull.

Samuel Skeen = Jemima Newberry.

Jacob Hatfield = Eleanor Skeen.

Charles William Kuhnle = Rachel Hatfield.

John Adam Boger = Mary Anna Kuhnle.

Edwin Lucien Boger = Anna Mae Roop.

HERMON BATTERSON BOGER

Bosler

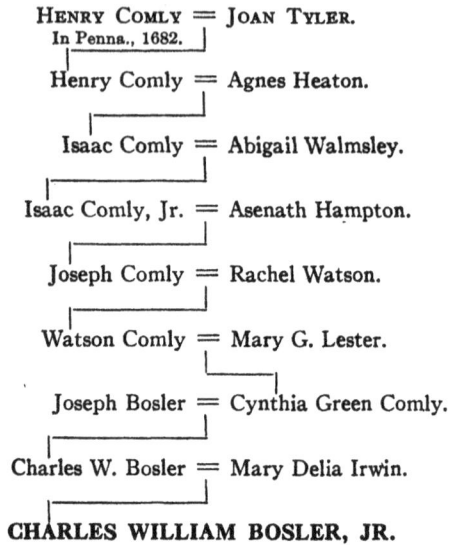

HENRY COMLY = JOAN TYLER.
In Penna., 1682.

Henry Comly = Agnes Heaton.

Isaac Comly = Abigail Walmsley.

Isaac Comly, Jr. = Asenath Hampton.

Joseph Comly = Rachel Watson.

Watson Comly = Mary G. Lester.

Joseph Bosler = Cynthia Green Comly.

Charles W. Bosler = Mary Delia Irwin.

CHARLES WILLIAM BOSLER, JR.

Bradley

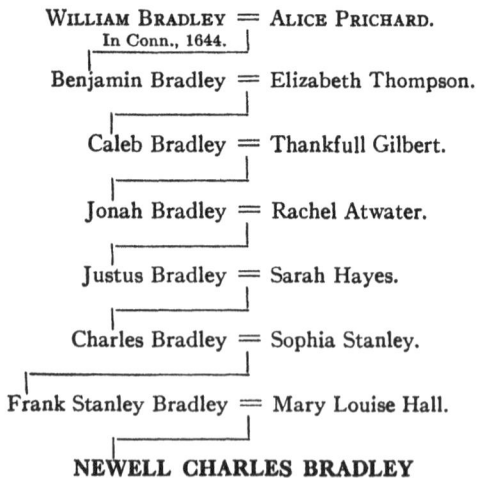

WILLIAM BRADLEY = ALICE PRICHARD.
In Conn., 1644.

Benjamin Bradley = Elizabeth Thompson.

Caleb Bradley = Thankfull Gilbert.

Jonah Bradley = Rachel Atwater.

Justus Bradley = Sarah Hayes.

Charles Bradley = Sophia Stanley.

Frank Stanley Bradley = Mary Louise Hall.

NEWELL CHARLES BRADLEY

𝔅𝔯𝔦𝔡𝔤𝔢𝔯

THOMAS CLARK = MARGARET DUHURST.
In West Jersey, 1685.

Thomas Clark = Hannah ——.

John Clark = Elizabeth Green.

Ephraim Clark = Mary Fygis.

Charles Clark = Martha R. Davis.

Ephraim Clark = Emma Neilson.

Robert Neilson Clark = Mary Ann Lewis.

William Reginald Pritchett Bridger = Minette Clark.

NEILSON CLARK BRIDGER

𝔅𝔯𝔦𝔫𝔱𝔬𝔫

WILLIAM BRINTON = ANN BAGLEY.
In Penna., 1684.

William Brinton = Jean Thatcher.

Joseph Brinton = Mary Pearce.

Moses Brinton = Elinor Varman.

William Brinton = Lydia Ferree.

Ferree Brinton = Elizabeth Sharpless.

Robert Morton Brinton = Octavia Eliza Fosdick.

CLARENCE CRESSON BRINTON

SUPPLEMENTALS

Eleventh in descent from William Mullins, in Plymouth Colony, 1620.
Tenth in descent from John Alden, in Plymouth Colony, 1620.
Tenth in descent from William Bullard, in Mass., 1636.
Tenth in descent from Hugh Churchman, in Mass., 1644.
Tenth in descent from Thomas Collier, in Mass., 1635.
Tenth in descent from Francis Cooke, in Plymouth Colony, 1620.
Tenth in descent from Robert Cutler, in Mass., 1637.
Tenth in descent from John Cutting, in Mass., 1642.
Tenth in descent from John Jenny, in Plymouth Colony, 1623.
Tenth in descent from William Moody, in Mass., 1634.
Tenth in descent from John Pabodie, in Plymouth Colony, 1635.
Tenth in descent from Francis Plumer, in Mass., 1635.
Tenth in descent from Thomas Rogers, in Plymouth Colony, 1620.
Tenth in descent from John Rolfe, in Mass., 1638.
Tenth in descent from Mark Symonds, in Mass., 1634.
Tenth in descent from John Whipple, in Mass., 1640.
Ninth in descent from John Allen, in Rhode Island, 1651.
Ninth in descent from John Ayres, in Mass., 1648.
Ninth in descent from Elizabeth Bacon, in Mass., 1650.
Ninth in descent from Nicholas Baker, in Mass., 1635.
Ninth in descent from Samuel Bidfield, in Mass., 1641.
Ninth in descent from William Bucknam, in Mass., 1647.
Ninth in descent from Edward Cottle, in Mass., 1652.
Ninth in descent from Zacceus Curtis, in Mass., 1635.
Ninth in descent from James Davis, in Rhode Island, 1639.
Ninth in descent from William Dixey, in Mass., 1629.
Ninth in descent from Abraham Errington, in Mass., 1649.
Ninth in descent from Stephen Fosdick, in Mass., 1635.
Ninth in descent from John Gatchell, in Mass., 1636.
Ninth in descent from Benjamin Gillam, in Mass., 1635.
Ninth in descent from Edward Goffe, in Mass., 1635.
Ninth in descent from Thomas Grant, in Mass., 1638.
Ninth in descent from Walter Haynes, in Mass., 1638.
Ninth in descent from Richard Ingersoll, in Mass., 1637.
Ninth in descent from Henry Kingman, in Mass., 1636.
Ninth in descent from George Lane, in Plymouth Colony, 1635.
Ninth in descent from George Lewis, in Plymouth Colony, 1633.
Ninth in descent from Thomas Loring, in Mass., 1634.
Ninth in descent from Henry Lunt, in Mass., 1635.
Ninth in descent from Experience Mitchell, in Plymouth Colony, 1623.
Ninth in descent from Francis Newcomb, in Mass., 1635.
Ninth in descent from Edmund Patteshall, in Mass., 1665.
Ninth in descent from William Pell, in Mass., 1634.
Ninth in descent from Samuel Poore, in Mass., 1638.
Ninth in descent from Thomas Pope, in Plymouth Colony, 1631.
Ninth in descent from John Richmond, in Plymouth Colony, 1637.
Ninth in descent from Richard Ring, in Mass., 1638.
Ninth in descent from William Scales, in Mass., 1640.

Ninth in descent from Nicholas Shapleigh, in Mass., 1635.
Ninth in descent from Henry Skerry, in Mass., 1629.
Ninth in descent from Thomas Smith, in Mass., 1637.
Ninth in descent from Ralph Sprague, in Mass., 1629.
Ninth in descent from John Trumbull, in Mass., 1636.
Ninth in descent from John Wheatley, in Mass., 1643.
Ninth in descent from Richard Woody, in Mass., 1642.
Ninth in descent from Lionel Worth, in Mass., before 1652.
Eighth in descent from Anthony Buxton, in Mass., 1637.
Eighth in descent from Mary Draper, in Mass., 1652.
Eighth in descent from Thomas Gwin, in Mass., 1660.
Eighth in descent from Edward Hazen, in Mass., 1649.
Eighth in descent from Thomas Hitchborn, in Mass., 1673.
Eighth in descent from Joseph Holton, in Mass., 1652.
Eighth in descent from Ann Hooper, in Mass., 1689.
Eighth in descent from Lewis Jones, in Mass., 1640.
Eighth in descent from Daniel Lincoln, in Plymouth Colony, 1644.
Eighth in descent from John Loker, in Mass., 1652.
Eighth in descent from Richard Martin, in Mass., 1665.
Eighth in descent from Richard Mason, in Penna., 1687.
Eighth in descent from John Moore, in Mass., 1643.
Eighth in descent from John Pearson, in Mass., 1643.
Eighth in descent from Robert Pennell, in Penna., 1686.
Eighth in descent from William Poat, in Mass., 1668.
Eighth in descent from William Randall, in Mass., 1649.
Eighth in descent from Joseph Richards, in Penna., 1685.
Eighth in descent from Edward Sheffield, in Mass., 1641.
Eighth in descent from Alexander Simpson, in Mass., 1659.
Eighth in descent from William Titcomb, in Mass., 1634.
Eighth in descent from Nathaniel Treadway, in Mass., before 1640.
Eighth in descent from Thomas Wheeler, in Mass., 1663.
Seventh in descent from John Baker, in Penna., 1685.
Seventh in descent from Richard Buffington, in West Jersey, 1677.
Seventh in descent from Oliver Cope, in Penna., 1683.
Seventh in descent from Ralph Lewis, in Penna., 1683.
Seventh in descent from Benjamin Mendenhall, in Penna., 1685.
Seventh in descent from Henry Nayle, in Penna., circa 1684.
Seventh in descent from Nicholas Newlin, in Penna., 1683.
Seventh in descent from Samuel Painter, in Penna., before 1700.
Seventh in descent from Owen Roberts, in Penna., 1695.
Seventh in descent from John Sharples, in Penna., 1682.
Seventh in descent from Richard Thatcher, in Penna., 1685.
Seventh in descent from Richard Woodward, in Penna., 1687.
Sixth in descent from Joel Baily, in Penna., 1685.
Sixth in descent from Joseph Gilpin, in Penna., 1695.
Sixth in descent from Ephraim Jackson, in Penna., 1687.
Sixth in descent from George Pearce, in Penna., 1684.
Sixth in descent from Ann Short, in Penna., 1687.
Sixth in descent from Philip Yarnall, in Penna., 1683.

Brown

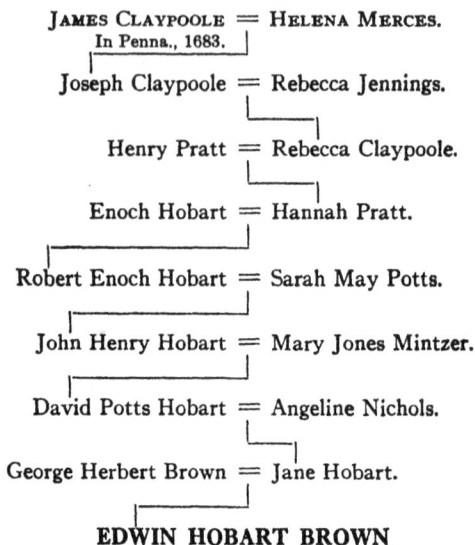

JAMES CLAYPOOLE = HELENA MERCES.
In Penna., 1683.

Joseph Claypoole = Rebecca Jennings.

Henry Pratt = Rebecca Claypoole.

Enoch Hobart = Hannah Pratt.

Robert Enoch Hobart = Sarah May Potts.

John Henry Hobart = Mary Jones Mintzer.

David Potts Hobart = Angeline Nichols.

George Herbert Brown = Jane Hobart.

EDWIN HOBART BROWN

Brown

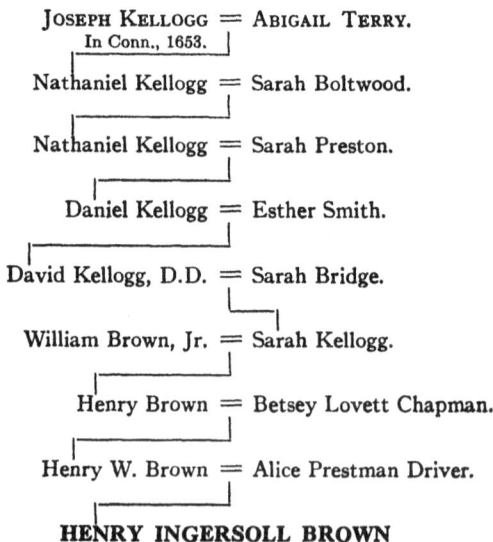

JOSEPH KELLOGG = ABIGAIL TERRY.
In Conn., 1653.

Nathaniel Kellogg = Sarah Boltwood.

Nathaniel Kellogg = Sarah Preston.

Daniel Kellogg = Esther Smith.

David Kellogg, D.D. = Sarah Bridge.

William Brown, Jr. = Sarah Kellogg.

Henry Brown = Betsey Lovett Chapman.

Henry W. Brown = Alice Prestman Driver.

HENRY INGERSOLL BROWN

𝔅𝔯𝔬𝔴𝔫

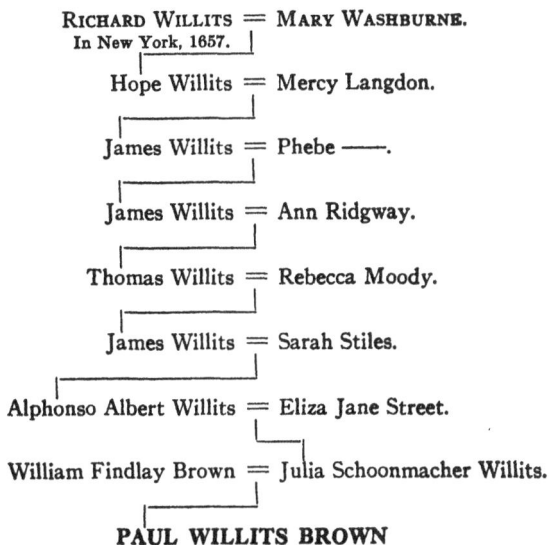

RICHARD WILLITS = MARY WASHBURNE.
In New York, 1657.

Hope Willits = Mercy Langdon.

James Willits = Phebe ——.

James Willits = Ann Ridgway.

Thomas Willits = Rebecca Moody.

James Willits = Sarah Stiles.

Alphonso Albert Willits = Eliza Jane Street.

William Findlay Brown = Julia Schoonmacher Willits.

PAUL WILLITS BROWN

𝔅𝔯𝔬𝔴𝔫𝔟𝔞𝔠𝔨

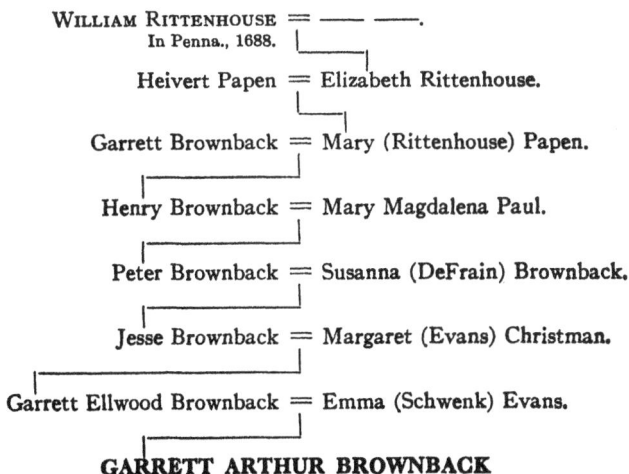

WILLIAM RITTENHOUSE = —— ——.
In Penna., 1688.

Heivert Papen = Elizabeth Rittenhouse.

Garrett Brownback = Mary (Rittenhouse) Papen.

Henry Brownback = Mary Magdalena Paul.

Peter Brownback = Susanna (DeFrain) Brownback.

Jesse Brownback = Margaret (Evans) Christman.

Garrett Ellwood Brownback = Emma (Schwenk) Evans.

GARRETT ARTHUR BROWNBACK

WILLEM STREYPERS = MERCKEN WILLEMSEN LUCKEN.
In Penna., 1683. | (widow of Jan Siemens.)

John Streper = Elizabeth Arets.

William Streper = Magdalene Kastner.

Jacob Neff = Sarah Streper.

Abraham Heydrick = Susanna Neff.

George Neff Heydrick = Ann Huston.

John William Buckenham = Loretta Susanna Heydrick.

JOHN EDGAR BURNETT BUCKENHAM, M.D.

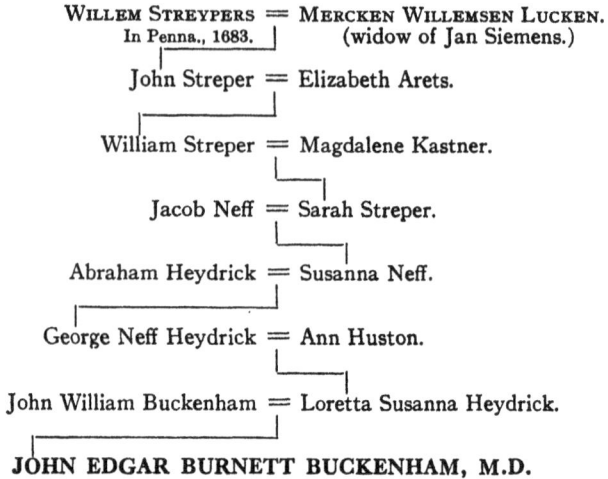

SUPPLEMENTALS

Seventh in descent from Lenert Arets, in Penna., 1683.
Seventh in descent from Paul Kastner, in Penna., 1690.

𝕭unting

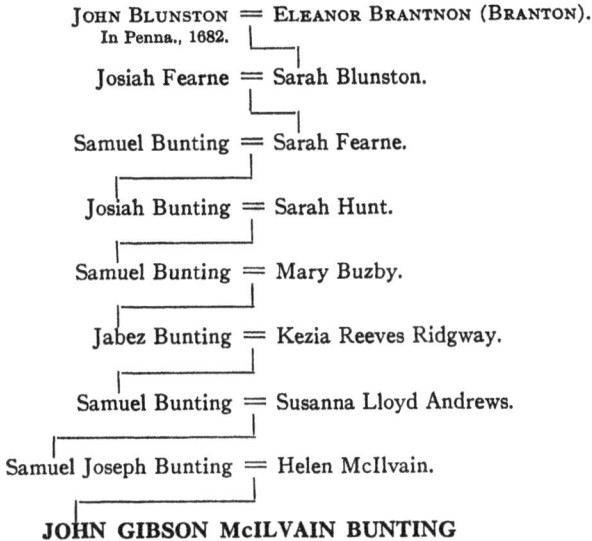

JOHN BLUNSTON = ELEANOR BRANTNON (BRANTON).
In Penna., 1682.

Josiah Fearne = Sarah Blunston.

Samuel Bunting = Sarah Fearne.

Josiah Bunting = Sarah Hunt.

Samuel Bunting = Mary Buzby.

Jabez Bunting = Kezia Reeves Ridgway.

Samuel Bunting = Susanna Lloyd Andrews.

Samuel Joseph Bunting = Helen McIlvain.

JOHN GIBSON McILVAIN BUNTING

𝕭urpee

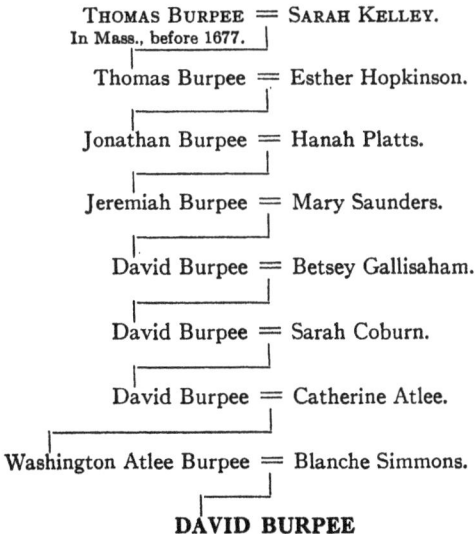

THOMAS BURPEE = SARAH KELLEY.
In Mass., before 1677.

Thomas Burpee = Esther Hopkinson.

Jonathan Burpee = Hanah Platts.

Jeremiah Burpee = Mary Saunders.

David Burpee = Betsey Gallisaham.

David Burpee = Sarah Coburn.

David Burpee = Catherine Atlee.

Washington Atlee Burpee = Blanche Simmons.

DAVID BURPEE

𝔅urpee

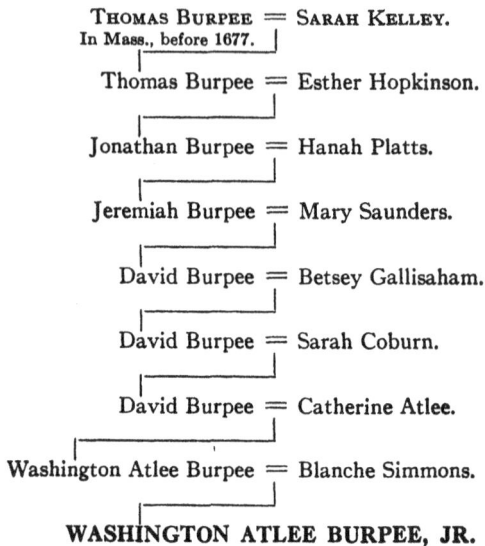

THOMAS BURPEE = SARAH KELLEY.
In Mass., before 1677.

Thomas Burpee = Esther Hopkinson.

Jonathan Burpee = Hanah Platts.

Jeremiah Burpee = Mary Saunders.

David Burpee = Betsey Gallisaham.

David Burpee = Sarah Coburn.

David Burpee = Catherine Atlee.

Washington Atlee Burpee = Blanche Simmons.

WASHINGTON ATLEE BURPEE, JR.

Cadwalader

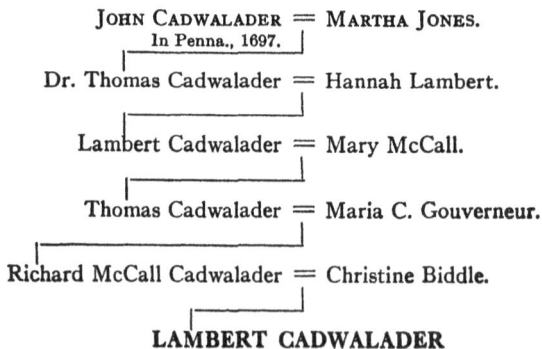

JOHN CADWALADER = MARTHA JONES.
In Penna., 1697.

Dr. Thomas Cadwalader = Hannah Lambert.

Lambert Cadwalader = Mary McCall.

Thomas Cadwalader = Maria C. Gouverneur.

Richard McCall Cadwalader = Christine Biddle.

LAMBERT CADWALADER

Campbell

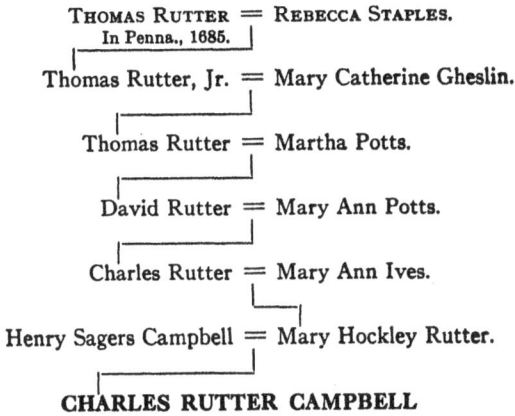

THOMAS RUTTER = REBECCA STAPLES.
In Penna., 1685.

Thomas Rutter, Jr. = Mary Catherine Gheslin.

Thomas Rutter = Martha Potts.

David Rutter = Mary Ann Potts.

Charles Rutter = Mary Ann Ives.

Henry Sagers Campbell = Mary Hockley Rutter.

CHARLES RUTTER CAMPBELL

Canby

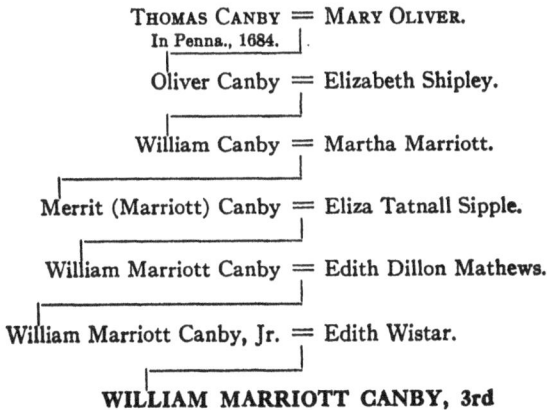

THOMAS CANBY = MARY OLIVER.
In Penna., 1684.

Oliver Canby = Elizabeth Shipley.

William Canby = Martha Marriott.

Merrit (Marriott) Canby = Eliza Tatnall Sipple.

William Marriott Canby = Edith Dillon Mathews.

William Marriott Canby, Jr. = Edith Wistar.

WILLIAM MARRIOTT CANBY, 3rd

John Howland = Elizabeth Tilley.
In Plymouth Colony, 1620.

John Gorham = Desire Howland.

Shubael Gorham = Puella Hussey.

Joseph Worth = Lydia Gorham.

Benjamin Bunker = Abigail (Worth) Bunker.

Timothy Bunker = Dinah Coffin.

Thomas Stitt = Ann Bunker.

Seth Bunker Stitt = Sarah Wilkinson Wall.

William Musser Capp, M.D. = Ida Estella Stitt.

SETH BUNKER CAPP

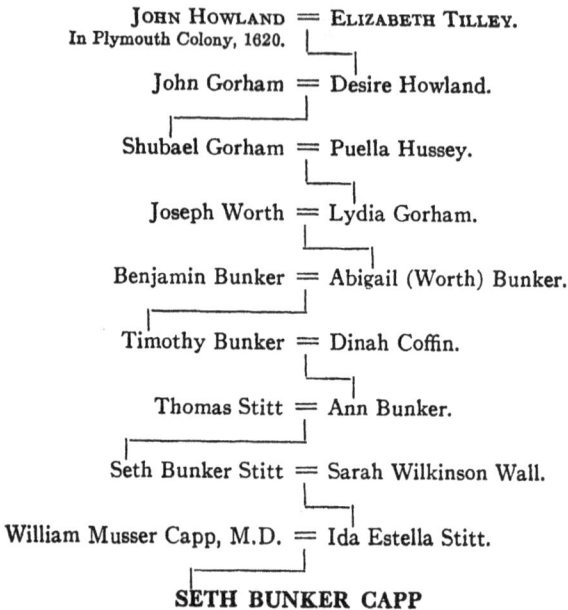

SUPPLEMENTALS

Tenth in descent from Rev. Stephen Bachiler, in Mass., 1632.
Tenth in descent from John Tilley, in Plymouth Colony, 1620.
Ninth in descent from Tristram Coffin, in Mass., 1642.
Ninth in descent from Ralph Farnum, in Mass., 1635.
Ninth in descent from Thomas Gardner, in Mass., 1623.
Ninth in descent from William Hayward, in Mass., 1648.
Ninth in descent from Christopher Hussey, in Mass., 1632.
Ninth in descent from Stephen Kent, in Mass., 1638.
Ninth in descent from Thomas King, in Mass., 1635.
Ninth in descent from Thomas Look, in Mass., circa. 1646.
Ninth in descent from Robert Paddock, in Plymouth Colony, 1643.
Ninth in descent from John Severance, in Mass., 1636.
Ninth in descent from Christopher Smith, in Rhode Island, 1650.
Ninth in descent from Thomas Thayer, in Mass., 1645.
Eighth in descent from George Aldrich, in Mass., 1631.
Eighth in descent from George Bunker, in Mass., before 1658.
Eighth in descent from John Gorham, in Mass., 1643.
Eighth in descent from Thomas Hatch, in Mass., 1634.
Eighth in descent from John Hewes, in Mass., 1632.

Eighth in descent from Thomas Macy, in Mass., 1639.
Eighth in descent from John Rogers, in Mass., 1643.
Eighth in descent from Rev. William Wickenden, in Rhode Island, 1637.
Eighth in descent from Lawrence Wilkinson, in Rhode Island, 1647.
Eighth in descent from William Worth, in Mass., 1665.

Elected
1940

Carr

No.
622

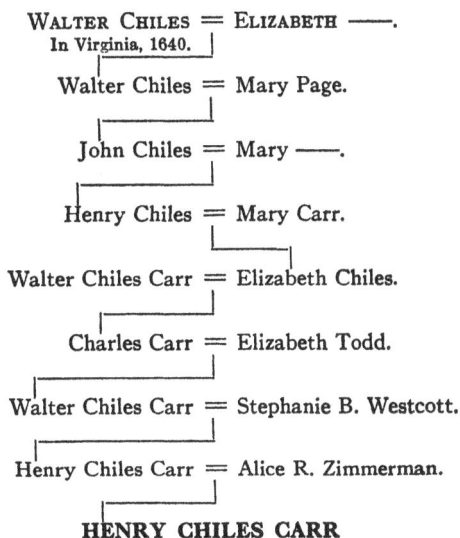

WALTER CHILES = ELIZABETH ——.
In Virginia, 1640.

Walter Chiles = Mary Page.

John Chiles = Mary ——.

Henry Chiles = Mary Carr.

Walter Chiles Carr = Elizabeth Chiles.

Charles Carr = Elizabeth Todd.

Walter Chiles Carr = Stephanie B. Westcott.

Henry Chiles Carr = Alice R. Zimmerman.

HENRY CHILES CARR

Carrigan

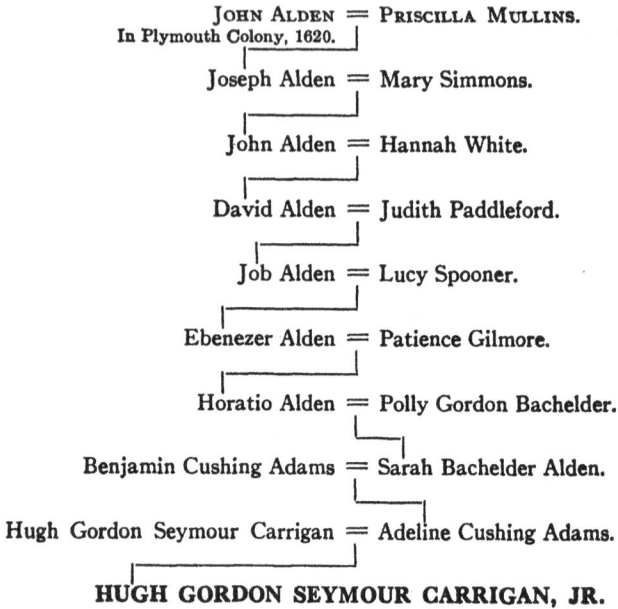

JOHN ALDEN = PRISCILLA MULLINS.
In Plymouth Colony, 1620.

Joseph Alden = Mary Simmons.

John Alden = Hannah White.

David Alden = Judith Paddleford.

Job Alden = Lucy Spooner.

Ebenezer Alden = Patience Gilmore.

Horatio Alden = Polly Gordon Bachelder.

Benjamin Cushing Adams = Sarah Bachelder Alden.

Hugh Gordon Seymour Carrigan = Adeline Cushing Adams.

HUGH GORDON SEYMOUR CARRIGAN, JR.

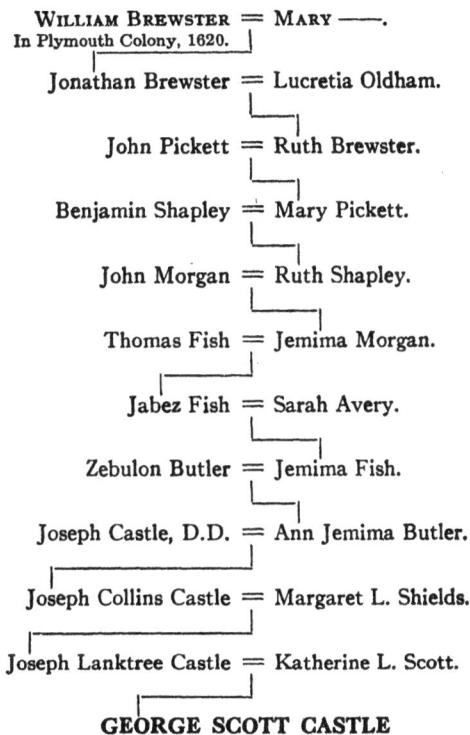

WILLIAM BREWSTER = MARY ——.
In Plymouth Colony, 1620.

Jonathan Brewster = Lucretia Oldham.

John Pickett = Ruth Brewster.

Benjamin Shapley = Mary Pickett.

John Morgan = Ruth Shapley.

Thomas Fish = Jemima Morgan.

Jabez Fish = Sarah Avery.

Zebulon Butler = Jemima Fish.

Joseph Castle, D.D. = Ann Jemima Butler.

Joseph Collins Castle = Margaret L. Shields.

Joseph Lanktree Castle = Katherine L. Scott.

GEORGE SCOTT CASTLE

Castner

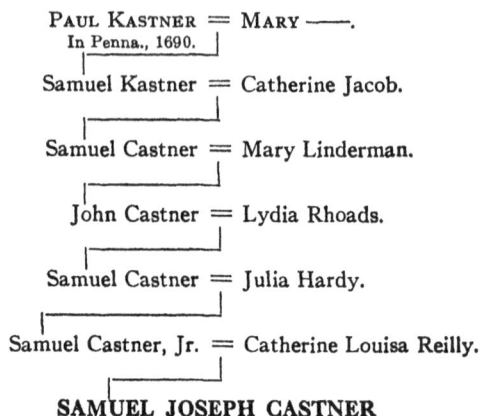

PAUL KASTNER = MARY ——.
In Penna., 1690.

Samuel Kastner = Catherine Jacob.

Samuel Castner = Mary Linderman.

John Castner = Lydia Rhoads.

Samuel Castner = Julia Hardy.

Samuel Castner, Jr. = Catherine Louisa Reilly.

SAMUEL JOSEPH CASTNER

SUPPLEMENTALS

Seventh in descent from John Rhoads, in Penna., before 1698.
Sixth in descent from John (Jan) Linderman, in Penna., 1698.

Chaffe

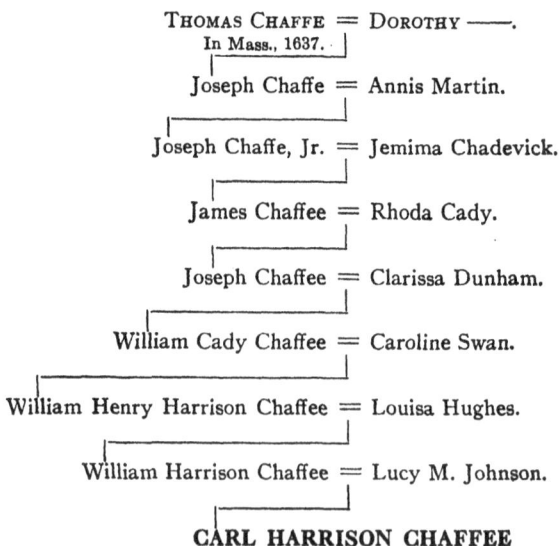

THOMAS CHAFFE = DOROTHY ——.
In Mass., 1637.

Joseph Chaffe = Annis Martin.

Joseph Chaffe, Jr. = Jemima Chadevick.

James Chaffee = Rhoda Cady.

Joseph Chaffee = Clarissa Dunham.

William Cady Chaffee = Caroline Swan.

William Henry Harrison Chaffee = Louisa Hughes.

William Harrison Chaffee = Lucy M. Johnson.

CARL HARRISON CHAFFEE

Claflin

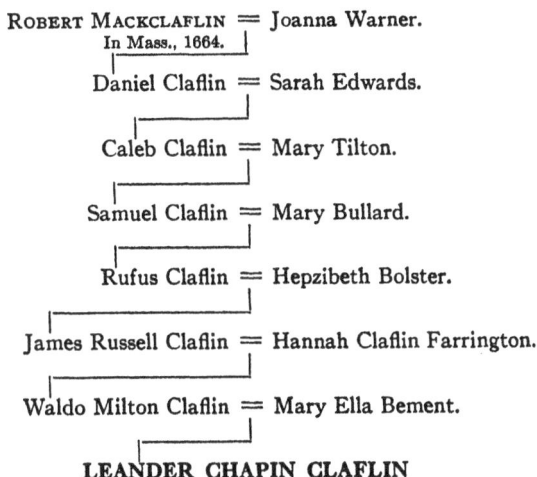

ROBERT MACKCLAFLIN = Joanna Warner.
In Mass., 1664.

Daniel Claflin = Sarah Edwards.

Caleb Claflin = Mary Tilton.

Samuel Claflin = Mary Bullard.

Rufus Claflin = Hepzibeth Bolster.

James Russell Claflin = Hannah Claflin Farrington.

Waldo Milton Claflin = Mary Ella Bement.

LEANDER CHAPIN CLAFLIN

Claghorn

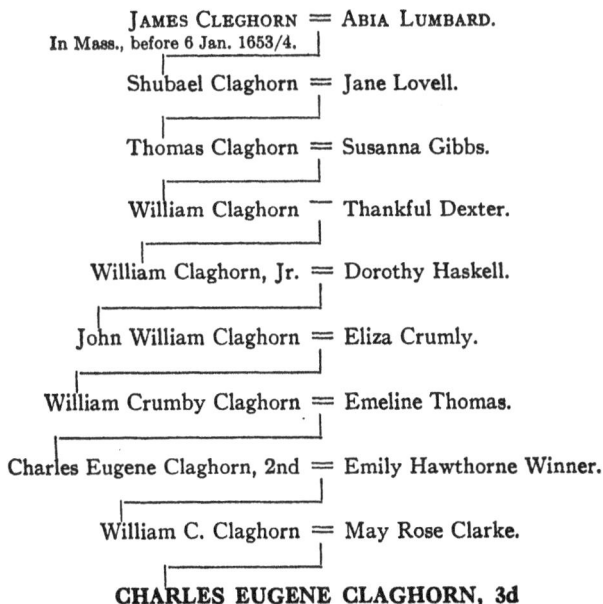

JAMES CLEGHORN = ABIA LUMBARD.
In Mass., before 6 Jan. 1653/4.

Shubael Claghorn = Jane Lovell.

Thomas Claghorn = Susanna Gibbs.

William Claghorn — Thankful Dexter.

William Claghorn, Jr. = Dorothy Haskell.

John William Claghorn = Eliza Crumly.

William Crumby Claghorn = Emeline Thomas.

Charles Eugene Claghorn, 2nd = Emily Hawthorne Winner.

William C. Claghorn = May Rose Clarke.

CHARLES EUGENE CLAGHORN, 3d

Clark

THOMAS CLARK = MARGARET DUHURST.
In West Jersey, 1685.

Thomas Clark = Hannah ——.

John Clark = Elizabeth Green.

Ephraim Clark = Mary Fygis.

Charles Clark = Martha Davis.

Ephraim Clark = Emma Neilson.

Robert Neilson Clark = Mary Ann Lewis.

LEWIS NEILSON CLARK

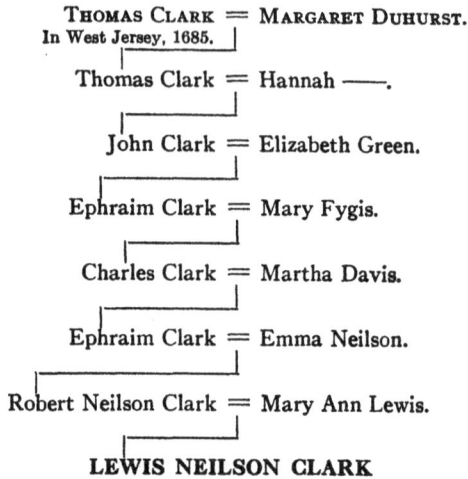

SUPPLEMENTALS

Ninth in descent from Henry Fleete, in Virginia, before 1623.
Eighth in descent from William Ball, in Virginia, before 1661.
Eighth in descent from Edwin Conway, in Virginia, before 1640.
Eighth in descent from Martha Eltonhead, in Virginia, 1652.
Eighth in descent from John Newton, in Virginia, before 1695.
Eighth in descent from John Oldham, in Virginia, 1635.

Clarkson

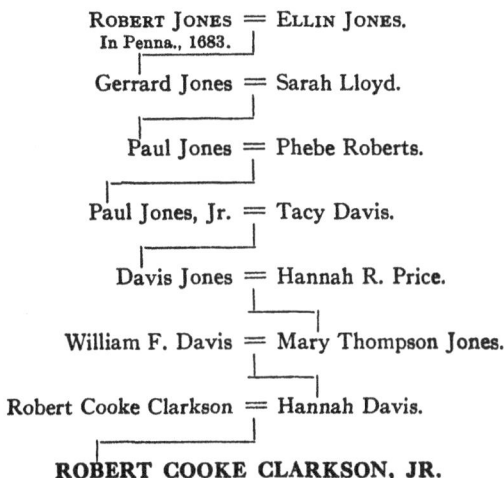

ROBERT JONES = ELLIN JONES.
In Penna., 1683.

Gerrard Jones = Sarah Lloyd.

Paul Jones = Phebe Roberts.

Paul Jones, Jr. = Tacy Davis.

Davis Jones = Hannah R. Price.

William F. Davis = Mary Thompson Jones.

Robert Cooke Clarkson = Hannah Davis.

ROBERT COOKE CLARKSON, JR.

Clement

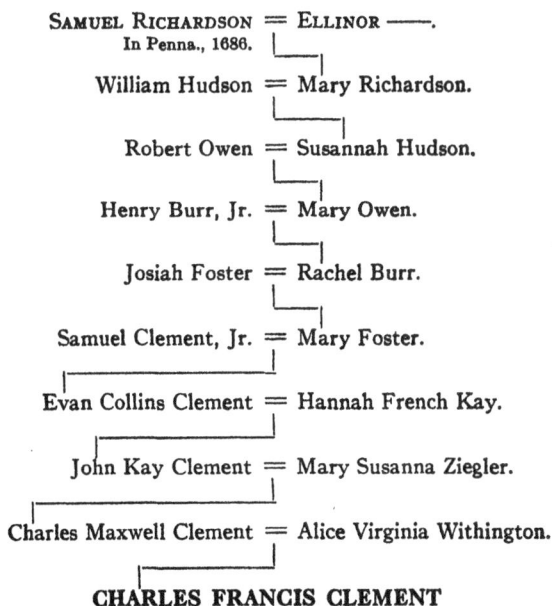

SAMUEL RICHARDSON = ELLINOR ——.
In Penna., 1686.

William Hudson = Mary Richardson.

Robert Owen = Susannah Hudson.

Henry Burr, Jr. = Mary Owen.

Josiah Foster = Rachel Burr.

Samuel Clement, Jr. = Mary Foster.

Evan Collins Clement = Hannah French Kay.

John Kay Clement = Mary Susanna Ziegler.

Charles Maxwell Clement = Alice Virginia Withington.

CHARLES FRANCIS CLEMENT

Clement

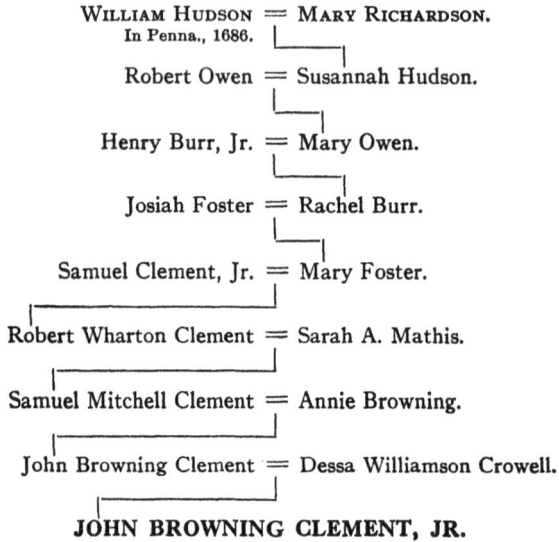

WILLIAM HUDSON = MARY RICHARDSON.
In Penna., 1686.

Robert Owen = Susannah Hudson.

Henry Burr, Jr. = Mary Owen.

Josiah Foster = Rachel Burr.

Samuel Clement, Jr. = Mary Foster.

Robert Wharton Clement = Sarah A. Mathis.

Samuel Mitchell Clement = Annie Browning.

John Browning Clement = Dessa Williamson Crowell.

JOHN BROWNING CLEMENT, JR.

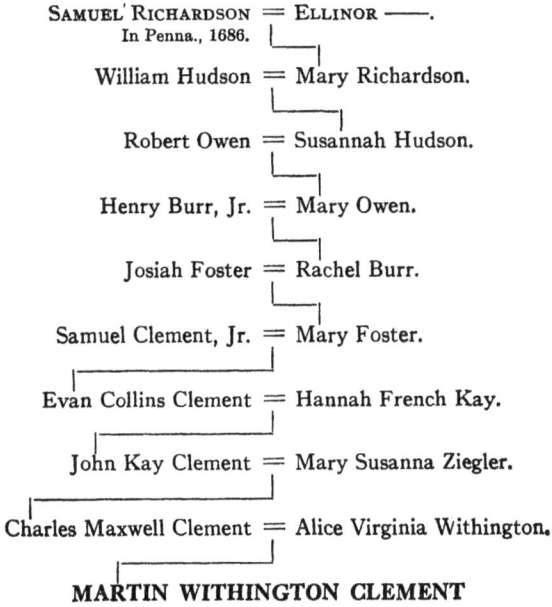

SAMUEL RICHARDSON = ELLINOR ——.
In Penna., 1686.

William Hudson = Mary Richardson.

Robert Owen = Susannah Hudson.

Henry Burr, Jr. = Mary Owen.

Josiah Foster = Rachel Burr.

Samuel Clement, Jr. = Mary Foster.

Evan Collins Clement = Hannah French Kay.

John Kay Clement = Mary Susanna Ziegler.

Charles Maxwell Clement = Alice Virginia Withington.

MARTIN WITHINGTON CLEMENT

Clement

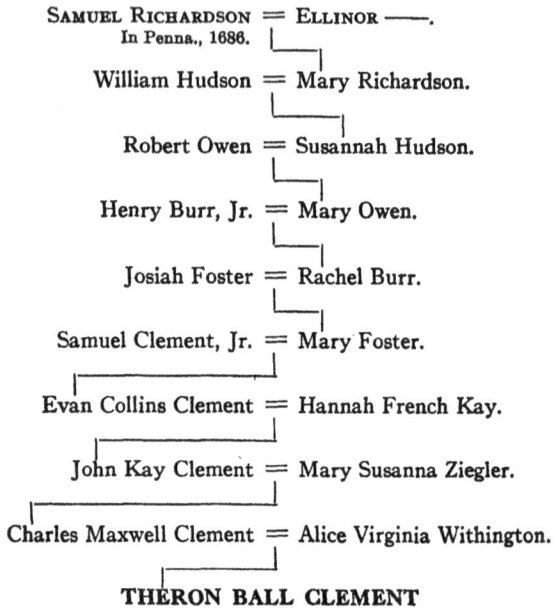

SAMUEL RICHARDSON = ELLINOR ——.
In Penna., 1686.

William Hudson = Mary Richardson.

Robert Owen = Susannah Hudson.

Henry Burr, Jr. = Mary Owen.

Josiah Foster = Rachel Burr.

Samuel Clement, Jr. = Mary Foster.

Evan Collins Clement = Hannah French Kay.

John Kay Clement = Mary Susanna Ziegler.

Charles Maxwell Clement = Alice Virginia Withington.

THERON BALL CLEMENT

Closson

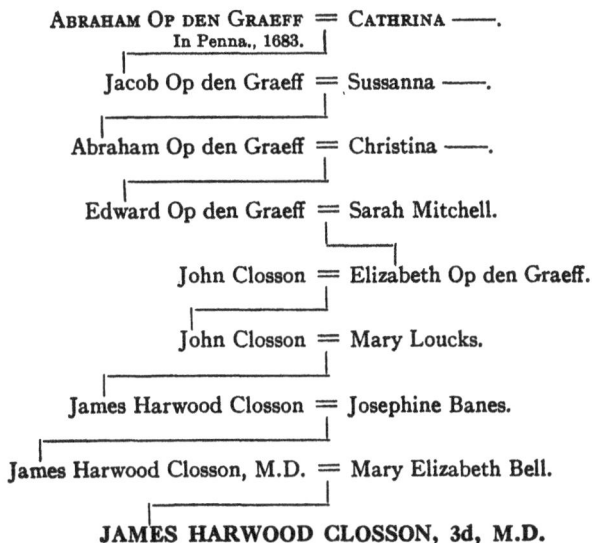

ABRAHAM OP DEN GRAEFF = CATHRINA ——.
In Penna., 1683.

Jacob Op den Graeff = Sussanna ——.

Abraham Op den Graeff = Christina ——.

Edward Op den Graeff = Sarah Mitchell.

John Closson = Elizabeth Op den Graeff.

John Closson = Mary Loucks.

James Harwood Closson = Josephine Banes.

James Harwood Closson, M.D. = Mary Elizabeth Bell.

JAMES HARWOOD CLOSSON, 3d, M.D.

Clothier

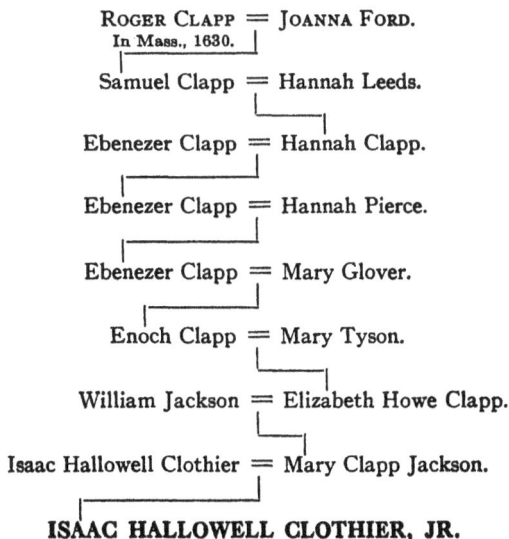

ROGER CLAPP = JOANNA FORD.
In Mass., 1630.

Samuel Clapp = Hannah Leeds.

Ebenezer Clapp = Hannah Clapp.

Ebenezer Clapp = Hannah Pierce.

Ebenezer Clapp = Mary Glover.

Enoch Clapp = Mary Tyson.

William Jackson = Elizabeth Howe Clapp.

Isaac Hallowell Clothier = Mary Clapp Jackson.

ISAAC HALLOWELL CLOTHIER, JR.

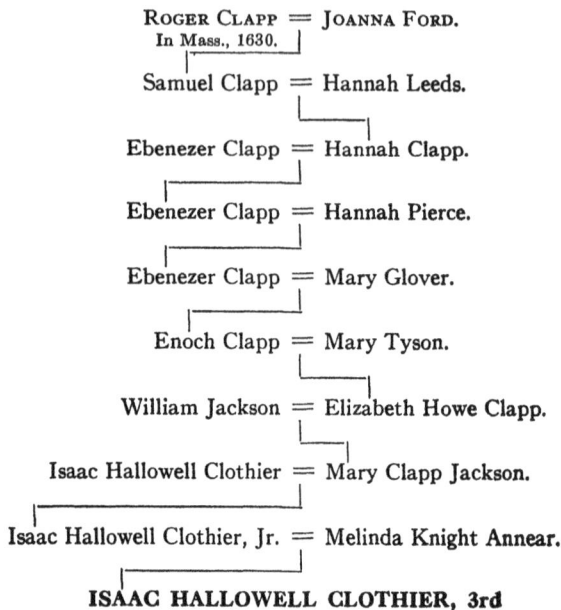

ROGER CLAPP = JOANNA FORD.
In Mass., 1630.

Samuel Clapp = Hannah Leeds.

Ebenezer Clapp = Hannah Clapp.

Ebenezer Clapp = Hannah Pierce.

Ebenezer Clapp = Mary Glover.

Enoch Clapp = Mary Tyson.

William Jackson = Elizabeth Howe Clapp.

Isaac Hallowell Clothier = Mary Clapp Jackson.

Isaac Hallowell Clothier, Jr. = Melinda Knight Annear.

ISAAC HALLOWELL CLOTHIER, 3rd

Clothier

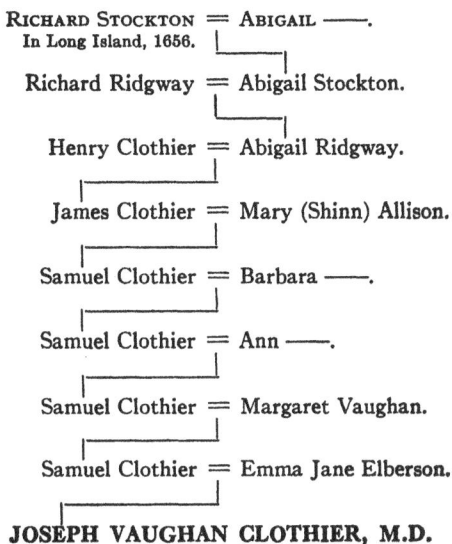

RICHARD STOCKTON = ABIGAIL ——.
In Long Island, 1656.

Richard Ridgway = Abigail Stockton.

Henry Clothier = Abigail Ridgway.

James Clothier = Mary (Shinn) Allison.

Samuel Clothier = Barbara ——.

Samuel Clothier = Ann ——.

Samuel Clothier = Margaret Vaughan.

Samuel Clothier = Emma Jane Elberson.

JOSEPH VAUGHAN CLOTHIER, M.D.

Clothier

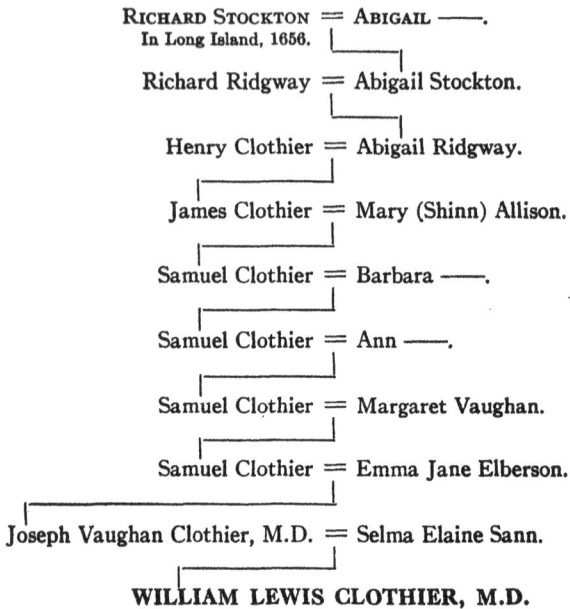

RICHARD STOCKTON = ABIGAIL ——.
In Long Island, 1656.

Richard Ridgway = Abigail Stockton.

Henry Clothier = Abigail Ridgway.

James Clothier = Mary (Shinn) Allison.

Samuel Clothier = Barbara ——.

Samuel Clothier = Ann ——.

Samuel Clothier = Margaret Vaughan.

Samuel Clothier = Emma Jane Elberson.

Joseph Vaughan Clothier, M.D. = Selma Elaine Sann.

WILLIAM LEWIS CLOTHIER, M.D.

Coates

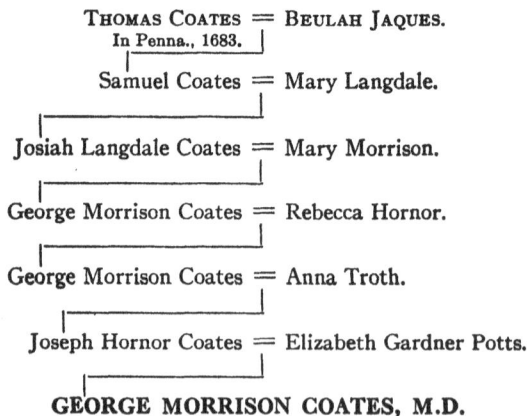

THOMAS COATES = BEULAH JAQUES.
In Penna., 1683.

Samuel Coates = Mary Langdale.

Josiah Langdale Coates = Mary Morrison.

George Morrison Coates = Rebecca Hornor.

George Morrison Coates = Anna Troth.

Joseph Hornor Coates = Elizabeth Gardner Potts.

GEORGE MORRISON COATES, M.D.

Coleman

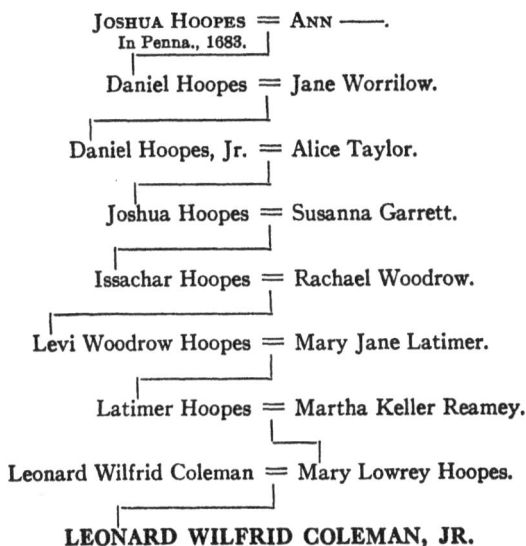

JOSHUA HOOPES = ANN ——.
In Penna., 1683.

Daniel Hoopes = Jane Worrilow.

Daniel Hoopes, Jr. = Alice Taylor.

Joshua Hoopes = Susanna Garrett.

Issachar Hoopes = Rachael Woodrow.

Levi Woodrow Hoopes = Mary Jane Latimer.

Latimer Hoopes = Martha Keller Reamey.

Leonard Wilfrid Coleman = Mary Lowrey Hoopes.

LEONARD WILFRID COLEMAN, JR.

Colket

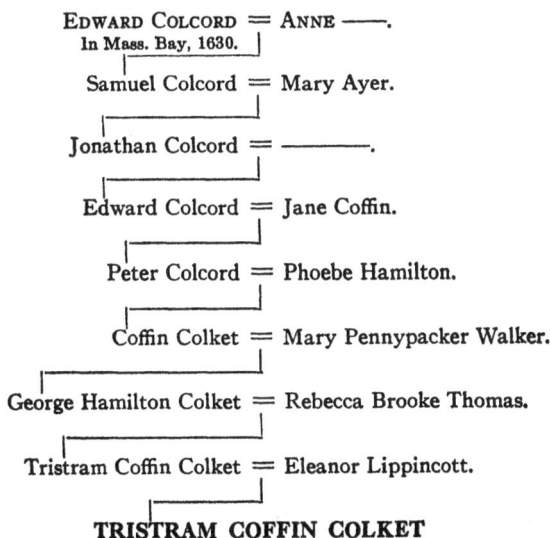

EDWARD COLCORD = ANNE ——.
In Mass. Bay, 1630.

Samuel Colcord = Mary Ayer.

Jonathan Colcord = ———.

Edward Colcord = Jane Coffin.

Peter Colcord = Phoebe Hamilton.

Coffin Colket = Mary Pennypacker Walker.

George Hamilton Colket = Rebecca Brooke Thomas.

Tristram Coffin Colket = Eleanor Lippincott.

TRISTRAM COFFIN COLKET

Colket

EDWARD COLCORD = ANN ——.
In Mass., 1630.

Samuel Colcord = Mary Ayer.

Jonathan Colcord = —— ——.

Edward Colcord = Jane Coffin.

Peter Colcord = Phœbe Hamilton.

Coffin Colket = Mary Pennypacker Walker.

Charles Howard Colket = Almira Little Peterson.

TRISTRAM COFFIN COLKET, 2nd

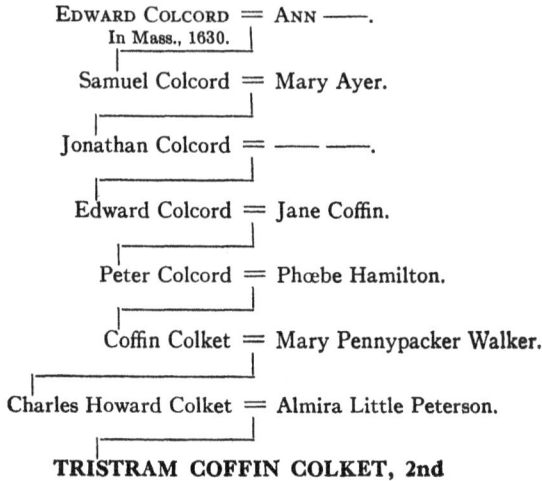

SUPPLEMENTALS

Ninth in descent from John Alden, in Plymouth Colony, 1620.
Ninth in descent from Joan (Kember) Coffin, in Mass., 1642.
Ninth in descent from Richard Warren, in Plymouth Colony, 1620.
Eighth in descent from John Ayer, in Mass., 1640.
Eighth in descent from Tristram Coffin, in Mass., 1642.
Eighth in descent from Thomas Croasdale, in Penna., 1682.
Eighth in descent from Agnes Hathernthwaite, in Penna., 1682.
Eighth in descent from John Heard, in Mass., 1640.
Eighth in descent from John Hutchins, in Mass., 1640.
Eighth in descent from Thomas Little, in Plymouth Colony, 1630.
Eighth in descent from Catherine Reynolds, in Mass., 1640.
Eighth in descent from Edward Starbuck, in Mass., 1640.
Seventh in descent from Nicholas Cole, in Mass., 1658.
Seventh in descent from Edward Jerman, in Penna., before 1688.
Seventh in descent from John Jerman, in Penna., 1683.
Seventh in descent from Mary Morris, in Penna., 1687.
Seventh in descent from Olaf (William) Peterson, in New Sweden, 1658.
Seventh in descent from Elizabeth Philips, in Penna., 1694.
Seventh in descent from David Potts, in Penna., 1690.
Seventh in descent from Hendrick Sellen, in Penna., 1689.
Seventh in descent from William Thomas, in Penna., circa 1690.
Seventh in descent from Cornelius Tyson, in Penna., before 1699.
Seventh in descent from Hans Peter Umstat, in Penna., 1685.
Seventh in descent from Lewis Walker, in Penna., 1687.
Sixth in descent from Hendrick Pannebecker, in Penna., before 1699.

Connell

CORNELIS MAESSEN VAN BUREN = CATALYNTJE MARTENSE.
In New Netherland, 1631.

Marten Cornelissen Van Buren = Maritje Quackenbosch.

Pieter Martense Van Buren = Ariaantje Barentse.

Marten Pieterse Van Buren = Dirckje Van Alstyne.

Pieter Van Buren = Catharine Quackenbosch.

Martin Pieter Van Buren = Catherine, or Getty, Goes (Hoes).

Daniel Hurd = Eliza Van Buren.

William Penn Connell = Alida Hurd.

Frederick Connell = Emma Augusta Baxter.

FREDERICK VAN BUREN CONNELL.

Cooper

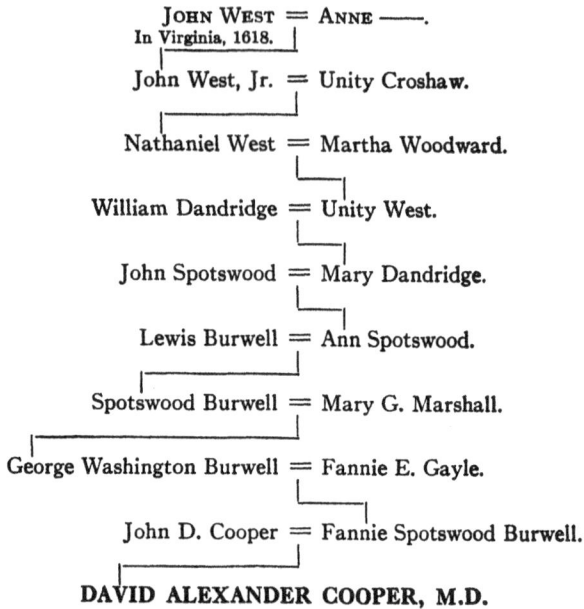

JOHN WEST = ANNE ——.
In Virginia, 1618.

John West, Jr. = Unity Croshaw.

Nathaniel West = Martha Woodward.

William Dandridge = Unity West.

John Spotswood = Mary Dandridge.

Lewis Burwell = Ann Spotswood.

Spotswood Burwell = Mary G. Marshall.

George Washington Burwell = Fannie E. Gayle.

John D. Cooper = Fannie Spotswood Burwell.

DAVID ALEXANDER COOPER, M.D.

Cope

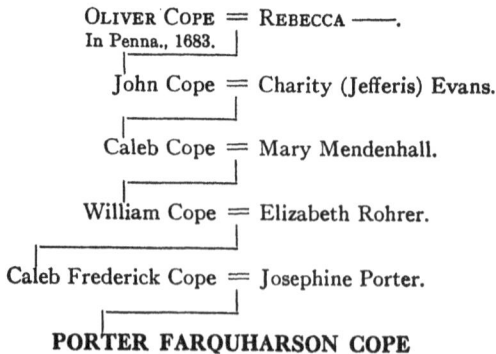

OLIVER COPE = REBECCA ——.
In Penna., 1683.

John Cope = Charity (Jefferis) Evans.

Caleb Cope = Mary Mendenhall.

William Cope = Elizabeth Rohrer.

Caleb Frederick Cope = Josephine Porter.

PORTER FARQUHARSON COPE

SUPPLEMENTALS

Seventh in descent from Henry Dixson, in Penna., now Delaware, 1690.
Seventh in descent from George Maris, in Penna., 1683.
Sixth in descent from John Mendenhall, in Penna., 1683.
Sixth in descent from Thomas Pierson, in Maryland, 1676.
Fifth in descent from Jane Chandler, in Penna., 1687.
Fifth in descent from Robert Jefferis, in Penna., 1685.

<table>
<tr><td>Elected
1941</td><td style="text-align:center">𝕮𝖔𝖗𝖘𝖔𝖓</td><td>No.
651</td></tr>
</table>

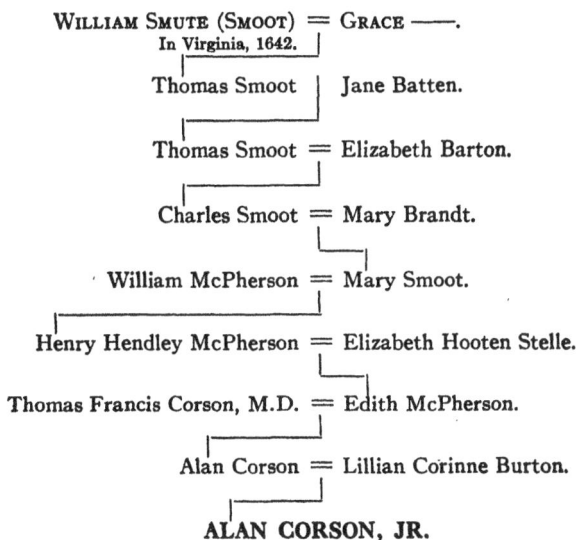

WILLIAM SMUTE (SMOOT) = GRACE ——.
In Virginia, 1642.

Thomas Smoot | Jane Batten.

Thomas Smoot = Elizabeth Barton.

Charles Smoot = Mary Brandt.

William McPherson = Mary Smoot.

Henry Hendley McPherson = Elizabeth Hooten Stelle.

Thomas Francis Corson, M.D. = Edith McPherson.

Alan Corson = Lillian Corinne Burton.

ALAN CORSON, JR.

Crispin

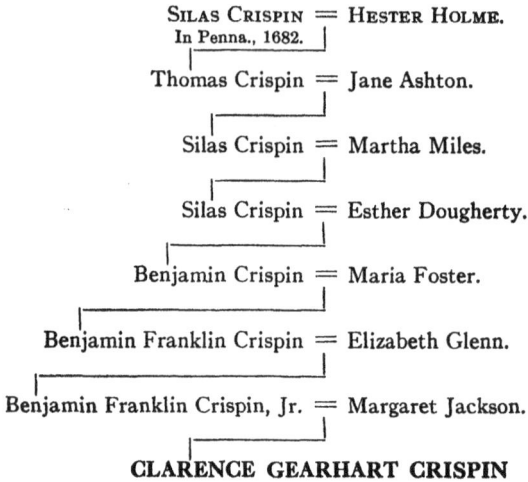

SILAS CRISPIN = HESTER HOLME.
In Penna., 1682.

Thomas Crispin = Jane Ashton.

Silas Crispin = Martha Miles.

Silas Crispin = Esther Dougherty.

Benjamin Crispin = Maria Foster.

Benjamin Franklin Crispin = Elizabeth Glenn.

Benjamin Franklin Crispin, Jr. = Margaret Jackson.

CLARENCE GEARHART CRISPIN

Croskey

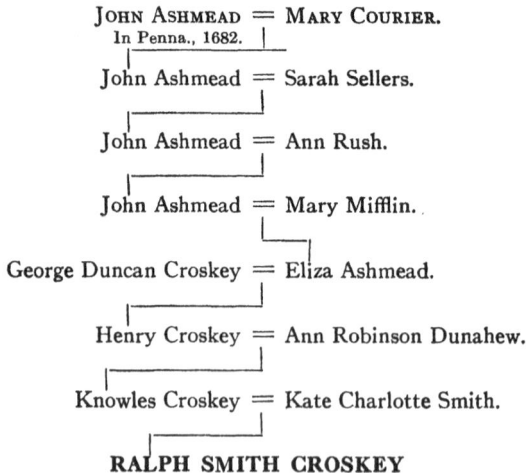

JOHN ASHMEAD = MARY COURIER.
In Penna., 1682.

John Ashmead = Sarah Sellers.

John Ashmead = Ann Rush.

John Ashmead = Mary Mifflin.

George Duncan Croskey = Eliza Ashmead.

Henry Croskey = Ann Robinson Dunahew.

Knowles Croskey = Kate Charlotte Smith.

RALPH SMITH CROSKEY

𝔇𝔞𝔟𝔦𝔰

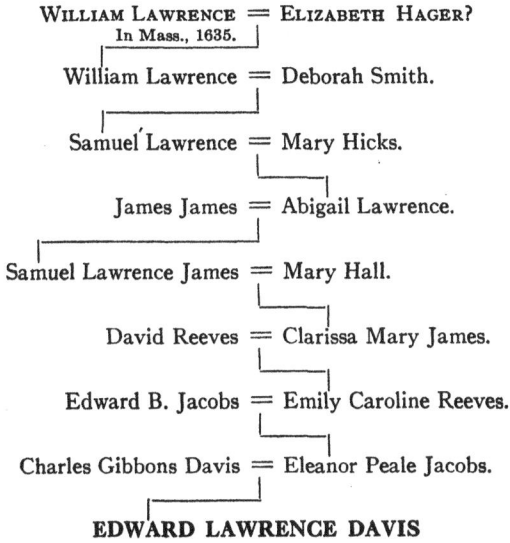

WILLIAM LAWRENCE = ELIZABETH HAGER?
In Mass., 1635.

William Lawrence = Deborah Smith.

Samuel Lawrence = Mary Hicks.

James James = Abigail Lawrence.

Samuel Lawrence James = Mary Hall.

David Reeves = Clarissa Mary James.

Edward B. Jacobs = Emily Caroline Reeves.

Charles Gibbons Davis = Eleanor Peale Jacobs.

EDWARD LAWRENCE DAVIS

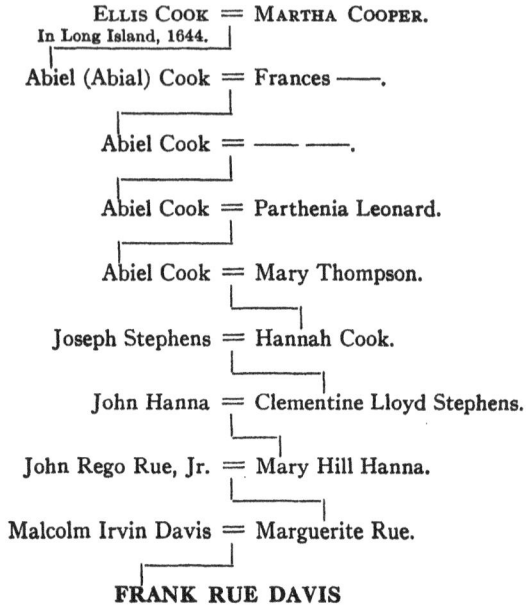

ELLIS COOK = MARTHA COOPER.
In Long Island, 1644.

Abiel (Abial) Cook = Frances ——.

Abiel Cook = —— ——.

Abiel Cook = Parthenia Leonard.

Abiel Cook = Mary Thompson.

Joseph Stephens = Hannah Cook.

John Hanna = Clementine Lloyd Stephens.

John Rego Rue, Jr. = Mary Hill Hanna.

Malcolm Irvin Davis = Marguerite Rue.

FRANK RUE DAVIS

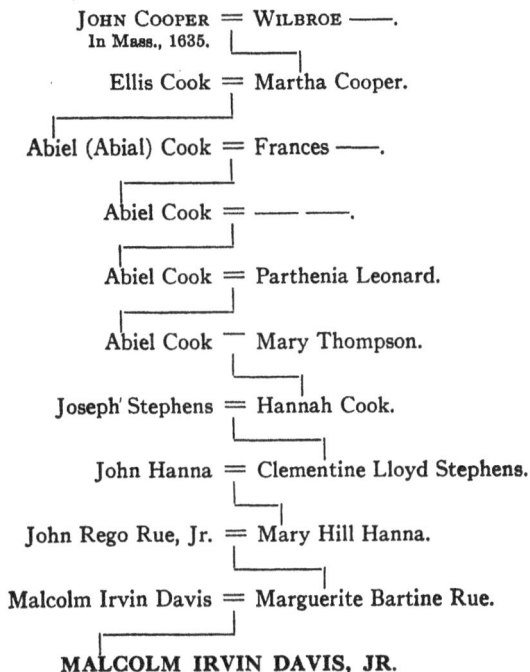

John Cooper = Wilbroe ——.
In Mass., 1635.

Ellis Cook = Martha Cooper.

Abiel (Abial) Cook = Frances ——.

Abiel Cook = —— ——.

Abiel Cook = Parthenia Leonard.

Abiel Cook — Mary Thompson.

Joseph Stephens = Hannah Cook.

John Hanna = Clementine Lloyd Stephens.

John Rego Rue, Jr. = Mary Hill Hanna.

Malcolm Irvin Davis = Marguerite Bartine Rue.

MALCOLM IRVIN DAVIS, JR.

Elected 1947

Davis

No. 725

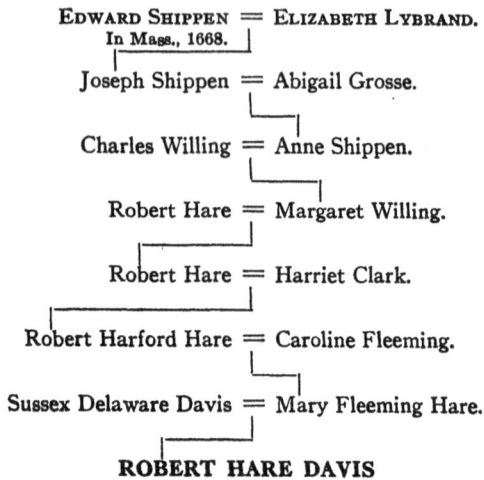

EDWARD SHIPPEN = ELIZABETH LYBRAND.
In Mass., 1668.

Joseph Shippen = Abigail Grosse.

Charles Willing = Anne Shippen.

Robert Hare = Margaret Willing.

Robert Hare = Harriet Clark.

Robert Harford Hare = Caroline Fleeming.

Sussex Delaware Davis = Mary Fleeming Hare.

ROBERT HARE DAVIS

JOHN COOPER = WILBROE ——.
In Mass., 1635.

Ellis Cook = Martha Cooper.

Abiel (Abial) Cook = Frances ——.

Abiel Cook = —— ——.

Abiel Cook = Parthenia Leonard.

Abiel Cook = Mary Thompson.

Joseph Stephens = Hannah Cook.

John Hanna = Clementine Lloyd Stephens.

Benjamin Mulford Day = Martha Elizabeth Hanna.

BENJAMIN MULFORD DAY

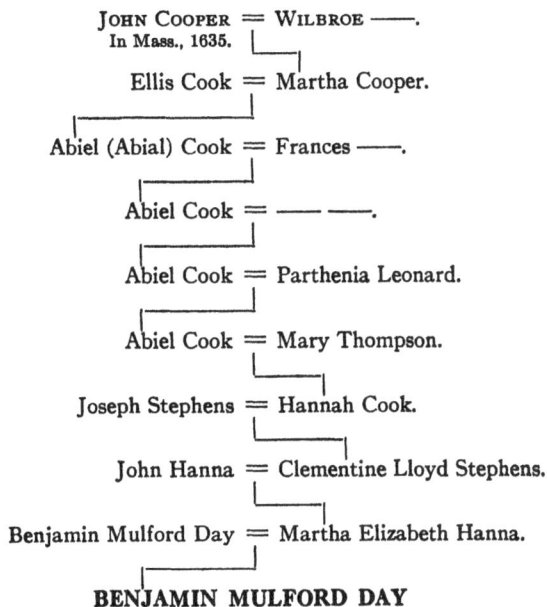

SUPPLEMENTAL

Eighth in descent from Ellis Cook, in Long Island, 1644.

Dilks

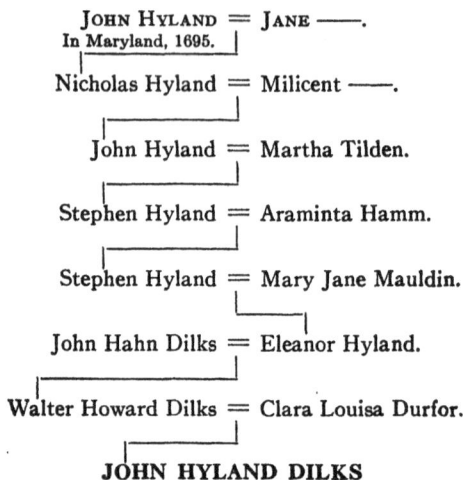

JOHN HYLAND = JANE ——.
In Maryland, 1695.

Nicholas Hyland = Milicent ——.

John Hyland = Martha Tilden.

Stephen Hyland = Araminta Hamm.

Stephen Hyland = Mary Jane Mauldin.

John Hahn Dilks = Eleanor Hyland.

Walter Howard Dilks = Clara Louisa Durfor.

JOHN HYLAND DILKS

Dilks

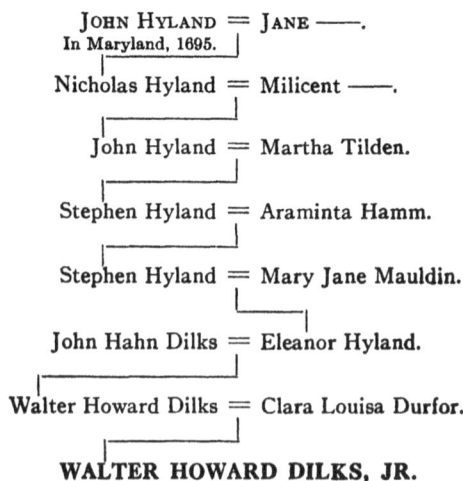

JOHN HYLAND = JANE ——.
In Maryland, 1695.

Nicholas Hyland = Milicent ——.

John Hyland = Martha Tilden.

Stephen Hyland = Araminta Hamm.

Stephen Hyland = Mary Jane Mauldin.

John Hahn Dilks = Eleanor Hyland.

Walter Howard Dilks = Clara Louisa Durfor.

WALTER HOWARD DILKS, JR.

RICHARD RIDGWAY = ELIZABETH CHAMBERLAIN.
In West Jersey, 1679.

Josiah Ridgway = Sarah ——.

Lott Ridgway = Susannah Peat.

John Dobbins = Susannah Ridgway.

Joseph Ridgway Dobbins = Mary Ann Hilyard.

Murrell Dobbins = Emily Munroe.

THOMAS MUNROE DOBBINS

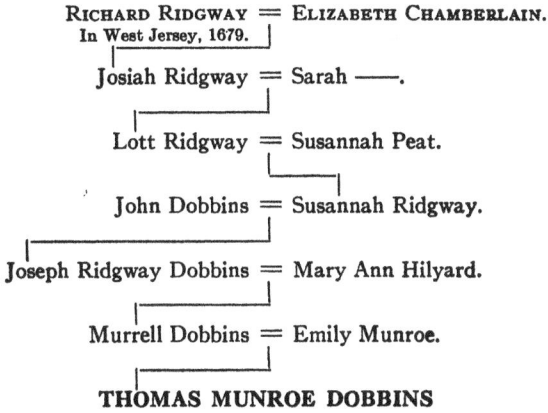

SUPPLEMENTALS

Seventh in descent from Barnard Devonish, in West Jersey, 1677.
Seventh in descent from Richard Haines, in West Jersey, 1682.
Sixth in descent from John Hilliard, in West Jersey, 1689.

GEORGE PALMER ═ ELIZABETH ———.
In Penna., 1682.

Thomas Palmer ═ Sarah Michener.

John Palmer ═ Mary Lukens.

Samuel McNeill ═ Mary Palmer.

Joseph Heaton ═ Sarah McNeill.

Reuben Ayres Heaton ═ Mary Carter.

William Francis Donaldson ═ Elizabeth Ayres Heaton.

FRANCIS DONALDSON

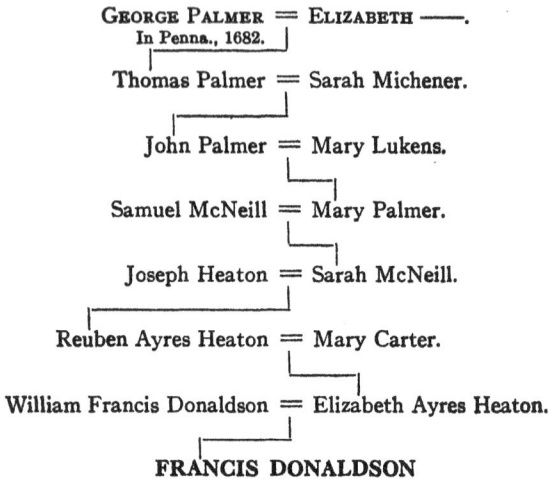

SUPPLEMENTALS

Seventh in descent from Jan Lucken, in Penna., 1683.
Seventh in descent from John Michener, in Penna., 1686.

𝕯uff

THOMAS MINOR = GRACE PALMER.
In Mass. and Conn., 1630.

Manasseh Minor = Lydia Moore.

Elnathan Minor = Rebecca Baldwin.

Manasseh Minor = Keziah Geer.

Moses Robbins = Keziah Minor.

Brintnel Robbins = Mary Boardman.

William Newlin = Keziah Robbins.

Joseph Miller = Mary Newlin.

Dr. James H. Duff = Susannah Miller.

Rev. Joseph Miller Duff = Margaret Morgan.

JAMES HENDERSON DUFF

JOHN ASHMEAD = MARY COURIER.
In Penna., 1682.

John Ashmead = Sarah Sellers.

John Ashmead = Ann Rush.

John Ashmead = Mary Mifflin.

William Ashmead = Margaret McKinley.

John Wayne Ashmead = Henrietta Graham Flower.

John Edward Dyer = Lavinia Lawrence Ashmead.

WILLIAM ASHMEAD DYER

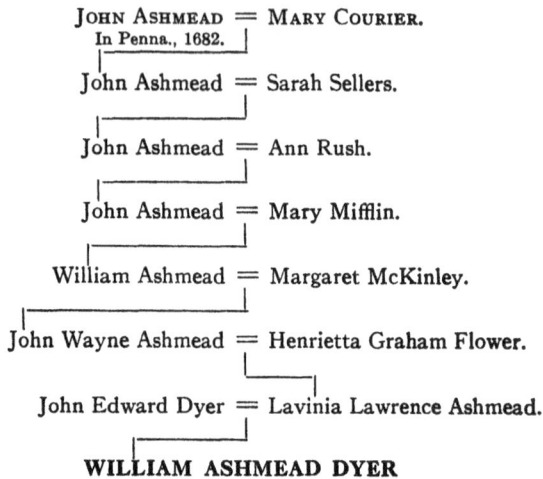

SUPPLEMENTALS

Eighth in descent from John Baker, in Penna., 1685.
Eighth in descent from Henry Gibbons, in Penna., 1682.
Eighth in descent from John Mifflin, in West Jersey, 1679.
Eighth in descent from John Rush, in Penna., 1683.
Seventh in descent from Thomas Mercer, in Penna., 1687.
Seventh in descent from Bryan Peart, in Maryland, 1686.
Seventh in descent from Robert Pennell, in Penna., 1686.
Seventh in descent from Samuel Sellers, in Penna., 1682.
Seventh in descent from Daniel Williamson, in Penna., 1682.
Seventh in descent from Philip Yarnall, in Penna., 1683.
Sixth in descent from John Buckley, in Penna., 1682.
Sixth in descent from William Flower, in Penna., 1692.
Sixth in descent from John Grubb, in Upland, now Penna., 1679.

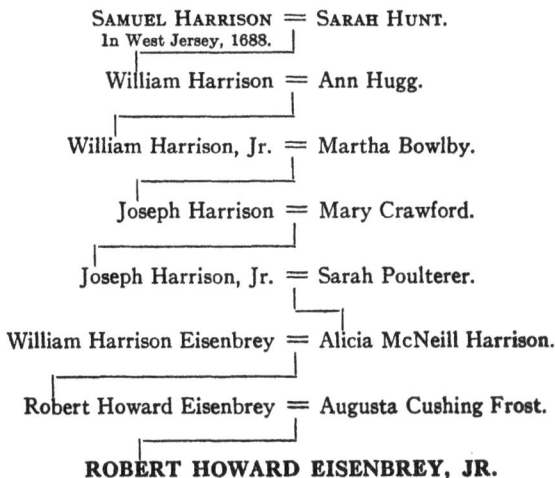

SAMUEL HARRISON ═ SARAH HUNT.
In West Jersey, 1688.

William Harrison ═ Ann Hugg.

William Harrison, Jr. ═ Martha Bowlby.

Joseph Harrison ═ Mary Crawford.

Joseph Harrison, Jr. ═ Sarah Poulterer.

William Harrison Eisenbrey ═ Alicia McNeill Harrison.

Robert Howard Eisenbrey ═ Augusta Cushing Frost.

ROBERT HOWARD EISENBREY, JR.

¢lⅾreⅾge

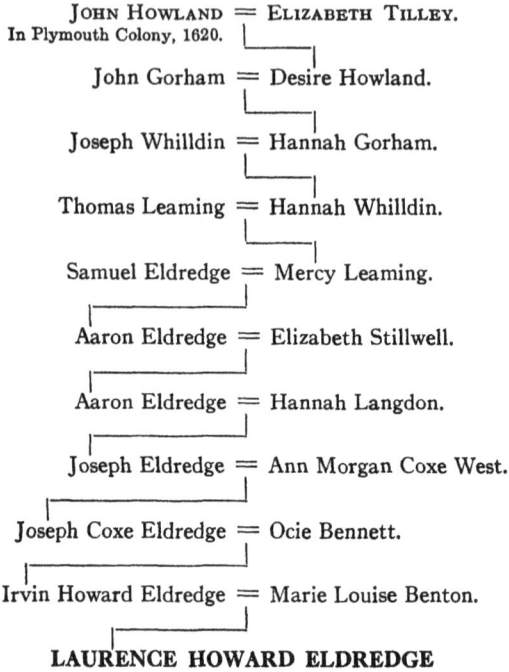

JOHN HOWLAND = ELIZABETH TILLEY.
In Plymouth Colony, 1620.

John Gorham = Desire Howland.

Joseph Whilldin = Hannah Gorham.

Thomas Leaming = Hannah Whilldin.

Samuel Eldredge = Mercy Leaming.

Aaron Eldredge = Elizabeth Stillwell.

Aaron Eldredge = Hannah Langdon.

Joseph Eldredge = Ann Morgan Coxe West.

Joseph Coxe Eldredge = Ocie Bennett.

Irvin Howard Eldredge = Marie Louise Benton.

LAURENCE HOWARD ELDREDGE

Elmer

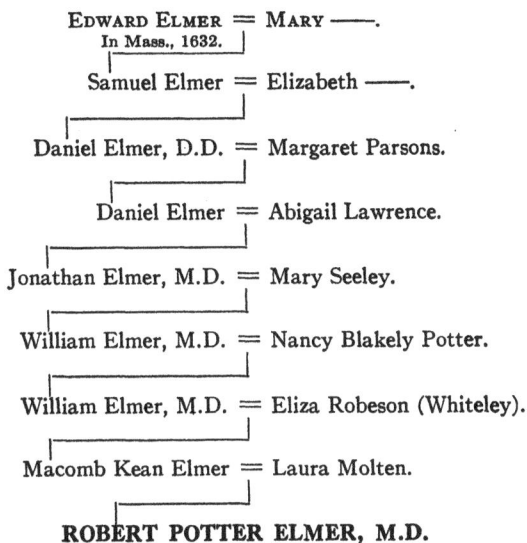

EDWARD ELMER = MARY ——.
In Mass., 1632.

Samuel Elmer = Elizabeth ——.

Daniel Elmer, D.D. = Margaret Parsons.

Daniel Elmer = Abigail Lawrence.

Jonathan Elmer, M.D. = Mary Seeley.

William Elmer, M.D. = Nancy Blakely Potter.

William Elmer, M.D. = Eliza Robeson (Whiteley).

Macomb Kean Elmer = Laura Molten.

ROBERT POTTER ELMER, M.D.

Esler

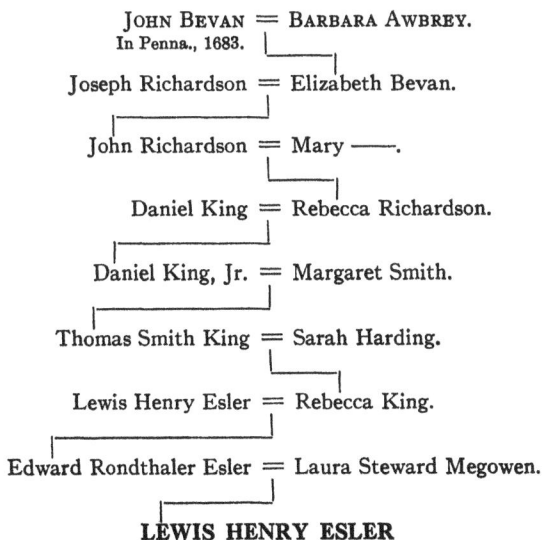

JOHN BEVAN = BARBARA AWBREY.
In Penna., 1683.

Joseph Richardson = Elizabeth Bevan.

John Richardson = Mary ——.

Daniel King = Rebecca Richardson.

Daniel King, Jr. = Margaret Smith.

Thomas Smith King = Sarah Harding.

Lewis Henry Esler = Rebecca King.

Edward Rondthaler Esler = Laura Steward Megowen.

LEWIS HENRY ESLER

Estlack

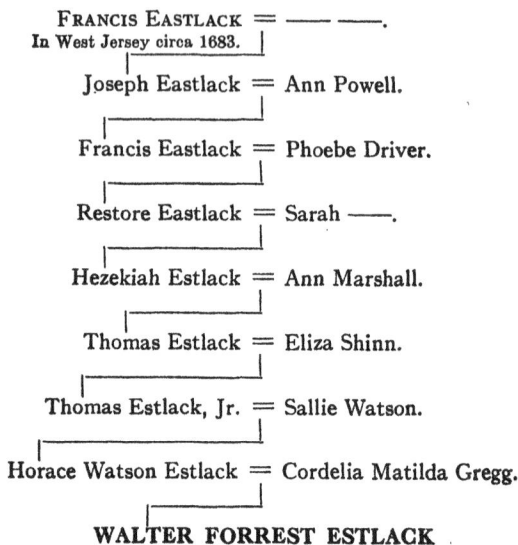

FRANCIS EASTLACK = ——— ———.
In West Jersey circa 1683.

Joseph Eastlack = Ann Powell.

Francis Eastlack = Phoebe Driver.

Restore Eastlack = Sarah ———.

Hezekiah Estlack = Ann Marshall.

Thomas Estlack = Eliza Shinn.

Thomas Estlack, Jr. = Sallie Watson.

Horace Watson Estlack = Cordelia Matilda Gregg.

WALTER FORREST ESTLACK

Evans

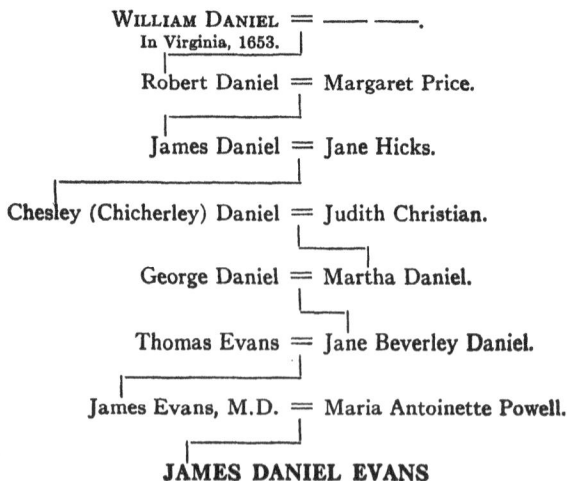

WILLIAM DANIEL = ——— ———.
In Virginia, 1653.

Robert Daniel = Margaret Price.

James Daniel = Jane Hicks.

Chesley (Chicherley) Daniel = Judith Christian.

George Daniel = Martha Daniel.

Thomas Evans = Jane Beverley Daniel.

James Evans, M.D. = Maria Antoinette Powell.

JAMES DANIEL EVANS

SUPPLEMENTALS

Eighth in descent from Richard Ferris, in Virginia, 1636.
Eighth in descent from Nicholas Fontaine, in Virginia, before 1663.
Eighth in descent from Samuel Tucker, in Virginia, 1654.
Eighth in descent from John Woodson, in Virginia, 1620.
Eighth in descent from Thomas Youell, in Maryland, 1634.
Seventh in descent from Thomas Christian, in Virginia, before 1687.
Seventh in descent from Burr Harrison, in Virginia, 1664.
Seventh in descent from George Lane, in Virginia, before 1662.
Seventh in descent from Andrew Monroe, in Maryland, 1640.
Seventh in descent from Henry Peyton, in Virginia, 1656.
Seventh in descent from Walter Powell, in Virginia, 1643.
Seventh in descent from Robert Price, in Virginia, before 1660.
Seventh in descent from Patrick Spence, in Virginia, 1657.
Sixth in descent from John Grayson, in Virginia, before 1700.

Elected
1941

Evans

No.
669

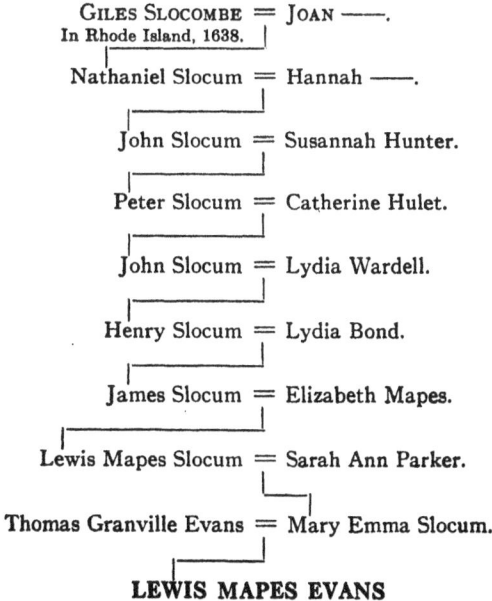

GILES SLOCOMBE = JOAN ——.
In Rhode Island, 1638.

Nathaniel Slocum = Hannah ——.

John Slocum = Susannah Hunter.

Peter Slocum = Catherine Hulet.

John Slocum = Lydia Wardell.

Henry Slocum = Lydia Bond.

James Slocum = Elizabeth Mapes.

Lewis Mapes Slocum = Sarah Ann Parker.

Thomas Granville Evans = Mary Emma Slocum.

LEWIS MAPES EVANS

Evans

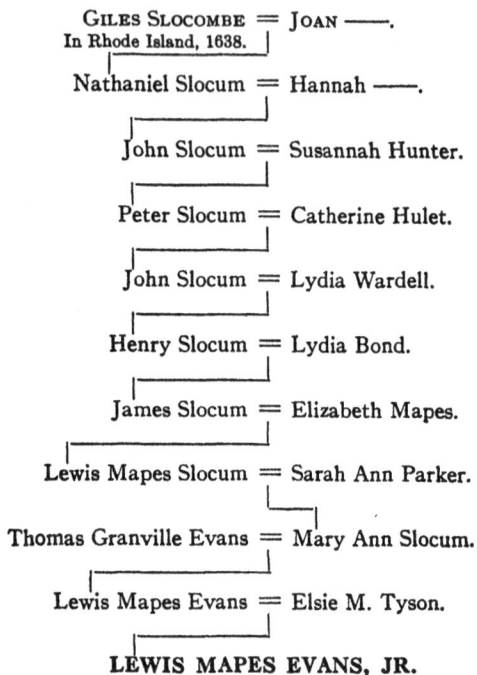

GILES SLOCOMBE = JOAN ——.
In Rhode Island, 1638.

Nathaniel Slocum = Hannah ——.

John Slocum = Susannah Hunter.

Peter Slocum = Catherine Hulet.

John Slocum = Lydia Wardell.

Henry Slocum = Lydia Bond.

James Slocum = Elizabeth Mapes.

Lewis Mapes Slocum = Sarah Ann Parker.

Thomas Granville Evans = Mary Ann Slocum.

Lewis Mapes Evans = Elsie M. Tyson.

LEWIS MAPES EVANS, JR.

Ewing

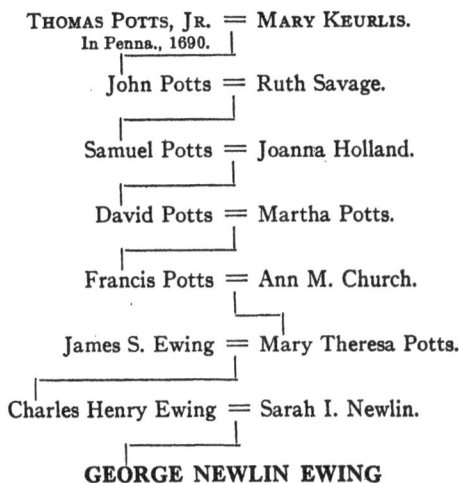

THOMAS POTTS, JR. = MARY KEURLIS.
In Penna., 1690.

John Potts = Ruth Savage.

Samuel Potts = Joanna Holland.

David Potts = Martha Potts.

Francis Potts = Ann M. Church.

James S. Ewing = Mary Theresa Potts.

Charles Henry Ewing = Sarah I. Newlin.

GEORGE NEWLIN EWING

Fell

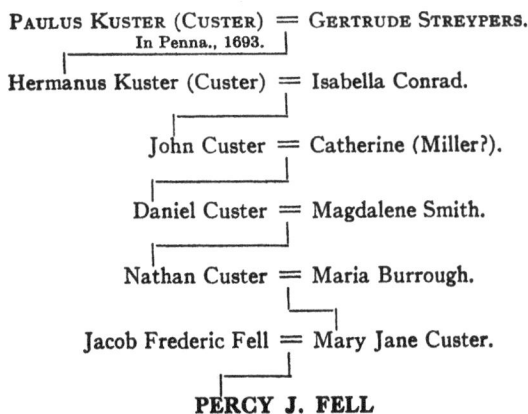

PAULUS KUSTER (CUSTER) = GERTRUDE STREYPERS.
In Penna., 1693.

Hermanus Kuster (Custer) = Isabella Conrad.

John Custer = Catherine (Miller?).

Daniel Custer = Magdalene Smith.

Nathan Custer = Maria Burrough.

Jacob Frederic Fell = Mary Jane Custer.

PERCY J. FELL

Ferguson

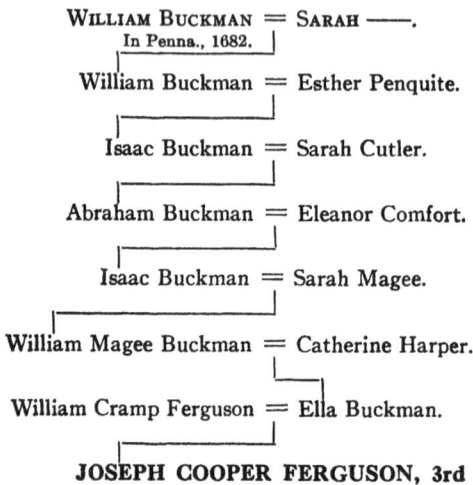

WILLIAM BUCKMAN = SARAH ——.
In Penna., 1682.

William Buckman = Esther Penquite.

Isaac Buckman = Sarah Cutler.

Abraham Buckman = Eleanor Comfort.

Isaac Buckman = Sarah Magee.

William Magee Buckman = Catherine Harper.

William Cramp Ferguson = Ella Buckman.

JOSEPH COOPER FERGUSON, 3rd

Ferguson

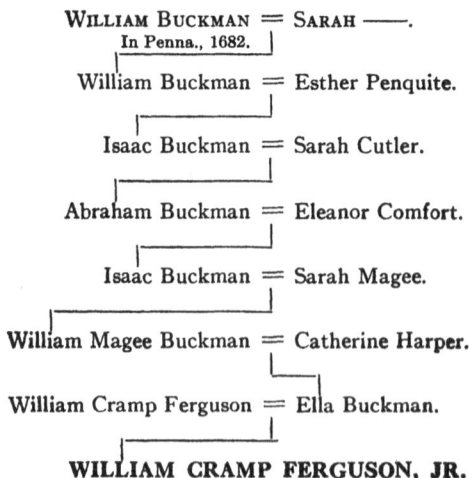

WILLIAM BUCKMAN = SARAH ——.
In Penna., 1682.

William Buckman = Esther Penquite.

Isaac Buckman = Sarah Cutler.

Abraham Buckman = Eleanor Comfort.

Isaac Buckman = Sarah Magee.

William Magee Buckman = Catherine Harper.

William Cramp Ferguson = Ella Buckman.

WILLIAM CRAMP FERGUSON, JR.

Fergusson

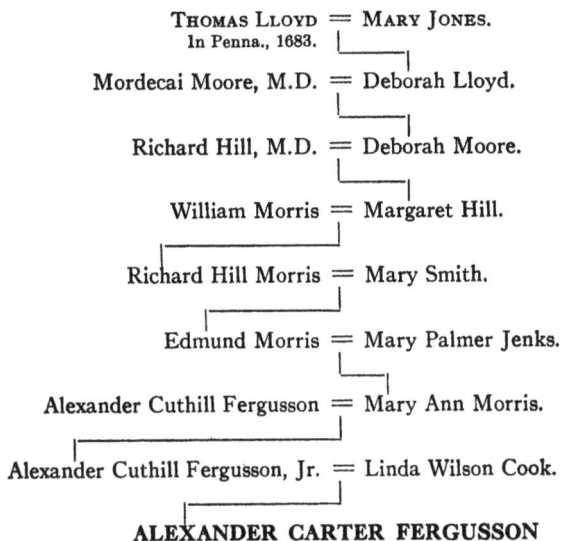

THOMAS LLOYD = MARY JONES.
In Penna., 1683.

Mordecai Moore, M.D. = Deborah Lloyd.

Richard Hill, M.D. = Deborah Moore.

William Morris = Margaret Hill.

Richard Hill Morris = Mary Smith.

Edmund Morris = Mary Palmer Jenks.

Alexander Cuthill Fergusson = Mary Ann Morris.

Alexander Cuthill Fergusson, Jr. = Linda Wilson Cook.

ALEXANDER CARTER FERGUSSON

Fergusson

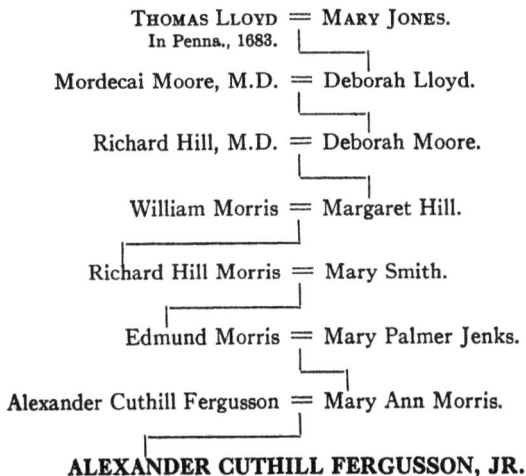

THOMAS LLOYD = MARY JONES.
In Penna., 1683.

Mordecai Moore, M.D. = Deborah Lloyd.

Richard Hill, M.D. = Deborah Moore.

William Morris = Margaret Hill.

Richard Hill Morris = Mary Smith.

Edmund Morris = Mary Palmer Jenks.

Alexander Cuthill Fergusson = Mary Ann Morris.

ALEXANDER CUTHILL FERGUSSON, JR.

JOHN DEGGE = —— ——.
In Virginia, 1673.

William Degge = Dorothea (Smith?).

John Digges (Degge) = Elizabeth Harris.

James Durrett = Nancy Digges.

Colson Heiskell = Nancy Durrett.

Nathan Myers = Margaret Ann Heiskell.

Edwin Henry Fitler, Jr. = Nannie Heiskell Myers.

DALE BAKER FITLER

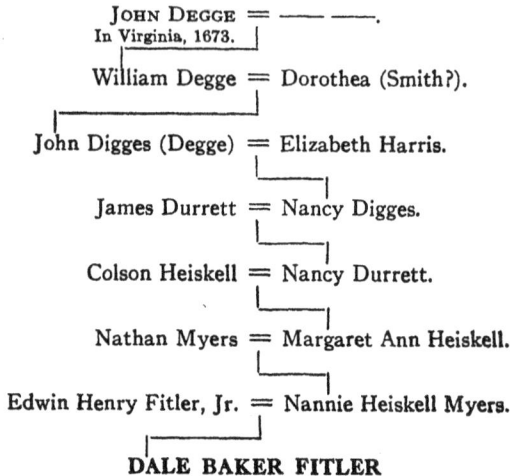

SUPPLEMENTALS

Tenth in descent from Joran Kyn, in New Sweden, 1643.

Ninth in descent from Jan Claassen, in New Sweden, 1666.

Ninth in descent from Samuel Harrison, in West Jersey, 1688.

Ninth in descent from Christina Toy, in Penna., 1684.

Eighth in descent from Joseph Ashton, in Penna., 1683.

Eighth in descent from Benjamin Duffield, in Penna., before 1685.

Eighth in descent from Jacob Hall, in Penna., 1684.

Eighth in descent from John Hinchman, in Long Island, 1673.

Eighth in descent from Thomas Rutter, in Penna., 1685.

Eighth in descent from James Steelman, in West Jersey, 1693.

Eighth in descent from John Swift, in Penna., before 1684.

jfitler

JÖRAN KYN = —— ——.
In New Sweden, 1643.

Hans Kyn or Keen = Willemka ——.

Matthias Keen = Henricka Claassen.

John Keen = Susannah Steelman.

James Keen = Mercy Ashton.

John Keen = Sarah Swift.

John Keen = Hannah Foster.

John Bispham Myers = Sarah Ann Keen.

Nathan Myers = Margaret Ann Heiskell.

Edwin Henry Fitler, Jr. = Nannie Heiskell Myers.

NATHAN MYERS FITLER

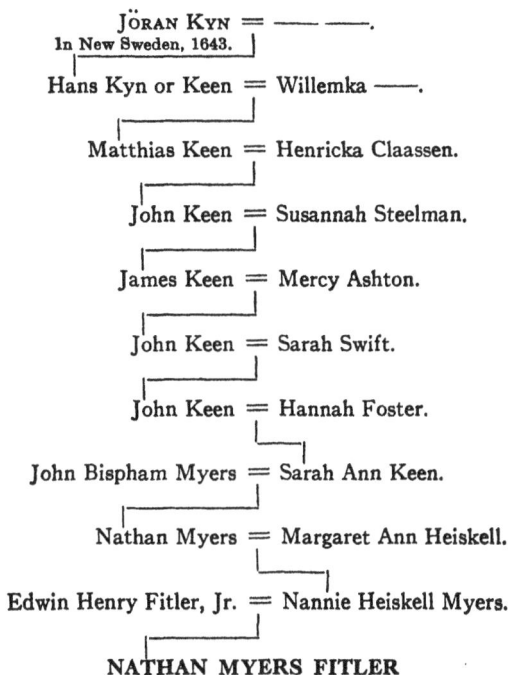

SUPPLEMENTALS

Ninth in descent from Jan Claassen, in New Sweden, 1666.
Ninth in descent from Samuel Harrison, in West Jersey, 1688.
Ninth in descent from Christina Toy, in Penna., 1684.
Eighth in descent from Benjamin Duffield, in Penna., before 1685.
Eighth in descent from Jacob Hall, in Penna., 1684.
Eighth in descent from John Hinchman, in Long Island, 1673.
Eighth in descent from Thomas Rutter, in Penna., 1685.
Eighth in descent from James Steelman, in West Jersey, 1693.
Eighth in descent from John Swift, in Penna., before 1684.

ꟊitler

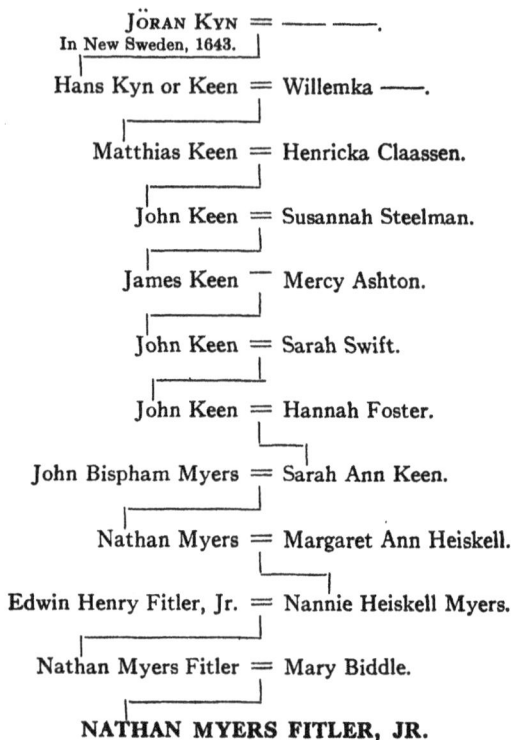

JÖRAN KYN = —— ——.
In New Sweden, 1643.

Hans Kyn or Keen = Willemka ——.

Matthias Keen = Henricka Claassen.

John Keen = Susannah Steelman.

James Keen — Mercy Ashton.

John Keen = Sarah Swift.

John Keen = Hannah Foster.

John Bispham Myers = Sarah Ann Keen.

Nathan Myers = Margaret Ann Heiskell.

Edwin Henry Fitler, Jr. = Nannie Heiskell Myers.

Nathan Myers Fitler = Mary Biddle.

NATHAN MYERS FITLER, JR.

Fitler

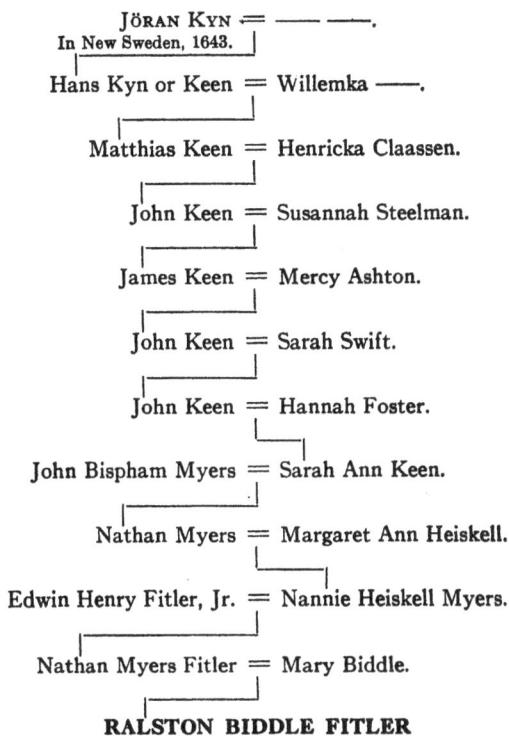

JÖRAN KYN = —— ——.
In New Sweden, 1643.

Hans Kyn or Keen = Willemka ——.

Matthias Keen = Henricka Claassen.

John Keen = Susannah Steelman.

James Keen = Mercy Ashton.

John Keen = Sarah Swift.

John Keen = Hannah Foster.

John Bispham Myers = Sarah Ann Keen.

Nathan Myers = Margaret Ann Heiskell.

Edwin Henry Fitler, Jr. = Nannie Heiskell Myers.

Nathan Myers Fitler = Mary Biddle.

RALSTON BIDDLE FITLER

𝔉lagg

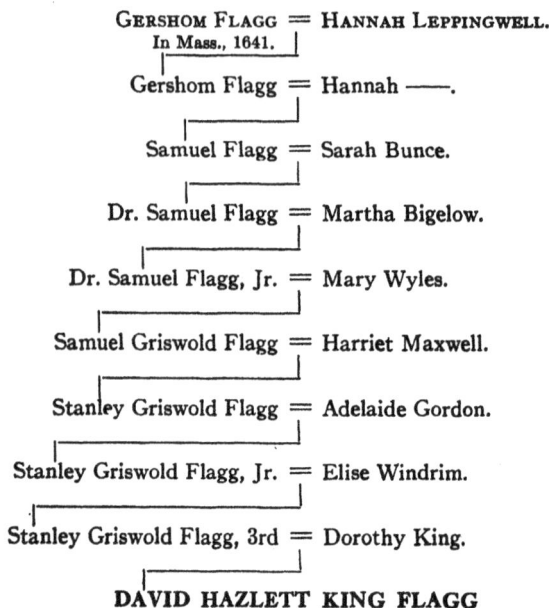

GERSHOM FLAGG = HANNAH LEPPINGWELL.
In Mass., 1641.

Gershom Flagg = Hannah ——.

Samuel Flagg = Sarah Bunce.

Dr. Samuel Flagg = Martha Bigelow.

Dr. Samuel Flagg, Jr. = Mary Wyles.

Samuel Griswold Flagg = Harriet Maxwell.

Stanley Griswold Flagg = Adelaide Gordon.

Stanley Griswold Flagg, Jr. = Elise Windrim.

Stanley Griswold Flagg, 3rd = Dorothy King.

DAVID HAZLETT KING FLAGG

𝔉lagg

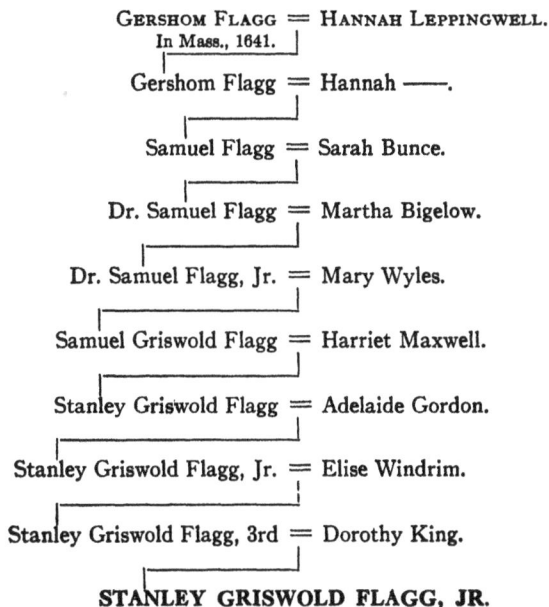

GERSHOM FLAGG = HANNAH LEPPINGWELL.
In Mass., 1641.

Gershom Flagg = Hannah ——.

Samuel Flagg = Sarah Bunce.

Dr. Samuel Flagg = Martha Bigelow.

Dr. Samuel Flagg, Jr. = Mary Wyles.

Samuel Griswold Flagg = Harriet Maxwell.

Stanley Griswold Flagg = Adelaide Gordon.

Stanley Griswold Flagg, Jr. = Elise Windrim.

Stanley Griswold Flagg, 3rd = Dorothy King.

STANLEY GRISWOLD FLAGG, JR.

𝕱𝖑𝖆𝖌𝖌

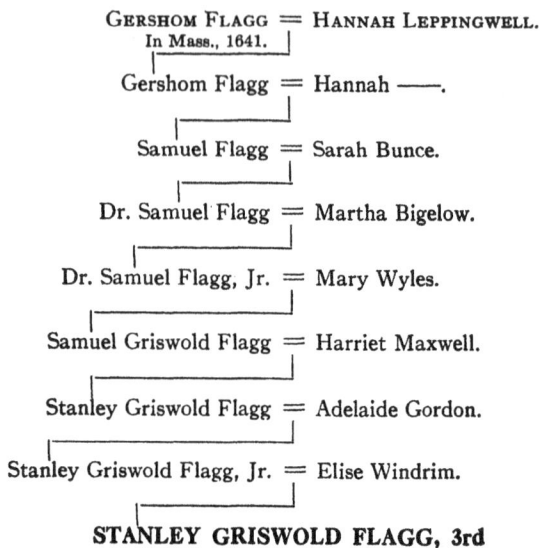

GERSHOM FLAGG = HANNAH LEPPINGWELL.
In Mass., 1641.

Gershom Flagg = Hannah ——.

Samuel Flagg = Sarah Bunce.

Dr. Samuel Flagg = Martha Bigelow.

Dr. Samuel Flagg, Jr. = Mary Wyles.

Samuel Griswold Flagg = Harriet Maxwell.

Stanley Griswold Flagg = Adelaide Gordon.

Stanley Griswold Flagg, Jr. = Elise Windrim.

STANLEY GRISWOLD FLAGG, 3rd

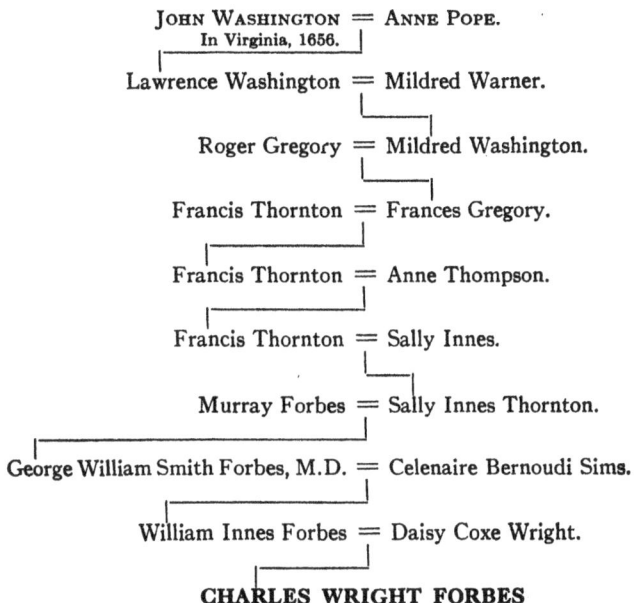

JOHN WASHINGTON = ANNE POPE.
In Virginia, 1656.

Lawrence Washington = Mildred Warner.

Roger Gregory = Mildred Washington.

Francis Thornton = Frances Gregory.

Francis Thornton = Anne Thompson.

Francis Thornton = Sally Innes.

Murray Forbes = Sally Innes Thornton.

George William Smith Forbes, M.D. = Celenaire Bernoudi Sims.

William Innes Forbes = Daisy Coxe Wright.

CHARLES WRIGHT FORBES

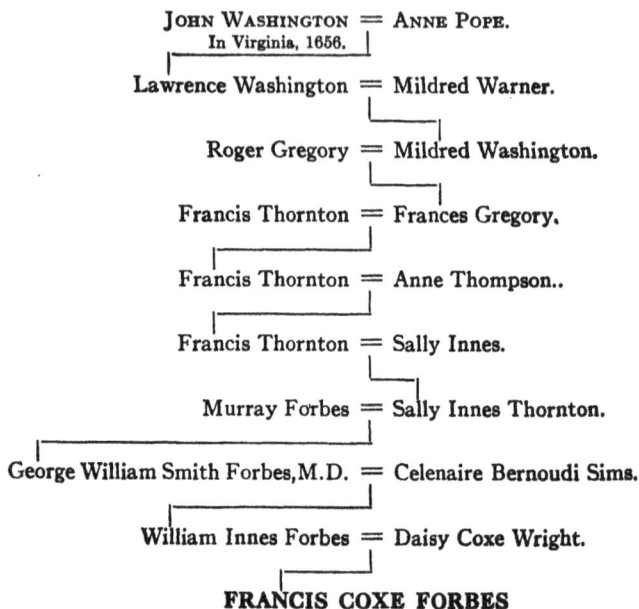

JOHN WASHINGTON = ANNE POPE.
In Virginia, 1656.

Lawrence Washington = Mildred Warner.

Roger Gregory = Mildred Washington.

Francis Thornton = Frances Gregory.

Francis Thornton = Anne Thompson..

Francis Thornton = Sally Innes.

Murray Forbes = Sally Innes Thornton.

George William Smith Forbes, M.D. = Celenaire Bernoudi Sims.

William Innes Forbes = Daisy Coxe Wright.

FRANCIS COXE FORBES

JOHN WASHINGTON = ANNE POPE.
In Virginia, 1656.

Lawrence Washington = Mildred Warner.

Roger Gregory = Mildred Washington.

Francis Thornton = Frances Gregory.

Francis Thornton = Anne Thompson.

Francis Thornton = Sally Innes.

Murray Forbes = Sally Innes Thornton.

George William Smith Forbes, M.D. = Celenaire Bernoudi Sims.

WILLIAM INNES FORBES

Forbes

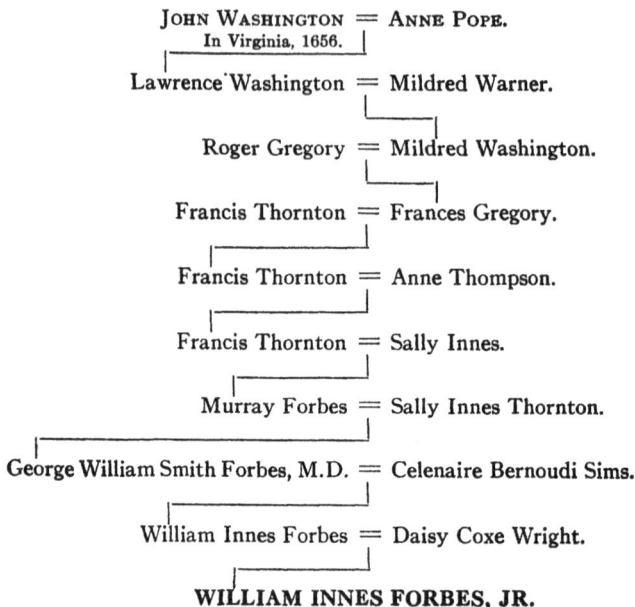

JOHN WASHINGTON = ANNE POPE.
In Virginia, 1656.

Lawrence Washington = Mildred Warner.

Roger Gregory = Mildred Washington.

Francis Thornton = Frances Gregory.

Francis Thornton = Anne Thompson.

Francis Thornton = Sally Innes.

Murray Forbes = Sally Innes Thornton.

George William Smith Forbes, M.D. = Celenaire Bernoudi Sims.

William Innes Forbes = Daisy Coxe Wright.

WILLIAM INNES FORBES, JR.

Fornance

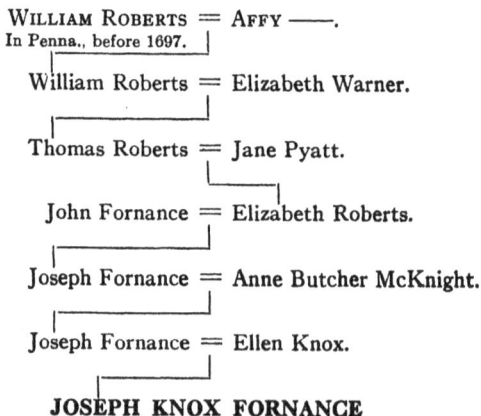

WILLIAM ROBERTS = AFFY ——.
In Penna., before 1697.

William Roberts = Elizabeth Warner.

Thomas Roberts = Jane Pyatt.

John Fornance = Elizabeth Roberts.

Joseph Fornance = Anne Butcher McKnight.

Joseph Fornance = Ellen Knox.

JOSEPH KNOX FORNANCE

WILLIAM REDFIN = REBECCA ——.
In Mass., 1642.

James Redfield (Redfin) = Elizabeth How.

Theophilus Redfield = Priscilla Grinnell.

William Redfield = Elizabeth Starr.

Samuel Redfield = Ann Heritage.

William Redfield = Deborah Skill.

John W. Frazier = Anna Maria Redfield.

BERTRAM GRAEME FRAZIER

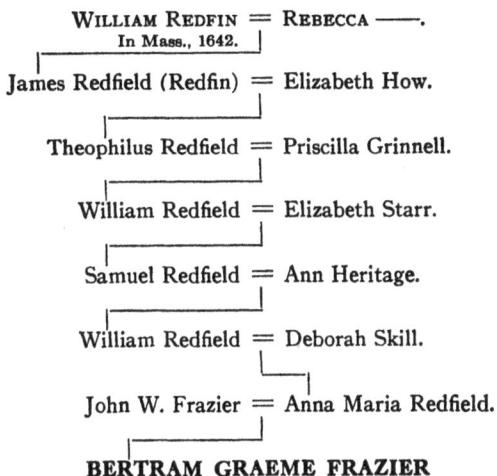

SUPPLEMENTALS

Ninth in descent from William Mullins, in Plymouth Colony, 1620.
Eighth in descent from John Alden, in Plymouth Colony, 1620.
Eighth in descent from Matthew Grinnell, in Rhode Island, 1638.
Eighth in descent from John Pabodie, in Plymouth Colony, 1636-7.
Eighth in descent from William Wodell, in Rhode Island, 1642.

Frazier

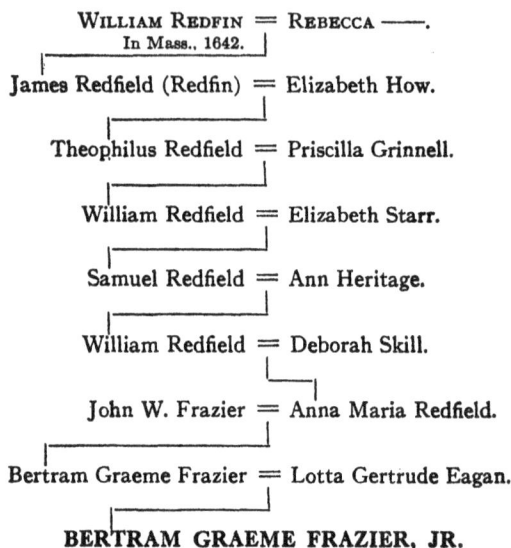

WILLIAM REDFIN = REBECCA ——.
In Mass., 1642.

James Redfield (Redfin) = Elizabeth How.

Theophilus Redfield = Priscilla Grinnell.

William Redfield = Elizabeth Starr.

Samuel Redfield = Ann Heritage.

William Redfield = Deborah Skill.

John W. Frazier = Anna Maria Redfield.

Bertram Graeme Frazier = Lotta Gertrude Eagan.

BERTRAM GRAEME FRAZIER, JR.

Fuller

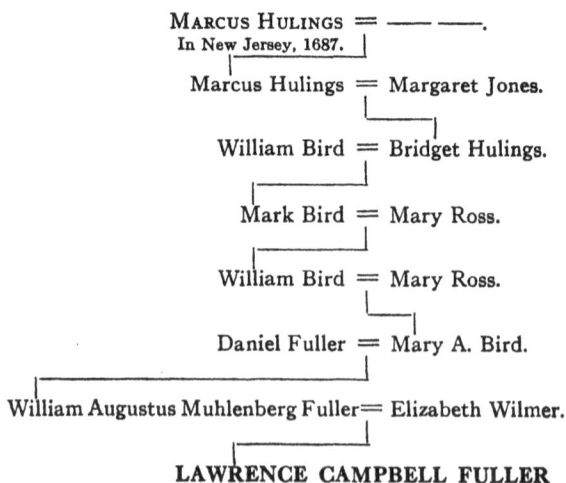

MARCUS HULINGS = —— ——.
In New Jersey, 1687.

Marcus Hulings = Margaret Jones.

William Bird = Bridget Hulings.

Mark Bird = Mary Ross.

William Bird = Mary Ross.

Daniel Fuller = Mary A. Bird.

William Augustus Muhlenberg Fuller= Elizabeth Wilmer.

LAWRENCE CAMPBELL FULLER

𝔉uller

MARCUS HULINGS = —— ——.
In New Jersey, 1687.

Marcus Hulings = Margaret Jones.

William Bird = Bridget Hulings.

Mark Bird = Mary Ross.

William Bird = Mary Ross.

Daniel Fuller = Mary A. Bird.

William Augustus Muhlenberg Fuller= Elizabeth Wilmer.

Lawrence Campbell Fuller = Constance Peabody.

LAWRENCE CAMPBELL FULLER, JR.

𝔉uller

MARCUS HULINGS = —— ——.
In New Jersey, 1687.

Marcus Hulings = Margaret Jones.

William Bird = Bridget Hulings.

Mark Bird = Mary Ross.

William Bird = Mary Ross.

Daniel Fuller = Mary A. Bird.

William Augustus Muhlenberg Fuller= Elizabeth Wilmer.

WILLIAM AUGUSTUS MUHLENBERG FULLER

𝔉unk

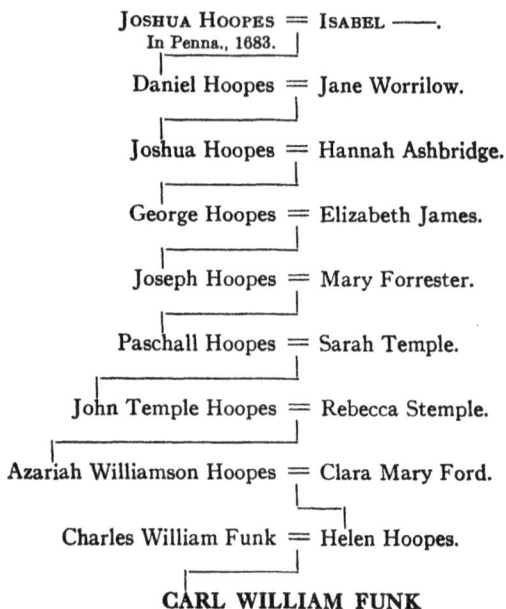

JOSHUA HOOPES = ISABEL ——.
In Penna., 1683.

Daniel Hoopes = Jane Worrilow.

Joshua Hoopes = Hannah Ashbridge.

George Hoopes = Elizabeth James.

Joseph Hoopes = Mary Forrester.

Paschall Hoopes = Sarah Temple.

John Temple Hoopes = Rebecca Stemple.

Azariah Williamson Hoopes = Clara Mary Ford.

Charles William Funk = Helen Hoopes.

CARL WILLIAM FUNK

𝔊arrett

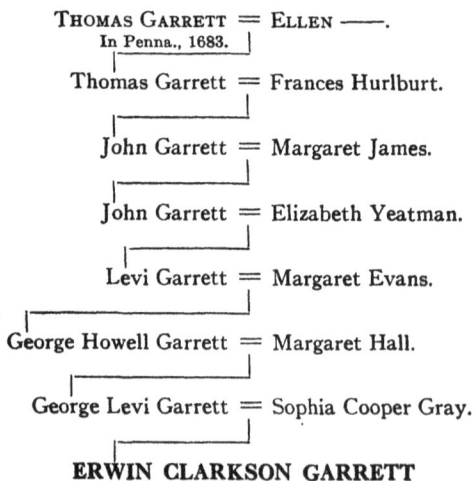

THOMAS GARRETT = ELLEN ——.
In Penna., 1683.

Thomas Garrett = Frances Hurlburt.

John Garrett = Margaret James.

John Garrett = Elizabeth Yeatman.

Levi Garrett = Margaret Evans.

George Howell Garrett = Margaret Hall.

George Levi Garrett = Sophia Cooper Gray.

ERWIN CLARKSON GARRETT

SUPPLEMENTALS

Ninth in descent from Henry Gibbons, in Penna., 1682.

Eighth in descent from John Ashmead, in Penna., 1682.

Eighth in descent from Gerrit Bancker, in New Netherland, 1657.

Eighth in descent from Johannes De Peyster, in New Netherland, 1649.

Eighth in descent from William Powell, in Penna., 1696.

Eighth in descent from Samuel Sellers, in Penna., 1682.

Eighth in descent from Gerrite Goosen Van Schaick, in New Netherland, 1649.

Seventh in descent from Matthew Clarkson, in New York, 1690.

Seventh in descent from Thomas Shute, in Penna., 1690.

Elected
1929

𝕲𝖆𝖙𝖊𝖘

No.
459

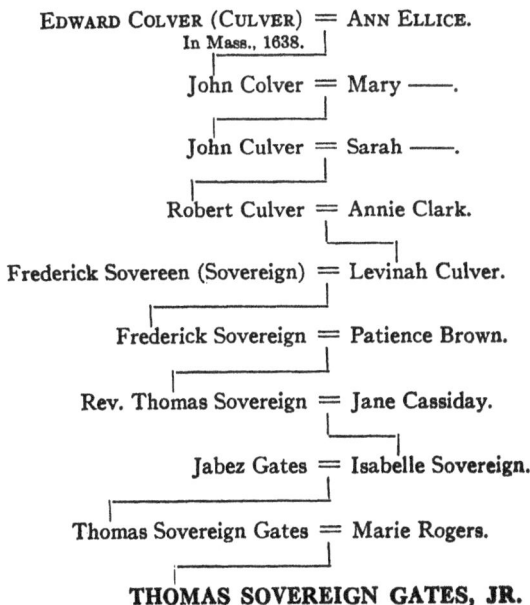

EDWARD COLVER (CULVER) = ANN ELLICE.
In Mass., 1638.

John Colver = Mary ——.

John Culver = Sarah ——.

Robert Culver = Annie Clark.

Frederick Sovereen (Sovereign) = Levinah Culver.

Frederick Sovereign = Patience Brown.

Rev. Thomas Sovereign = Jane Cassiday.

Jabez Gates = Isabelle Sovereign.

Thomas Sovereign Gates = Marie Rogers.

THOMAS SOVEREIGN GATES, JR.

⚙ïllíngham

YEAMANS GILLINGHAM = MARY TAYLOR.
In Penna., 1690.

James Gillingham = Martha Canby.

Yeamans Gillingham = Bridget Moon.

Joseph Gillingham = Rebecca Harrold.

Samuel Harrold Gillingham = Louisa Maria Hubbs.

Frank Clemens Gillingham = Tacy Shoemaker Morris.

HARROLD EDGAR GILLINGHAM

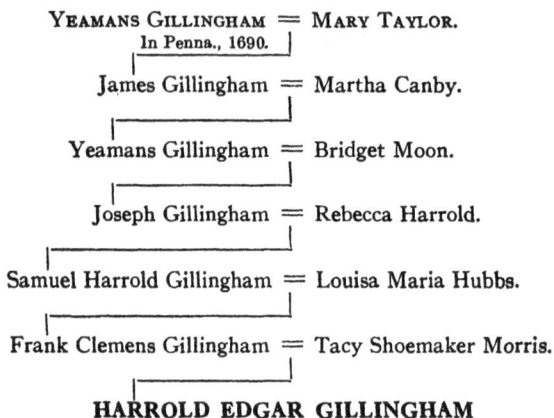

SUPPLEMENTALS

Tenth in descent from Henry Chamberlain, in Mass., 1638.
Ninth in descent from William Almy, in Mass., 1631.
Ninth in descent from Nicholas Brown, in Rhode Island, 1638.
Ninth in descent from Thomas Cornell, in Mass., 1638.
Ninth in descent from Toby Leech, in Penna., 1682.
Ninth in descent from Edward Patterson, in Mass., 1643.
Ninth in descent from Richard Wall, in Penna., 1682.
Eighth in descent from Henry Comly, in Penna., 1683.
Eighth in descent from Peter Ellet, in Penna., 1686.
Eighth in descent from Robert Heaton, in Penna., 1682.
Eighth in descent from William Lawrence, in East Jersey, 1666.
Eighth in descent from William North, in New Jersey, 1687.
Eighth in descent from Thomas Potter, in Rhode Island, 1664.
Eighth in descent from Abraham Shotwell, in East Jersey, 1665.
Eighth in descent from John Tilton, in New York, 1640.
Eighth in descent from Robert White, in New York, 1694.
Seventh in descent from Samuel Allen, in Penna., 1681.
Seventh in descent from Henry Baker, in Penna., 1684.
Seventh in descent from Elizabeth Burton, in New York, 1679.
Seventh in descent from Peter Clever, in Penna., 1691.
Seventh in descent from Thomas Croasdale, in Penna., 1682.
Seventh in descent from Agnes Hathernthwaite, in Penna., 1682.
Seventh in descent from John Kirk, in Penna., 1687.
Seventh in descent from John Laing, in East Jersey, 1685.
Seventh in descent from William Levering, in Penna., 1685.
Seventh in descent from Robert Lucas, in Penna., 1679.

Seventh in descent from Lewis Morris, in New Jersey, 1689.
Seventh in descent from Benjamin Scott, in West Jersey, 1677.
Seventh in descent from George Shoemaker, in Penna., 1686.
Seventh in descent from Reynier Tyson, in Penna., 1683.
Seventh in descent from Nicholas Waln, in Penna., 1682.
Seventh in descent from John Willson, in New Jersey, 1676–77.
Sixth in descent from Mary Bradwell, in Penna., 1685.
Sixth in descent from Thomas Canby, in Penna., 1684.
Sixth in descent from Sarah Jarvis, in Penna., 1693.
Sixth in descent from William Smith, in Penna., 1682.
Sixth in descent from Stephen Wilson, in Penna., 1692.

Elected
1931

Green

No.
536

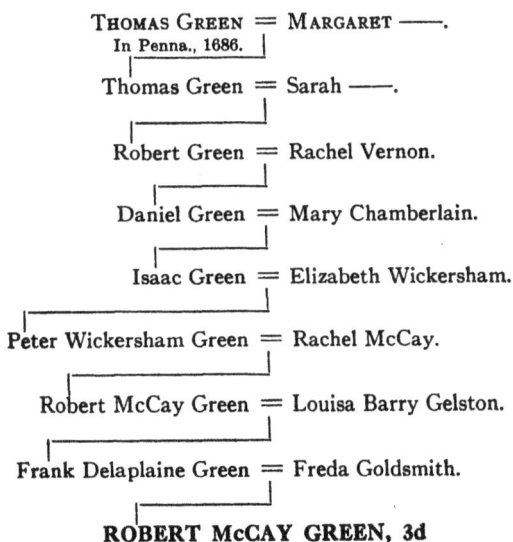

THOMAS GREEN = MARGARET ——.
In Penna., 1686.

Thomas Green = Sarah ——.

Robert Green = Rachel Vernon.

Daniel Green = Mary Chamberlain.

Isaac Green = Elizabeth Wickersham.

Peter Wickersham Green = Rachel McCay.

Robert McCay Green = Louisa Barry Gelston.

Frank Delaplaine Green = Freda Goldsmith.

ROBERT McCAY GREEN, 3d

RICHARD STOCKTON = ABIGAIL ———.
In Long Island, 1656.

Richard Ridgway = Abigail Stockton.

Job Ridgway = Rebecca Butcher.

Solomon Ridgway = Mary Burr.

Benjamin Earl Ridgway = Prudence Borton.

Benjamin Ridgway = Margaret Bispham Fenimore.

William Hulme Grundy = Mary Lamb Ridgway.

JOSEPH RIDGWAY GRUNDY

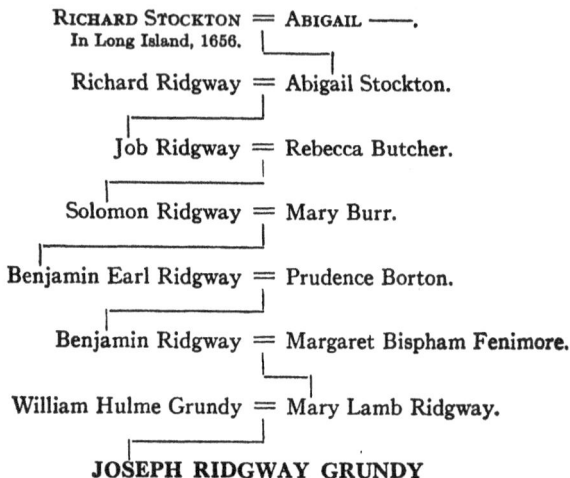

SUPPLEMENTALS

Ninth in descent from Thomas Philbrick, in Mass., 1636.
Eighth in descent from William Cooper, in West Jersey, 1679.
Eighth in descent from Thomas Croasdale, in Penna., 1682.
Eighth in descent from Isaac Perkins, in New Hampshire, 1642.
Seventh in descent from Giles Knight, in Penna., 1682.
Seventh in descent from Mahlon Stacy, in West Jersey, 1678.
Seventh in descent from John Woolston, in West Jersey, 1677.
Sixth in descent from John Butcher, in West Jersey, 1680.
Sixth in descent from Richard Ridgway, in West Jersey, 1679.

ð’ð®ðžð«ð§ð¬ðžð²

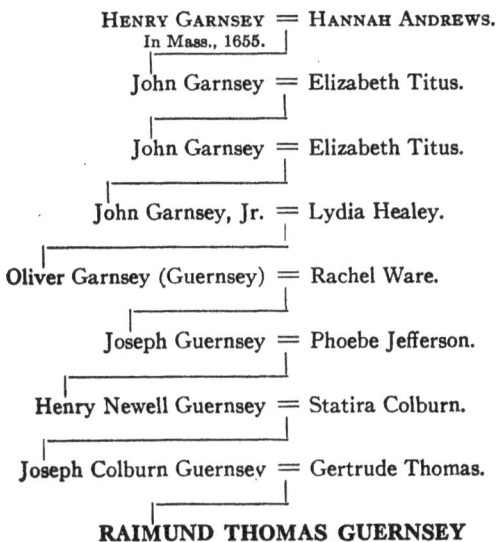

HENRY GARNSEY = HANNAH ANDREWS.
In Mass., 1655.

John Garnsey = Elizabeth Titus.

John Garnsey = Elizabeth Titus.

John Garnsey, Jr. = Lydia Healey.

Oliver Garnsey (Guernsey) = Rachel Ware.

Joseph Guernsey = Phoebe Jefferson.

Henry Newell Guernsey = Statira Colburn.

Joseph Colburn Guernsey = Gertrude Thomas.

RAIMUND THOMAS GUERNSEY

ð‡ð€ð¢ð§ðžð¬

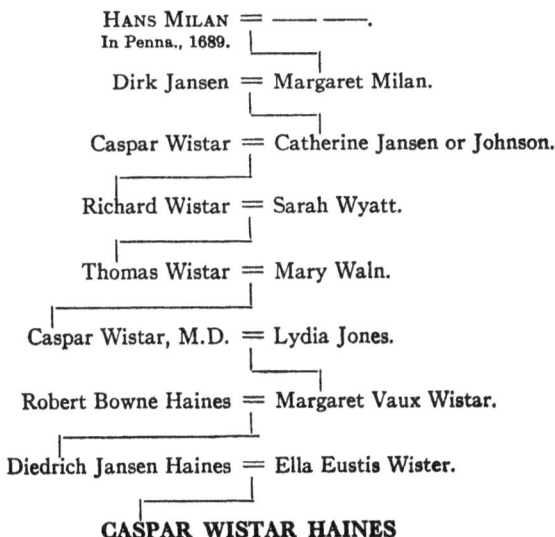

HANS MILAN = —— ——.
In Penna., 1689.

Dirk Jansen = Margaret Milan.

Caspar Wistar = Catherine Jansen or Johnson.

Richard Wistar = Sarah Wyatt.

Thomas Wistar = Mary Waln.

Caspar Wistar, M.D. = Lydia Jones.

Robert Bowne Haines = Margaret Vaux Wistar.

Diedrich Jansen Haines = Ella Eustis Wister.

CASPAR WISTAR HAINES

𝕳anna

WILLIAM ROBERTS = AFFY ——.
In Penna., 1697.

William Roberts = Elizabeth Warner.

Thomas Roberts = Jane Pyatt.

George Vanderslice = Janette Roberts.

Samuel Mickle Hopper = Deborah Lavina Vanderslice.

William Brantly Hanna = Mary Vanderslice Hopper.

MEREDITH HANNA

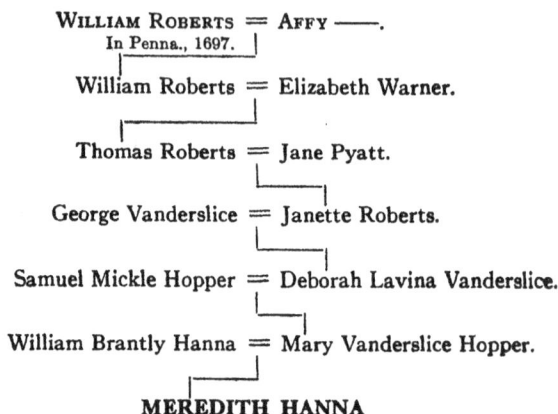

SUPPLEMENTALS

Ninth in descent from Joseph Andrews, in Mass., 1635.
Ninth in descent from John Cooper, in Mass., 1635.
Eighth in descent from Ellis Cook, in Long Island, 1644.
Eighth in descent from John Denn, in West Jersey, 1678.
Eighth in descent from Peter Ellet, in Penna., 1686.
Eighth in descent from Hans Peter Umstat, in Penna., 1685.
Eighth in descent from William Warner, in Penna., 1679.
Seventh in descent from Richard Hancock, in West Jersey, 1675.
Seventh in descent from John Kirk, in Penna., 1687.
Sixth in descent from Thomas Garwood, in West Jersey, 1685.
Sixth in descent from John Hopper, in New Amsterdam, 1675.
Sixth in descent from Hendrick Pannebecker, in Penna., before 1699.

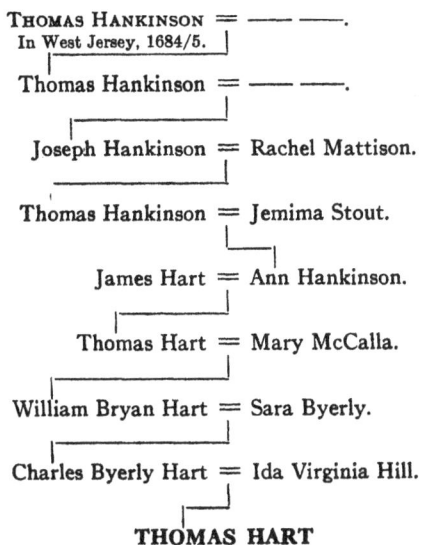

THOMAS HANKINSON = —— ——.
In West Jersey, 1684/5.

Thomas Hankinson = —— ——.

Joseph Hankinson = Rachel Mattison.

Thomas Hankinson = Jemima Stout.

James Hart = Ann Hankinson.

Thomas Hart = Mary McCalla.

William Bryan Hart = Sara Byerly.

Charles Byerly Hart = Ida Virginia Hill.

THOMAS HART

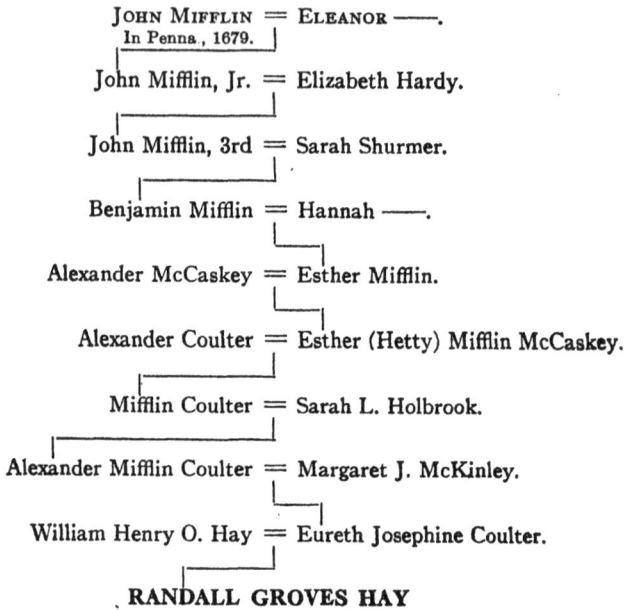

JOHN MIFFLIN = ELEANOR ———.
In Penna., 1679.

John Mifflin, Jr. = Elizabeth Hardy.

John Mifflin, 3rd = Sarah Shurmer.

Benjamin Mifflin = Hannah ———.

Alexander McCaskey = Esther Mifflin.

Alexander Coulter = Esther (Hetty) Mifflin McCaskey.

Mifflin Coulter = Sarah L. Holbrook.

Alexander Mifflin Coulter = Margaret J. McKinley.

William Henry O. Hay = Eureth Josephine Coulter.

RANDALL GROVES HAY

Henderson

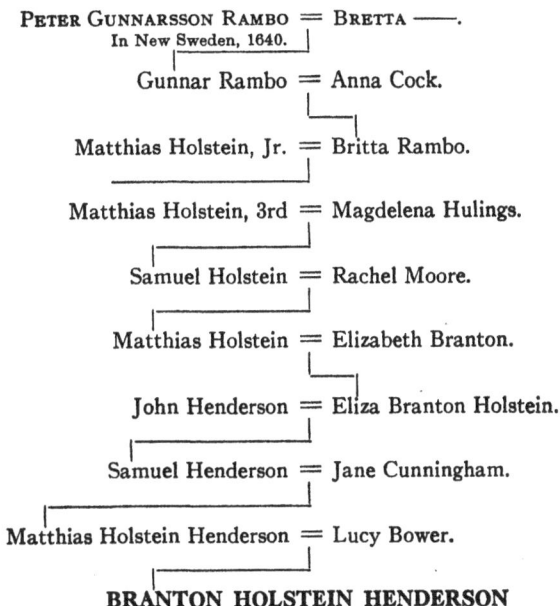

PETER GUNNARSSON RAMBO = BRETTA ——.
In New Sweden, 1640.

Gunnar Rambo = Anna Cock.

Matthias Holstein, Jr. = Britta Rambo.

Matthias Holstein, 3rd = Magdelena Hulings.

Samuel Holstein = Rachel Moore.

Matthias Holstein = Elizabeth Branton.

John Henderson = Eliza Branton Holstein.

Samuel Henderson = Jane Cunningham.

Matthias Holstein Henderson = Lucy Bower.

BRANTON HOLSTEIN HENDERSON

Henry

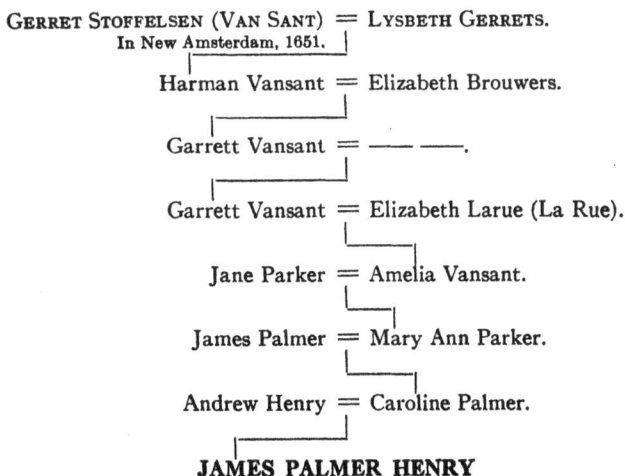

GERRET STOFFELSEN (VAN SANT) = LYSBETH GERRETS.
In New Amsterdam, 1651.

Harman Vansant = Elizabeth Brouwers.

Garrett Vansant = —— ——.

Garrett Vansant = Elizabeth Larue (La Rue).

Jane Parker = Amelia Vansant.

James Palmer = Mary Ann Parker.

Andrew Henry = Caroline Palmer.

JAMES PALMER HENRY

𝕳erkness

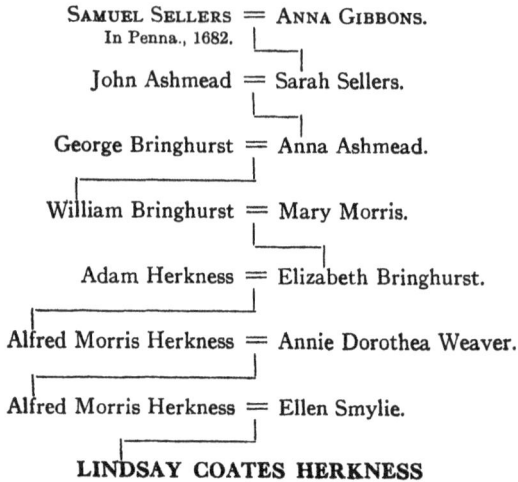

SAMUEL SELLERS = ANNA GIBBONS.
In Penna., 1682.

John Ashmead = Sarah Sellers.

George Bringhurst = Anna Ashmead.

William Bringhurst = Mary Morris.

Adam Herkness = Elizabeth Bringhurst.

Alfred Morris Herkness = Annie Dorothea Weaver.

Alfred Morris Herkness = Ellen Smylie.

LINDSAY COATES HERKNESS

ℌerndon

REV. WILLIAM WILKINSON = NAOMI ——.
In Virginia, 1635.

Thomas Dent = Rebecca Wilkinson.

Edmund Howard = Margaret Dent.

George Howard = Mrs. Sarah Hall.

William Woodcraft = Mary Howard.

William Jordan Hall = Sophia Woodcraft.

Adam Dale = Polly Hall.

Robert Turner = Sophia Woodcraft Dale.

Cotesworth Pinckney Herndon = Mahala Hall Turner.

John Goodwin Herndon = Florence Early Linton.

JOHN GOODWIN HERNDON

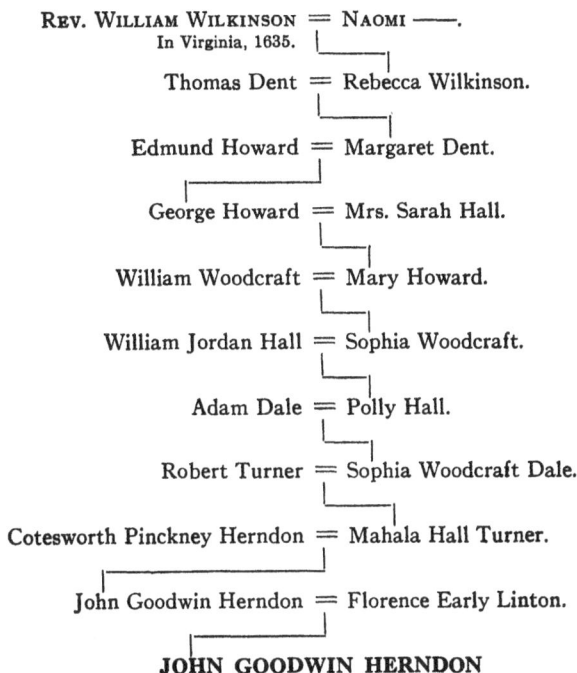

SUPPLEMENTALS

Eighth in descent from William Herndon, in Virginia, 1672.
Seventh in descent from James Dale, in Maryland, 1699.
Seventh in descent from John McKnitt, in Maryland, 1685.

Hinkson

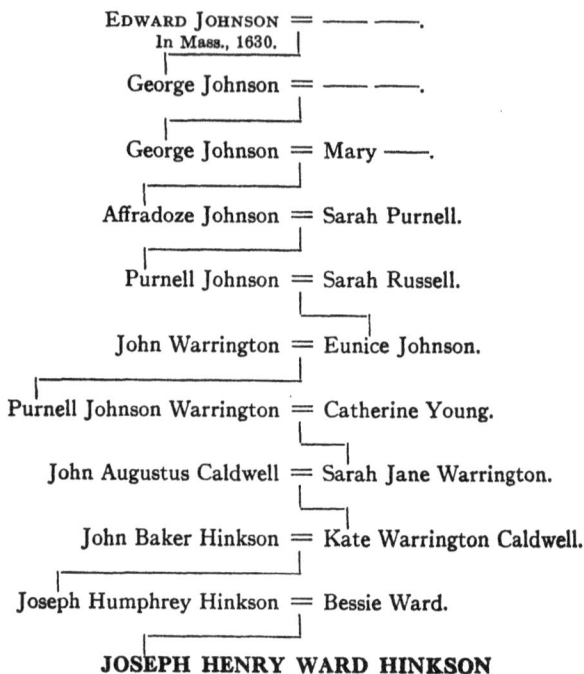

EDWARD JOHNSON = —— ——.
In Mass., 1630.

George Johnson = —— ——.

George Johnson = Mary ——.

Affradoze Johnson = Sarah Purnell.

Purnell Johnson = Sarah Russell.

John Warrington = Eunice Johnson.

Purnell Johnson Warrington = Catherine Young.

John Augustus Caldwell = Sarah Jane Warrington.

John Baker Hinkson = Kate Warrington Caldwell.

Joseph Humphrey Hinkson = Bessie Ward.

JOSEPH HENRY WARD HINKSON

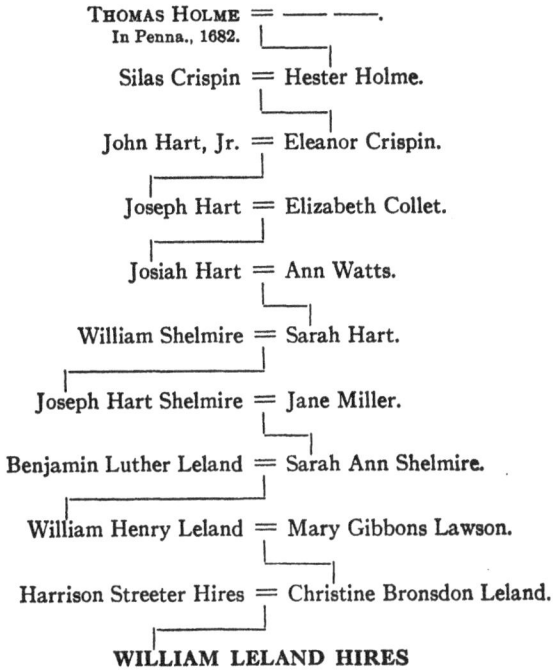

THOMAS HOLME = —— ——.
In Penna., 1682.

Silas Crispin = Hester Holme.

John Hart, Jr. = Eleanor Crispin.

Joseph Hart = Elizabeth Collet.

Josiah Hart = Ann Watts.

William Shelmire = Sarah Hart.

Joseph Hart Shelmire = Jane Miller.

Benjamin Luther Leland = Sarah Ann Shelmire.

William Henry Leland = Mary Gibbons Lawson.

Harrison Streeter Hires = Christine Bronsdon Leland.

WILLIAM LELAND HIRES

𝕳offman

WILLIAM JENKINS = ELIZABETH GRIFFITH.
In Penna., 1686.

Thomas Paschall = Margaret Jenkins.

William Paschall = Hannah (Lloyd) Roberts.

Joseph Sellers = Hannah Paschall.

William Rose = Hannah Sellers.

Jacob Hoffman = Hannah Rose.

Sellers Hoffman = Jessie Watson.

BENJAMIN ROSE HOFFMAN

𝕳𝖔𝖌𝖊𝖑𝖆𝖓𝖉

CORNELIUS DIERCKSEN HOOCHLANDT = ALTIE ARIENS.
In New Amsterdam, 1638.

Dirck Cornelius Hoochlandt = Elizabeth Rapalje.

Joris Hogeland = Catherine Richou.

Derck Hogeland = Maria Slot.

Daniel Hogeland = Elsie Krewsen.

Derrick K. Hogeland = Johanna Stevens.

Daniel Hogeland = Cornelia Van Sant.

Henry Hogeland = Elizabeth Randall.

John F. Hogeland = Anna Starm.

William Henry Hogeland = Ethel Miriam Freas.

RUSSELL FREAS HOGELAND

𝔥𝔬𝔩𝔩𝔬𝔴𝔞𝔭

WILLIAM RITTENHOUSE = —— ——.
In Penna., 1688.

Nicholas Rittenhouse = Wilhelmina Dewees.

Hendrick Highley = Susanna Rittenhouse.

John Highley = Elizabeth Taney.

Jacob Highley = Sarah Roberts.

John Starr Holloway = Mary Highley.

James Ner Holloway = Clara Knight.

JAMES DONALD HOLLOWAY

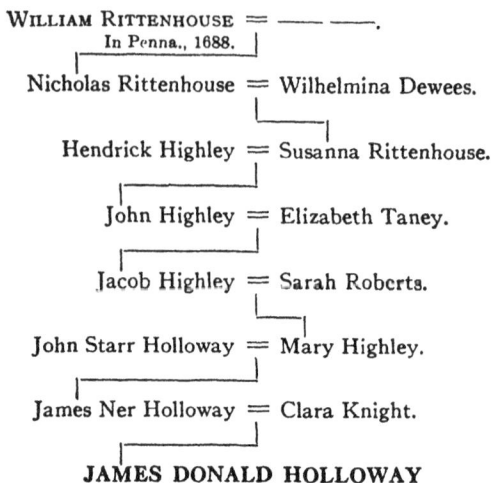

SUPPLEMENTALS

Ninth in descent from Peter Wright, in Plymouth Colony, 1638.
Eighth in descent from Samuel Andrews, in Long Island, 1661.
Eighth in descent from Thomas Butcher, in West Jersey, 1682.
Eighth in descent from John Day, in West Jersey, 1682.
Seventh in descent from Gerhard Hendricks Dewees, in Penna., circa 1690.
Seventh in descent from Thomas Knight, in Penna., 1686.
Seventh in descent from William Sharp, in West Jersey, 1694.

WILLIAM RITTENHOUSE = ―― ――.
In Penna., 1688.

Nicholas Rittenhouse = Wilhelmina Dewees.

Hendrick Highley = Susanna Rittenhouse.

John Highley = Elizabeth Taney.

Jacob Highley = Sarah Roberts.

John Starr Holloway = Mary Highley.

James Ner Holloway = Clara Knight.

JEROME KNIGHT HOLLOWAY

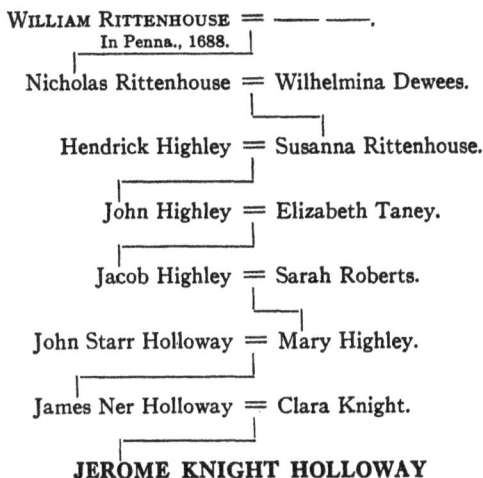

SUPPLEMENTALS

Ninth in descent from Peter Wright, in Plymouth Colony, 1638.
Eighth in descent from Samuel Andrews, in Long Island, 1661.
Eighth in descent from Thomas Butcher, in West Jersey, 1682.
Eighth in descent from John Day, in West Jersey, 1682.
Seventh in descent from Gerhard Hendricks Dewees, in Penna., circa 1690.
Seventh in descent from Thomas Knight, in Penna., 1686.
Seventh in descent from William Sharp, in West Jersey, 1694.

Hood

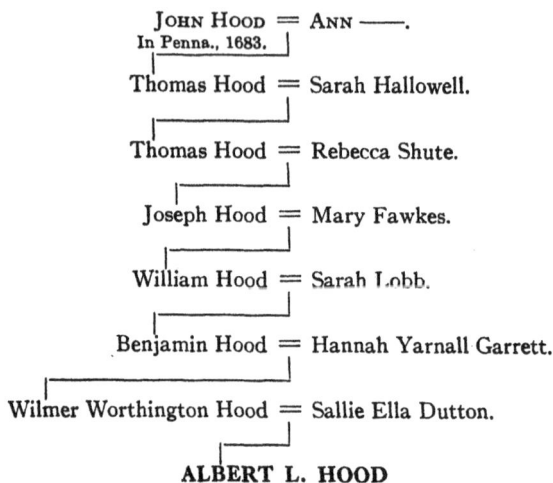

JOHN HOOD = ANN ———.
In Penna., 1683.

Thomas Hood = Sarah Hallowell.

Thomas Hood = Rebecca Shute.

Joseph Hood = Mary Fawkes.

William Hood = Sarah Lobb.

Benjamin Hood = Hannah Yarnall Garrett.

Wilmer Worthington Hood = Sallie Ella Dutton.

ALBERT L. HOOD

Hoopes

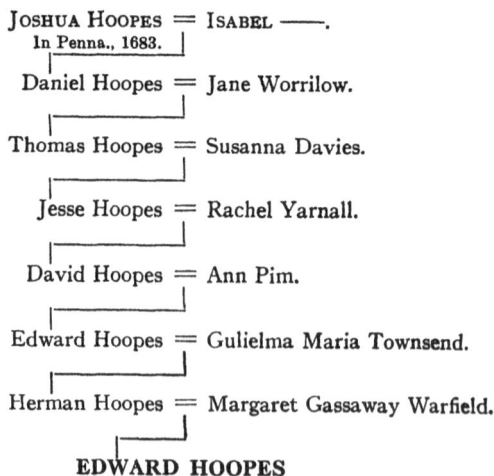

JOSHUA HOOPES = ISABEL ———.
In Penna., 1683.

Daniel Hoopes = Jane Worrilow.

Thomas Hoopes = Susanna Davies.

Jesse Hoopes = Rachel Yarnall.

David Hoopes = Ann Pim.

Edward Hoopes = Gulielma Maria Townsend.

Herman Hoopes = Margaret Gassaway Warfield.

EDWARD HOOPES

Hopkinson

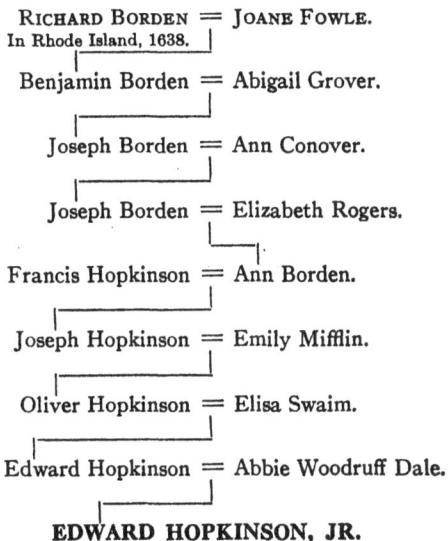

RICHARD BORDEN = JOANE FOWLE.
In Rhode Island, 1638.

Benjamin Borden = Abigail Grover.

Joseph Borden = Ann Conover.

Joseph Borden = Elizabeth Rogers.

Francis Hopkinson = Ann Borden.

Joseph Hopkinson = Emily Mifflin.

Oliver Hopkinson = Elisa Swaim.

Edward Hopkinson = Abbie Woodruff Dale.

EDWARD HOPKINSON, JR.

Hopper

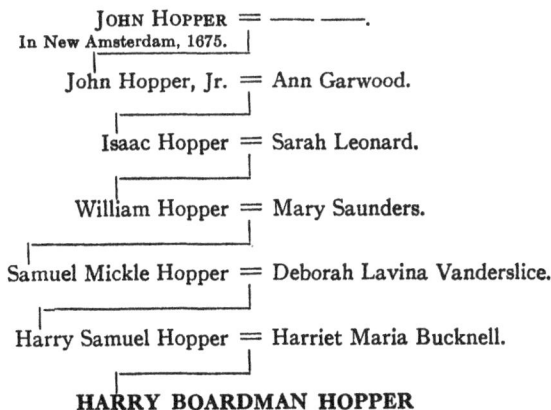

JOHN HOPPER = —— ——.
In New Amsterdam, 1675.

John Hopper, Jr. = Ann Garwood.

Isaac Hopper = Sarah Leonard.

William Hopper = Mary Saunders.

Samuel Mickle Hopper = Deborah Lavina Vanderslice.

Harry Samuel Hopper = Harriet Maria Bucknell.

HARRY BOARDMAN HOPPER

𝕳oward

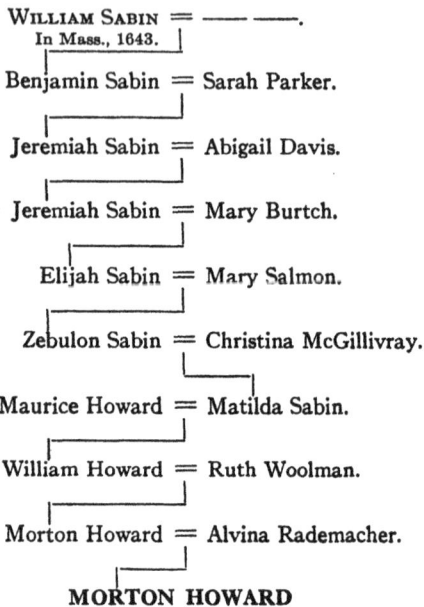

WILLIAM SABIN = —— ——.
In Mass., 1643.

Benjamin Sabin = Sarah Parker.

Jeremiah Sabin = Abigail Davis.

Jeremiah Sabin = Mary Burtch.

Elijah Sabin = Mary Salmon.

Zebulon Sabin = Christina McGillivray.

Maurice Howard = Matilda Sabin.

William Howard = Ruth Woolman.

Morton Howard = Alvina Rademacher.

MORTON HOWARD

Howard-Smith

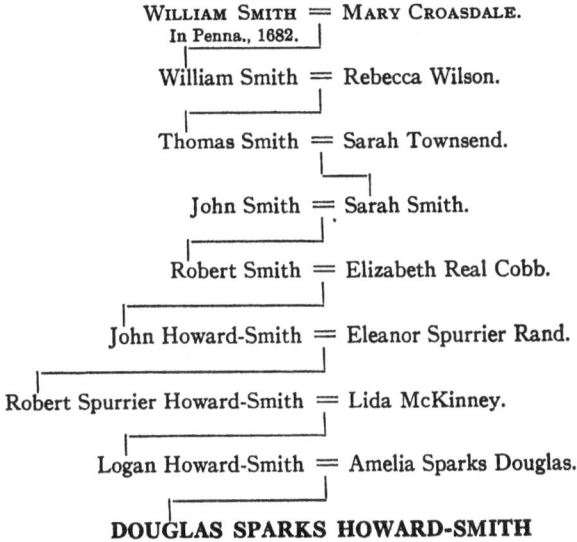

WILLIAM SMITH = MARY CROASDALE.
In Penna., 1682.

William Smith = Rebecca Wilson.

Thomas Smith = Sarah Townsend.

John Smith = Sarah Smith.

Robert Smith = Elizabeth Real Cobb.

John Howard-Smith = Eleanor Spurrier Rand.

Robert Spurrier Howard-Smith = Lida McKinney.

Logan Howard-Smith = Amelia Sparks Douglas.

DOUGLAS SPARKS HOWARD-SMITH

Howell

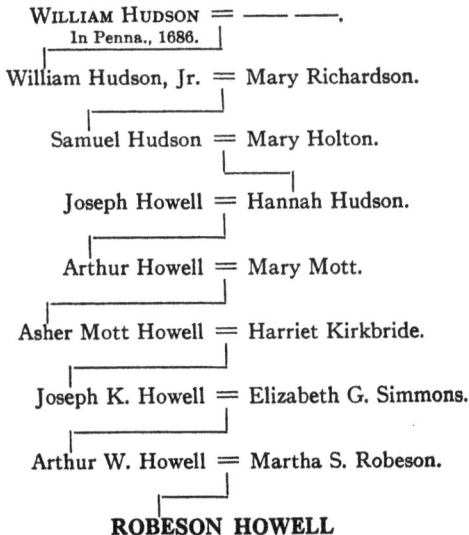

WILLIAM HUDSON = ——— ———.
In Penna., 1686.

William Hudson, Jr. = Mary Richardson.

Samuel Hudson = Mary Holton.

Joseph Howell = Hannah Hudson.

Arthur Howell = Mary Mott.

Asher Mott Howell = Harriet Kirkbride.

Joseph K. Howell = Elizabeth G. Simmons.

Arthur W. Howell = Martha S. Robeson.

ROBESON HOWELL

𝕳𝖚𝖊𝖕

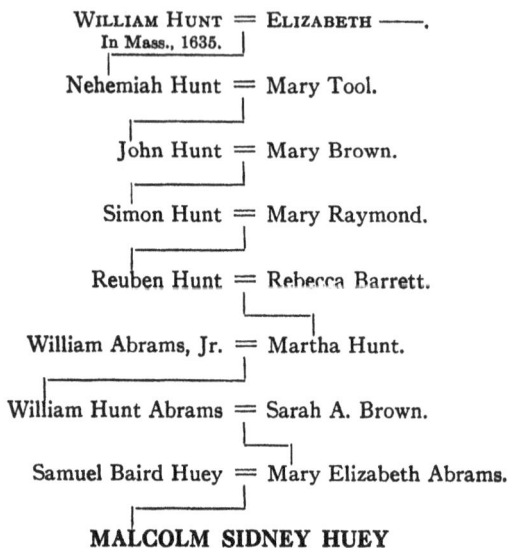

WILLIAM HUNT = ELIZABETH ———.
In Mass., 1635.

Nehemiah Hunt = Mary Tool.

John Hunt = Mary Brown.

Simon Hunt = Mary Raymond.

Reuben Hunt = Rebecca Barrett.

William Abrams, Jr. = Martha Hunt.

William Hunt Abrams = Sarah A. Brown.

Samuel Baird Huey = Mary Elizabeth Abrams.

MALCOLM SIDNEY HUEY

𝕳urlburt

THOMAS HURLBURT = MARY ——.
In Conn., 1637.

Nathan Hurlburt = Mary Blinn.

Gideon Hurlburt = Mary Deming.

Jeremiah Hurlburt = Esther Thompson.

Gideon Hurlburt = Ann Beach.

Ira Hurlburt = —— ——.

William Frederick Hurlburt = Adaline Eaton.

Henry Oscar Hurlburt = Susan Jane Butler.

William Henry Hurlburt = Emily Grant Merritt.

WILLIAM MERRITT HURLBURT

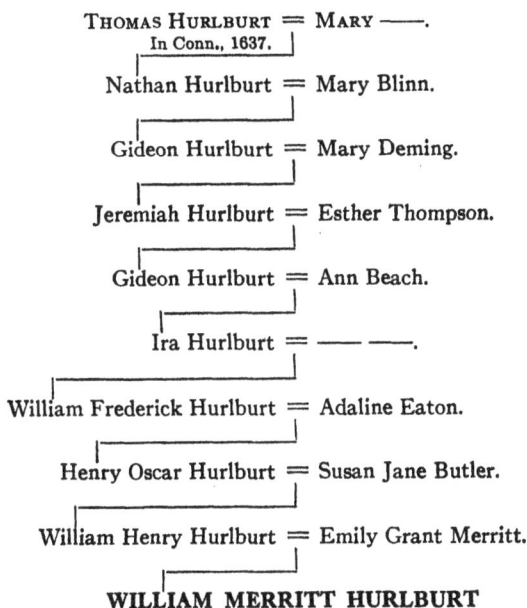

SUPPLEMENTALS

Tenth in descent from Isaac Allerton, in Plymouth Colony, 1620.
Ninth in descent from Peter Blinn, in Conn., 1675.
Ninth in descent from Thomas Merritt, in Conn., 1662.

EDWARD FOULKE = ELEANOR HUGH.
In Penna., 1698.

Hugh Foulke = Ann Williams.

Theophilus Foulke = Margaret Thomas.

Edward Jenkins = Sarah Foulke.

Charles Foulke Jenkins = Mary Lancaster.

Algernon Sidney Jenkins = Anna Maria Thomas.

Howard Malcolm Jenkins = Mary Anna Atkinson.

CHARLES FRANCIS JENKINS

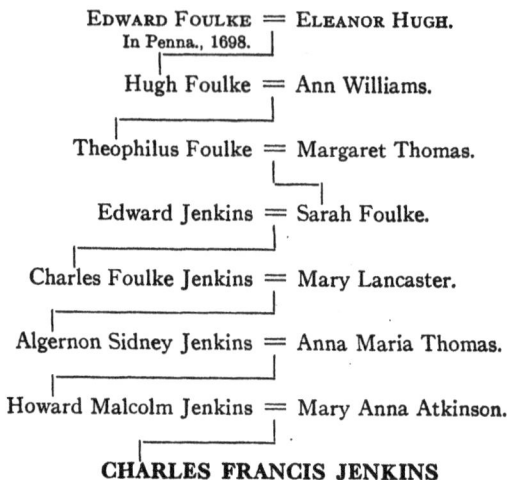

SUPPLEMENTALS

Tenth in descent from William Freeborn, in Mass., 1634.
Tenth in descent from Clement Weaver, in Rhode Island, 1655.
Ninth in descent from Matthew West, in Mass., 1636.
Eighth in descent from Thomas Dungan, in Rhode Island, 1637.
Eighth in descent from Peter Ellet, in Penna., 1686.
Eighth in descent from Thones Kunders, in Penna., 1683.
Eighth in descent from Jan Lucken, in Penna., 1683.
Eighth in descent from Evan Morris, in Penna., 1690.
Eighth in descent from Evan Thomas, in Penna., 1682.
Eighth in descent from Robert Whitton, in Penna., 1687.
Seventh in descent from George Brown, in Penna., 1679.
Seventh in descent from William Buckman, in Penna., 1682.
Seventh in descent from John Kirk, in Penna., 1687.
Seventh in descent from John Penquite, in Penna., 1683.
Seventh in descent from William Quinby, in Mass., 1638.
Seventh in descent from John Sotcher, in Penna., 1699.
Seventh in descent from Samuel Spencer, in Penna., 1699.
Seventh in descent from Reynier Tyson, in Penna., 1683.

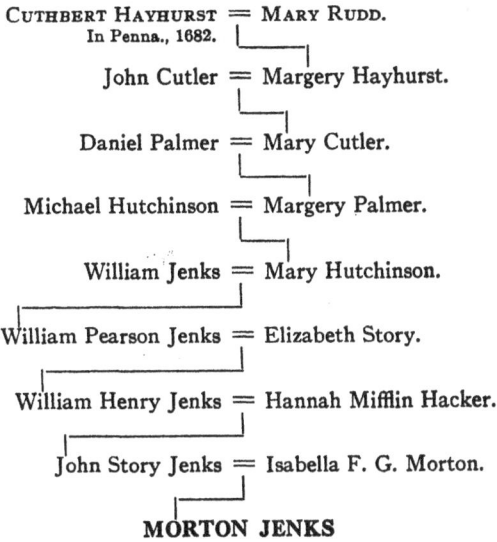

CUTHBERT HAYHURST = MARY RUDD.
In Penna., 1682.

John Cutler = Margery Hayhurst.

Daniel Palmer = Mary Cutler.

Michael Hutchinson = Margery Palmer.

William Jenks = Mary Hutchinson.

William Pearson Jenks = Elizabeth Story.

William Henry Jenks = Hannah Mifflin Hacker.

John Story Jenks = Isabella F. G. Morton.

MORTON JENKS

Johnson

CHRISTIAN BARENTSEN VAN HORN = JANNETJE JANS.
In New Amsterdam, 1653.

Barent Christiansen Van Horn = Geertje Dircks.

Christian Van Horn = Williamtje Van Dyck.

Henry Van Horn = Susanna Van Vleck.

Christian Van Horn = Sarah Van Zandt.

Isaiah Van Horn = Catherine Subers.

Aaron Winder = Sarah Van Horn.

Lawrence Johnson = Mary Winder.

Robert Winder Johnson = Rosalie Morris.

ROBERT WINDER JOHNSON, JR.

Jones

WILLIAM BRINTON = ANN BAGLEY.
In Penna., 1684.

William Brinton = Jane Thatcher.

Joseph Brinton = Mary Pierce.

William Jones = Mary Brinton.

Samuel Jones = Lydia Crossley.

William Jones = Catherine Ann Permar.

Charles Sharpless Jones = Rosina M. Herring.

CHARLES SHARPLESS JONES, JR.

𝕵𝖔𝖓𝖊𝖘

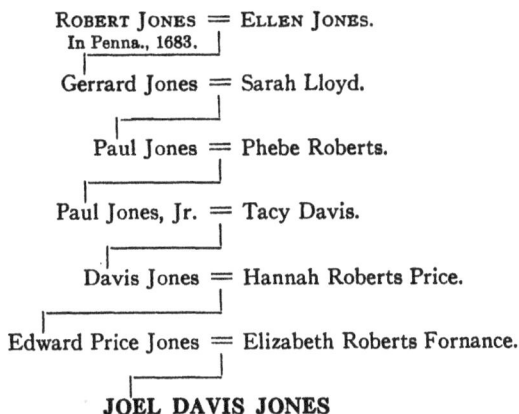

ROBERT JONES = ELLEN JONES.
In Penna., 1683.

Gerrard Jones = Sarah Lloyd.

Paul Jones = Phebe Roberts.

Paul Jones, Jr. = Tacy Davis.

Davis Jones = Hannah Roberts Price.

Edward Price Jones = Elizabeth Roberts Fornance.

JOEL DAVIS JONES

SUPPLEMENTAL

Seventh in descent from Edward Price or Rees, in Penna., 1682.

𝕵𝖚𝖒𝖕

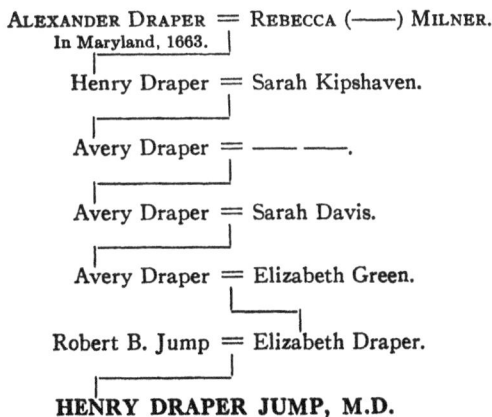

ALEXANDER DRAPER = REBECCA (——) MILNER.
In Maryland, 1663.

Henry Draper = Sarah Kipshaven.

Avery Draper = —— ——.

Avery Draper = Sarah Davis.

Avery Draper = Elizabeth Green.

Robert B. Jump = Elizabeth Draper.

HENRY DRAPER JUMP, M.D.

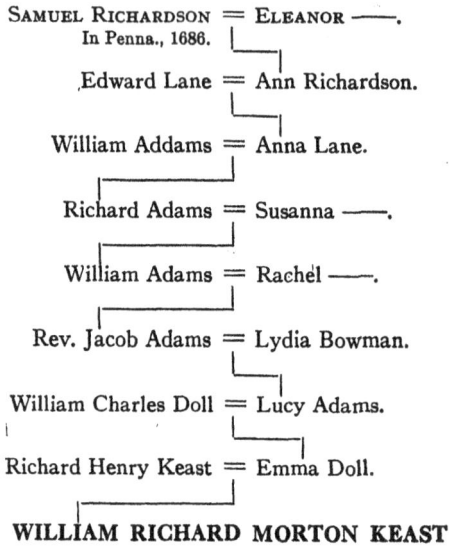

SAMUEL RICHARDSON = ELEANOR ——.
In Penna., 1686.

Edward Lane = Ann Richardson.

William Addams = Anna Lane.

Richard Adams = Susanna ——.

William Adams = Rachel ——.

Rev. Jacob Adams = Lydia Bowman.

William Charles Doll = Lucy Adams.

Richard Henry Keast = Emma Doll.

WILLIAM RICHARD MORTON KEAST

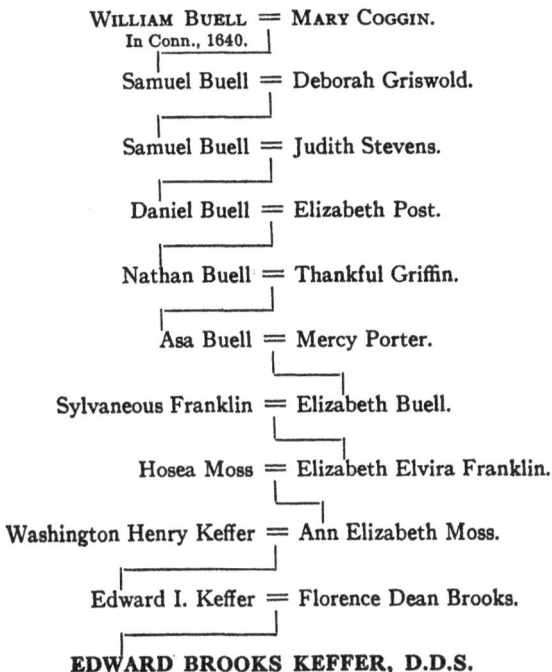

WILLIAM BUELL = MARY COGGIN.
In Conn., 1640.

Samuel Buell = Deborah Griswold.

Samuel Buell = Judith Stevens.

Daniel Buell = Elizabeth Post.

Nathan Buell = Thankful Griffin.

Asa Buell = Mercy Porter.

Sylvaneous Franklin = Elizabeth Buell.

Hosea Moss = Elizabeth Elvira Franklin.

Washington Henry Keffer = Ann Elizabeth Moss.

Edward I. Keffer = Florence Dean Brooks.

EDWARD BROOKS KEFFER, D.D.S.

RICHARD LIPPINCOTT = ABIGAIL ——.
In Mass., 1640.

Restore Lippincott = Hannah Shattock.

James Shinn = Abigail Lippincott.

Henry Reeves = Abigail Shinn.

Henry Reeves = Rachel Jess.

Abraham Reeves = Mary Matlack.

John James Lytle = Ann Reeves.

William Kennard = Ruth Anna Lytle.

WILLIAM KENNARD, JR.

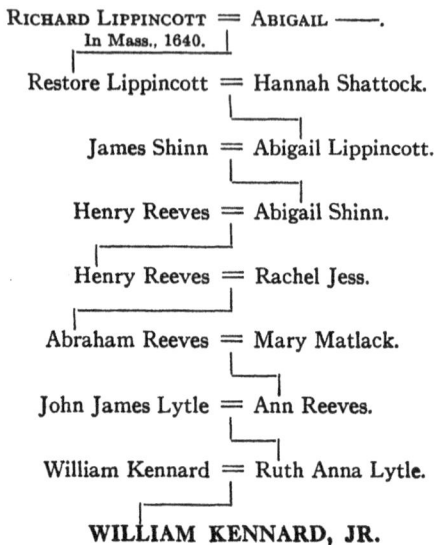

SUPPLEMENTAL

Seventh in descent from John Shinn, in West Jersey, in 1678.

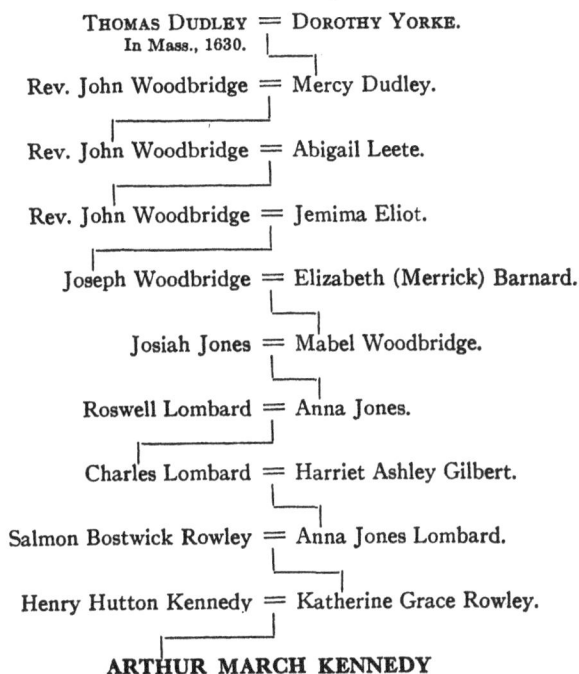

THOMAS DUDLEY = DOROTHY YORKE.
In Mass., 1630.

Rev. John Woodbridge = Mercy Dudley.

Rev. John Woodbridge = Abigail Leete.

Rev. John Woodbridge = Jemima Eliot.

Joseph Woodbridge = Elizabeth (Merrick) Barnard.

Josiah Jones = Mabel Woodbridge.

Roswell Lombard = Anna Jones.

Charles Lombard = Harriet Ashley Gilbert.

Salmon Bostwick Rowley = Anna Jones Lombard.

Henry Hutton Kennedy = Katherine Grace Rowley.

ARTHUR MARCH KENNEDY

143

𝕶lapp

JOHN CLAPP = —— ——.
In New York, 1690.

Elias Clapp = Ruth Allen.

Joseph Clapp = Mercy Carpenter.

Henry Klapp = Mary Ostrom.

Joseph Klapp, M.D. = Anna Milnor.

Joseph Klapp, M.D. = Anna Pauline Van Lew.

Wilbur Paddock Klapp, M.D. = Emma Fredericka Klemm.

EDWARD MEINEL KLEMM KLAPP

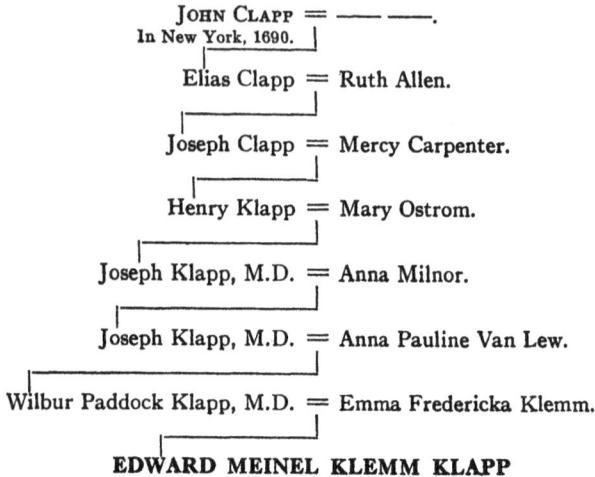

SUPPLEMENTALS

Ninth in descent from Richard Betts, in Mass., 1648.
Ninth in descent from Jan Jansen, in Long Island, 1681.
Ninth in descent from Louwrens Pieterse, in New Netherland, 1661.
Eighth in descent from Jan Van Cleef, in Long Island, 1653.
Eighth in descent from Frederick Hendricksen Van Leuwen, in Long
Island, 1681.
Seventh in descent from Henry Allen, in Long Island, before 1698.
Seventh in descent from Thomas French, in West Jersey, 1677.
Seventh in descent from Henry Pawlin, in Penna., before 1687.
Sixth in descent from David Breintnall, in Penna., 1683.
Sixth in descent from Joseph Milnor, in Penna., 1690.
Sixth in descent from Philip Taylor, in Penna., 1696.

𝕶lapp

JOHN CLAPP = —— ——.
In New York, 1690.

Elias Clapp = Ruth Allen.

Joseph Clapp = Mercy Carpenter.

Henry Klapp = Mary Ostrom.

Joseph Klapp, M.D. = Anna Milnor.

Joseph Klapp, M.D. = Anna Pauline Van Lew.

Wilbur Paddock Klapp, M.D. = Emma Fredricka Klemm.

WILBUR PADDOCK KLAPP, JR.

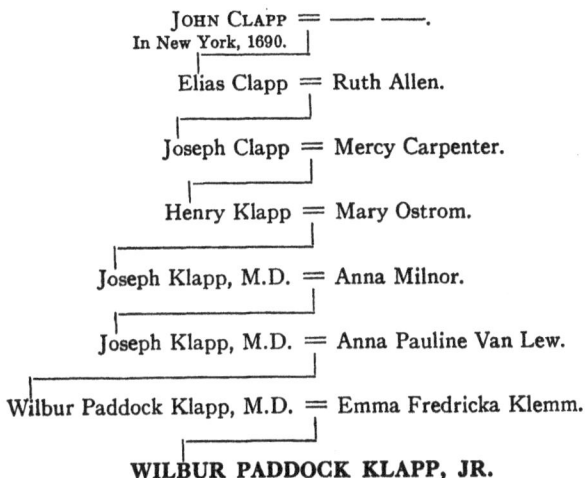

SUPPLEMENTALS

Ninth in descent from Richard Betts, in Mass., 1648.
Ninth in descent from Jan Jansen, in Long Island, 1681.
Ninth in descent from Louwrens Pieterse, in New Netherland, 1661.
Eight in descent from Jan Van Cleef, in Long Island, 1653.
Eighth in descent from Frederick Hendricksen Van Leuwen, in Long Island, 1681.
Seventh in descent from Henry Allen, in Long Island, before 1698.
Seventh in descent from Thomas French, in West Jersey, 1677.
Seventh in descent from Henry Pawlin, in Penna., before 1687.
Sixth in descent from David Breintnall, in Penna., 1683.
Sixth in descent from Joseph Milnor, in Penna., 1690.
Sixth in descent from Philip Taylor, in Penna., 1696.

𝕶night

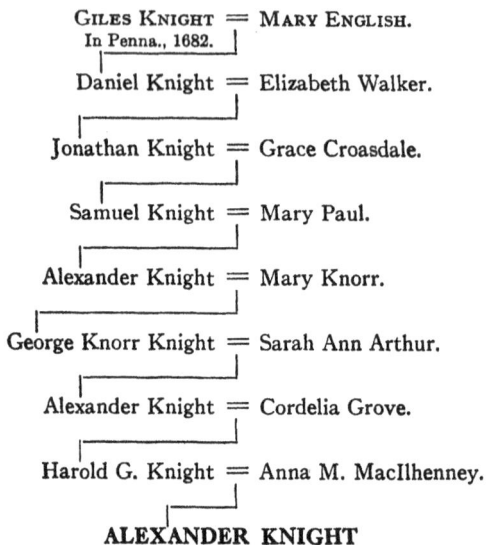

GILES KNIGHT = MARY ENGLISH.
In Penna., 1682.

Daniel Knight = Elizabeth Walker.

Jonathan Knight = Grace Croasdale.

Samuel Knight = Mary Paul.

Alexander Knight = Mary Knorr.

George Knorr Knight = Sarah Ann Arthur.

Alexander Knight = Cordelia Grove.

Harold G. Knight = Anna M. MacIlhenney.

ALEXANDER KNIGHT

𝕶night

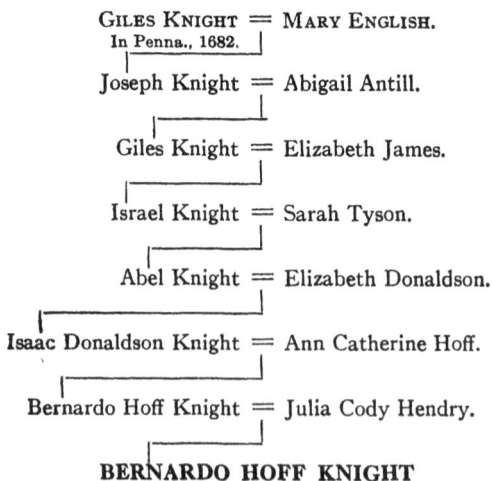

GILES KNIGHT = MARY ENGLISH.
In Penna., 1682.

Joseph Knight = Abigail Antill.

Giles Knight = Elizabeth James.

Israel Knight = Sarah Tyson.

Abel Knight = Elizabeth Donaldson.

Isaac Donaldson Knight = Ann Catherine Hoff.

Bernardo Hoff Knight = Julia Cody Hendry.

BERNARDO HOFF KNIGHT

Knowles

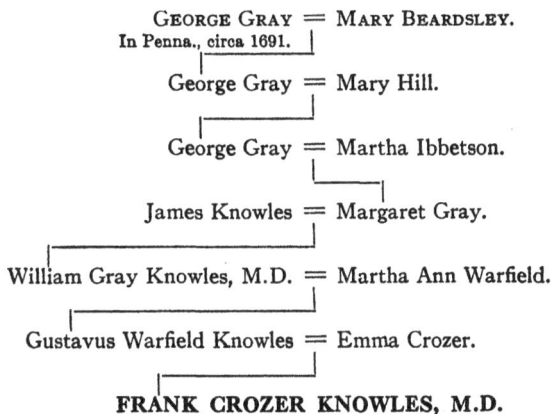

GEORGE GRAY = MARY BEARDSLEY.
In Penna., circa 1691.

George Gray = Mary Hill.

George Gray = Martha Ibbetson.

James Knowles = Margaret Gray.

William Gray Knowles, M.D. = Martha Ann Warfield.

Gustavus Warfield Knowles = Emma Crozer.

FRANK CROZER KNOWLES, M.D.

Laing

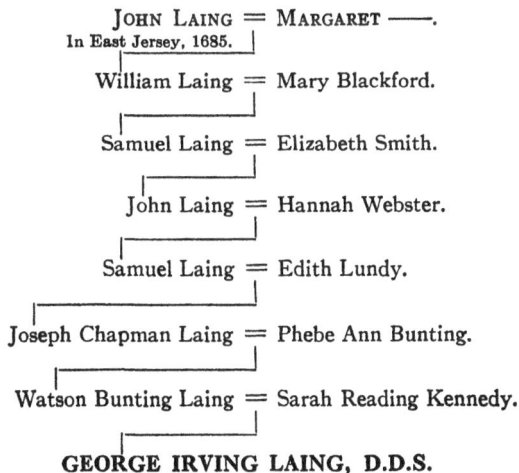

JOHN LAING = MARGARET ——.
In East Jersey, 1685.

William Laing = Mary Blackford.

Samuel Laing = Elizabeth Smith.

John Laing = Hannah Webster.

Samuel Laing = Edith Lundy.

Joseph Chapman Laing = Phebe Ann Bunting.

Watson Bunting Laing = Sarah Reading Kennedy.

GEORGE IRVING LAING, D.D.S.

SUPPLEMENTAL

Eighth in descent from Nicholas Stillwell, in New Netherland, 1638.

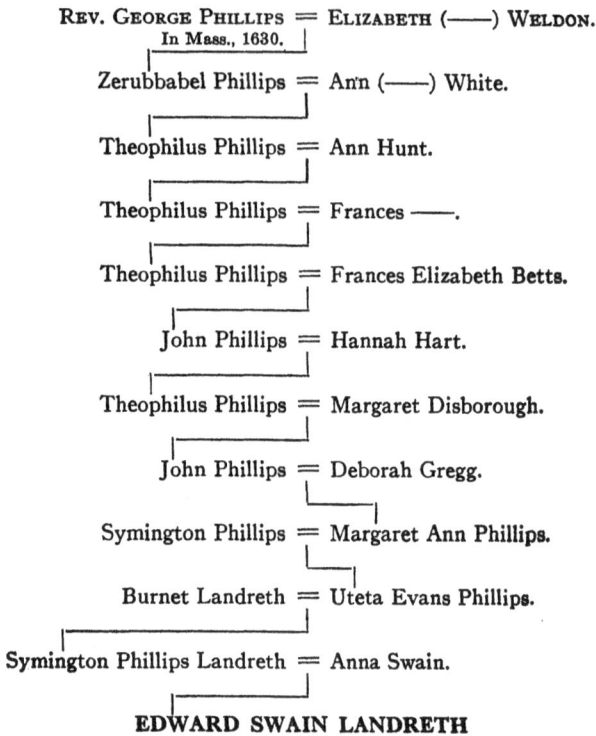

REV. GEORGE PHILLIPS = ELIZABETH (——) WELDON.
In Mass., 1630.

Zerubbabel Phillips = An'n (——) White.

Theophilus Phillips = Ann Hunt.

Theophilus Phillips = Frances ——.

Theophilus Phillips = Frances Elizabeth Betts.

John Phillips = Hannah Hart.

Theophilus Phillips = Margaret Disborough.

John Phillips = Deborah Gregg.

Symington Phillips = Margaret Ann Phillips.

Burnet Landreth = Uteta Evans Phillips.

Symington Phillips Landreth = Anna Swain.

EDWARD SWAIN LANDRETH

148

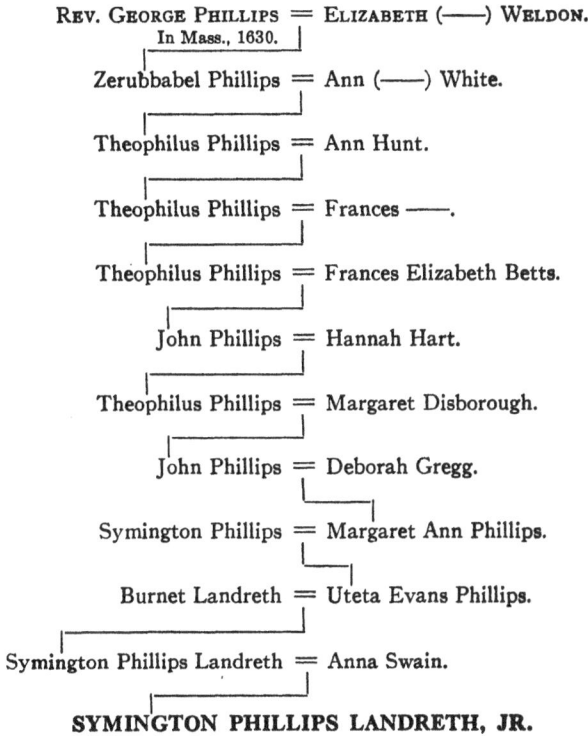

REV. GEORGE PHILLIPS = ELIZABETH (——) WELDON.
In Mass., 1630.

Zerubbabel Phillips = Ann (——) White.

Theophilus Phillips = Ann Hunt.

Theophilus Phillips = Frances ——.

Theophilus Phillips = Frances Elizabeth Betts.

John Phillips = Hannah Hart.

Theophilus Phillips = Margaret Disborough.

John Phillips = Deborah Gregg.

Symington Phillips = Margaret Ann Phillips.

Burnet Landreth = Uteta Evans Phillips.

Symington Phillips Landreth = Anna Swain.

SYMINGTON PHILLIPS LANDRETH, JR.

Lay

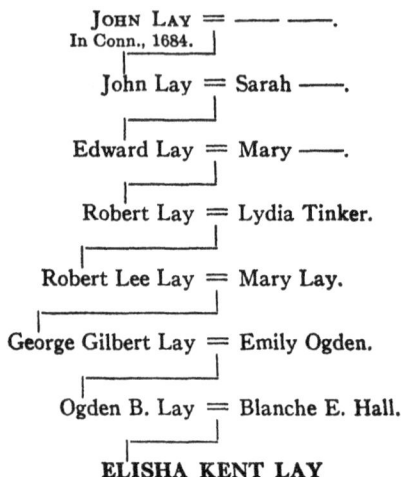

JOHN LAY = —— ——.
In Conn., 1684.

John Lay = Sarah ——.

Edward Lay = Mary ——.

Robert Lay = Lydia Tinker.

Robert Lee Lay = Mary Lay.

George Gilbert Lay = Emily Ogden.

Ogden B. Lay = Blanche E. Hall.

ELISHA KENT LAY

Leach

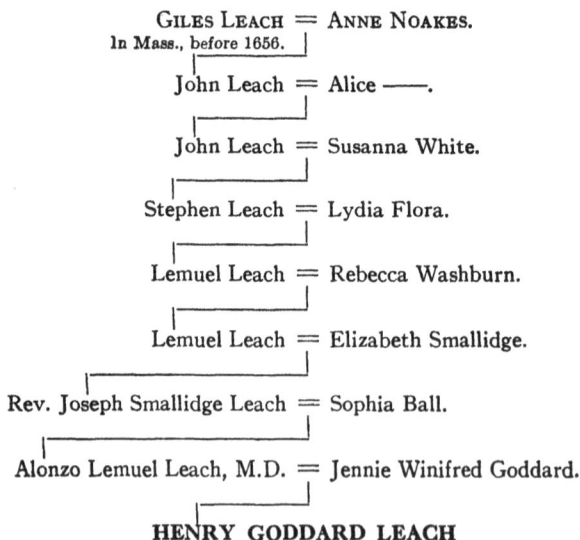

GILES LEACH = ANNE NOAKES.
In Mass., before 1656.

John Leach = Alice ——.

John Leach = Susanna White.

Stephen Leach = Lydia Flora.

Lemuel Leach = Rebecca Washburn.

Lemuel Leach = Elizabeth Smallidge.

Rev. Joseph Smallidge Leach = Sophia Ball.

Alonzo Lemuel Leach, M.D. = Jennie Winifred Goddard.

HENRY GODDARD LEACH

SUPPLEMENTALS

Tenth in descent from William Manning, in Mass., 1634.
Tenth in descent from Edmund Rice, in Mass., 1639.
Ninth in descent from John Ball, in Mass., before 1635.
Ninth in descent from Francis Cooke, in Plymouth Colony, 1620.
Ninth in descent from Ralph Earle, in Rhode Island, 1638.
Ninth in descent from Jacob Farrar, in Mass., 1653.
Ninth in descent from Abraham Howe, in Mass., 1638.
Ninth in descent from John Howe, in Mass., 1639.
Ninth in descent from Experience Mitchell, in Plymouth Colony, 1623.
Ninth in descent from Ralph Shepard, in Mass., 1635.
Ninth in descent from John Shipley, in Mass., 1637.
Ninth in descent from Isaac Stearns, in Mass., 1630.
Ninth in descent from Nathaniel Tilden, in Plymouth Colony, 1635.
Ninth in descent from John Washburn, in Plymouth Colony, 1632.
Ninth in descent from Ralph Wheelock, in Mass., 1637.
Ninth in descent from John Woods, in Mass., 1641.
Eighth in descent from Joseph Batchelder, in Mass., 1636.
Eight in descent from Robert Carr, in Rhode Island, 1635.
Eighth in descent from William Cheney, in Mass., 1635.
Eighth in descent from Richard Child, in Mass., before 1652.
Eighth in descent from John Perrin, in Mass., 1641.
Eighth in descent from Walter Powers, in Mass., 1660.
Eighth in descent from Samuel Richardson, in Mass., 1636.
Eighth in descent from John Thurston, in Mass., 1637.
Seventh in descent from Francis Curtis, in Mass., 1671.
Seventh in descent from William Goddard, in Mass., 1666.

Lee

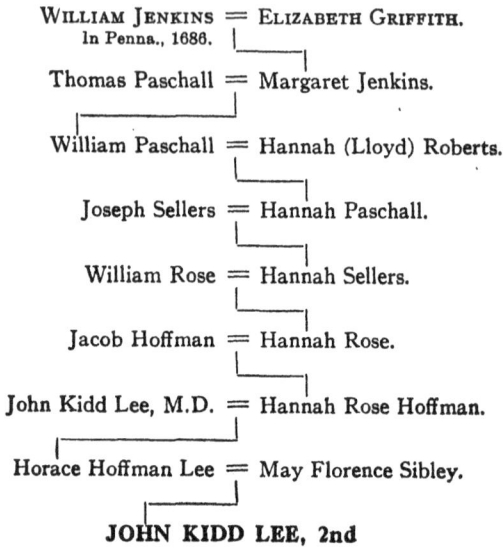

WILLIAM JENKINS = ELIZABETH GRIFFITH.
In Penna., 1686.

Thomas Paschall = Margaret Jenkins.

William Paschall = Hannah (Lloyd) Roberts.

Joseph Sellers = Hannah Paschall.

William Rose = Hannah Sellers.

Jacob Hoffman = Hannah Rose.

John Kidd Lee, M.D. = Hannah Rose Hoffman.

Horace Hoffman Lee = May Florence Sibley.

JOHN KIDD LEE, 2nd

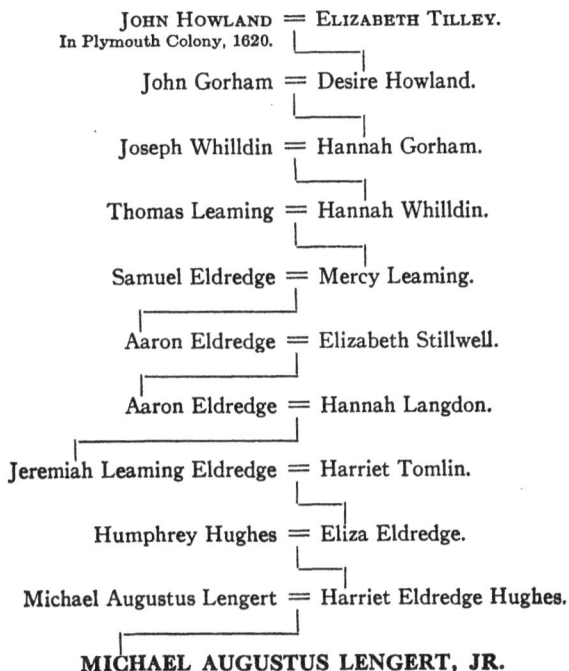

JOHN HOWLAND = ELIZABETH TILLEY.
In Plymouth Colony, 1620.

John Gorham = Desire Howland.

Joseph Whilldin = Hannah Gorham.

Thomas Leaming = Hannah Whilldin.

Samuel Eldredge = Mercy Leaming.

Aaron Eldredge = Elizabeth Stillwell.

Aaron Eldredge = Hannah Langdon.

Jeremiah Leaming Eldredge = Harriet Tomlin.

Humphrey Hughes = Eliza Eldredge.

Michael Augustus Lengert = Harriet Eldredge Hughes.

MICHAEL AUGUSTUS LENGERT, JR.

𝕷𝖊𝖇𝖎𝖘

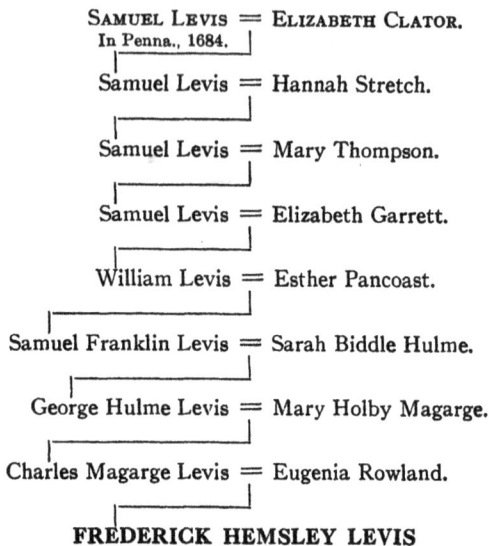

SAMUEL LEVIS = ELIZABETH CLATOR.
In Penna., 1684.

Samuel Levis = Hannah Stretch.

Samuel Levis = Mary Thompson.

Samuel Levis = Elizabeth Garrett.

William Levis = Esther Pancoast.

Samuel Franklin Levis = Sarah Biddle Hulme.

George Hulme Levis = Mary Holby Magarge.

Charles Magarge Levis = Eugenia Rowland.

FREDERICK HEMSLEY LEVIS

𝔏𝔢𝔴𝔦𝔰

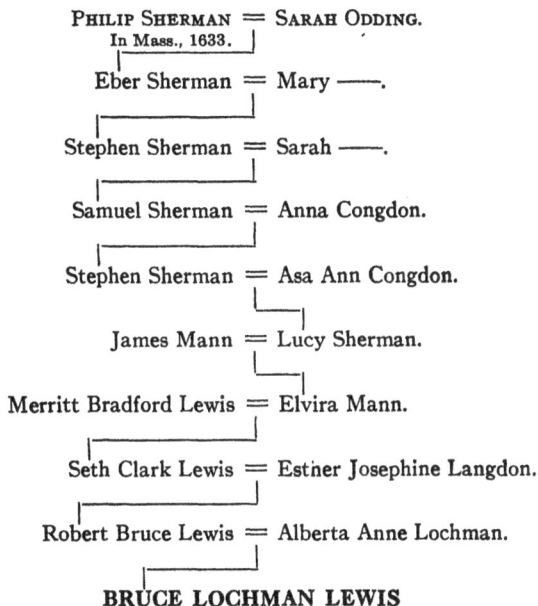

PHILIP SHERMAN = SARAH ODDING.
In Mass., 1633.

Eber Sherman = Mary ——.

Stephen Sherman = Sarah ——.

Samuel Sherman = Anna Congdon.

Stephen Sherman = Asa Ann Congdon.

James Mann = Lucy Sherman.

Merritt Bradford Lewis = Elvira Mann.

Seth Clark Lewis = Esther Josephine Langdon.

Robert Bruce Lewis = Alberta Anne Lochman.

BRUCE LOCHMAN LEWIS

𝔏𝔢𝔴𝔦𝔰

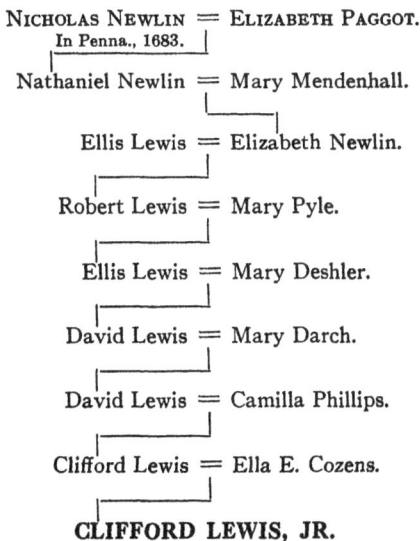

NICHOLAS NEWLIN = ELIZABETH PAGGOT.
In Penna., 1683.

Nathaniel Newlin = Mary Mendenhall.

Ellis Lewis = Elizabeth Newlin.

Robert Lewis = Mary Pyle.

Ellis Lewis = Mary Deshler.

David Lewis = Mary Darch.

David Lewis = Camilla Phillips.

Clifford Lewis = Ella E. Cozens.

CLIFFORD LEWIS, JR.

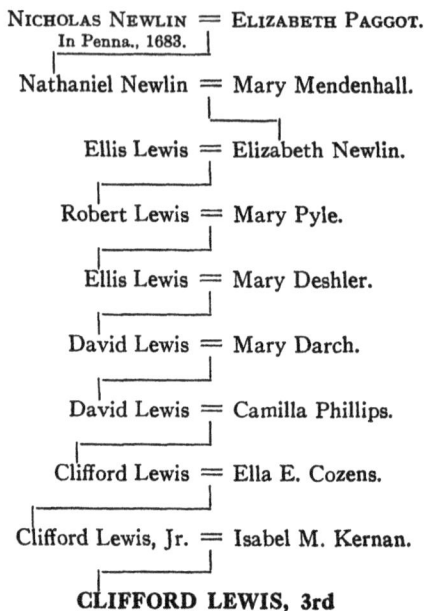

NICHOLAS NEWLIN = ELIZABETH PAGGOT.
In Penna., 1683.

Nathaniel Newlin = Mary Mendenhall.

Ellis Lewis = Elizabeth Newlin.

Robert Lewis = Mary Pyle.

Ellis Lewis = Mary Deshler.

David Lewis = Mary Darch.

David Lewis = Camilla Phillips.

Clifford Lewis = Ella E. Cozens.

Clifford Lewis, Jr. = Isabel M. Kernan.

CLIFFORD LEWIS, 3rd

Lewis

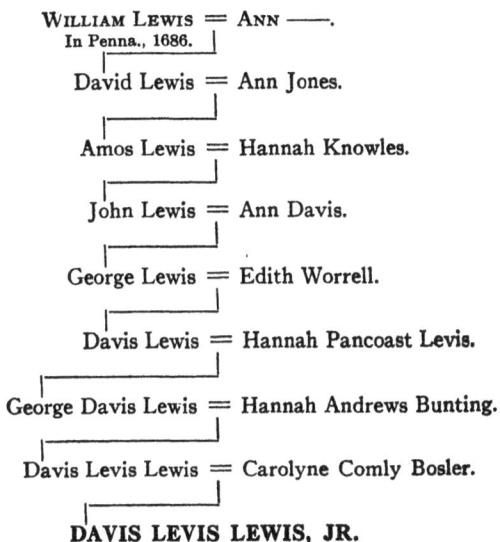

WILLIAM LEWIS = ANN ———.
In Penna., 1686.

David Lewis = Ann Jones.

Amos Lewis = Hannah Knowles.

John Lewis = Ann Davis.

George Lewis = Edith Worrell.

Davis Lewis = Hannah Pancoast Levis.

George Davis Lewis = Hannah Andrews Bunting.

Davis Levis Lewis = Carolyne Comly Bosler.

DAVIS LEVIS LEWIS, JR.

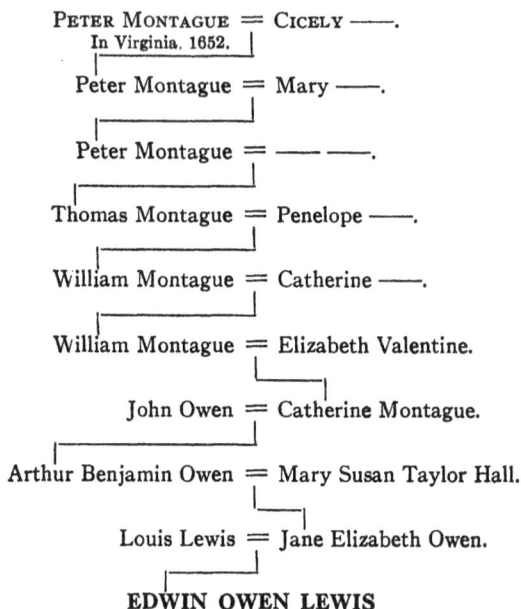

PETER MONTAGUE = CICELY ——.
In Virginia, 1652.

Peter Montague = Mary ——.

Peter Montague = —— ——.

Thomas Montague = Penelope ——.

William Montague = Catherine ——.

William Montague = Elizabeth Valentine.

John Owen = Catherine Montague.

Arthur Benjamin Owen = Mary Susan Taylor Hall.

Louis Lewis = Jane Elizabeth Owen.

EDWIN OWEN LEWIS

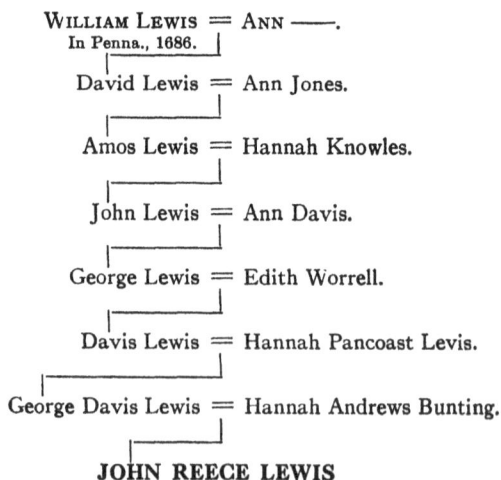

WILLIAM LEWIS = ANN ——.
In Penna., 1686.

David Lewis = Ann Jones.

Amos Lewis = Hannah Knowles.

John Lewis = Ann Davis.

George Lewis = Edith Worrell.

Davis Lewis = Hannah Pancoast Levis.

George Davis Lewis = Hannah Andrews Bunting.

JOHN REECE LEWIS

SUPPLEMENTALS

Ninth in descent from Edward Bradway, in West Jersey, 1677.
Ninth in descent from William Brinton, in Penna., 1684.
Ninth in descent from William Cooper, in West Jersey, 1679.
Eighth in descent from John Bennett, in Penna., 1685.
Eighth in descent from John Blunston, in Penna., 1682.
Eighth in descent from Peter Dicks, in Penna., 1686.
Eighth in descent from Walter Fausett, in Penna., 1684.
Eighth in descent from John Grubb, in Upland, now Penna., 1679.
Eighth in descent from William Jenkins, in Penna., 1686.
Eighth in descent from Thomas Paschall, in Penna., 1682.
Eighth in descent from Robert Pyle, in Penna., 1684.
Eighth in descent from Samuel Sellers, in Penna., 1682.
Seventh in descent from William Garrett, in Penna., 1684.
Seventh in descent from Samuel Levis, in Penna., 1684.
Seventh in descent from Robert Lloyd, in Penna., 1683.
Seventh in descent from Henry Oborn, in Penna., 1684.
Seventh in descent from Robert Taylor, in Penna., 1683.
Sixth in descent from David Ogden, in Penna., 1682.
Sixth in descent from John Pancoast, in West Jersey, before 1695.
Sixth in descent from John Worrall, in Penna., 1682.

Elected
1928

Lewis

No.
420

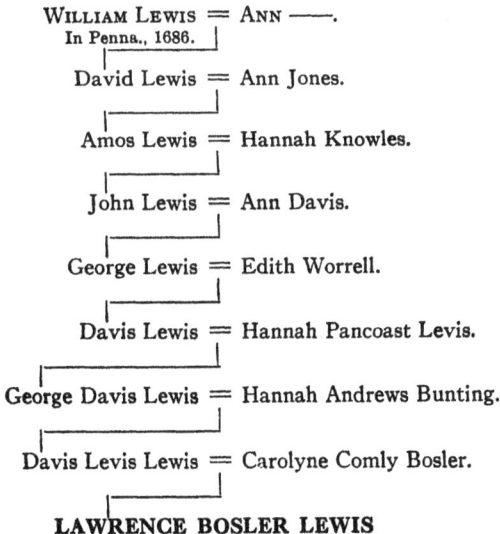

WILLIAM LEWIS = ANN ——.
In Penna., 1686.

David Lewis = Ann Jones.

Amos Lewis = Hannah Knowles.

John Lewis = Ann Davis.

George Lewis = Edith Worrell.

Davis Lewis = Hannah Pancoast Levis.

George Davis Lewis = Hannah Andrews Bunting.

Davis Levis Lewis = Carolyne Comly Bosler.

LAWRENCE BOSLER LEWIS

WILLIAM LEWIS = ANN ——.
In Penna. 1686.

David Lewis = Ann Jones.

Amos Lewis = Hannah Knowles.

John Lewis = Ann Davis.

George Lewis = Edith Worrell.

Davis Lewis = Hannah Pancoast Levis.

George Davis Lewis = Hannah Andrews Bunting.

SAMUEL BUNTING LEWIS

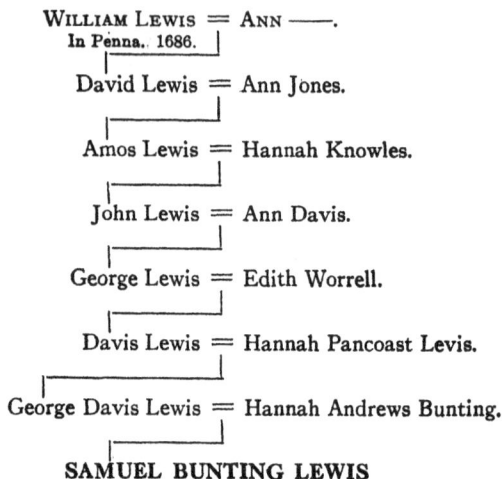

SUPPLEMENTALS

Ninth in descent from Edward Bradway, in West Jersey, 1677.
Ninth in descent from William Brinton, in Penna., 1684.
Ninth in descent from William Cooper, in West Jersey, 1679.
Eighth in descent from John Bennett, in Penna., 1685.
Eighth in descent from John Blunston, in Penna., 1682.
Eighth in descent from Peter Dicks, in Penna., 1686.
Eighth in descent from Walter Fausett, in Penna., 1684.
Eighth in descent from John Grubb, in Upland, now Penna., 1679.
Eighth in descent from William Jenkins, in Penna., 1686.
Eighth in descent from Thomas Paschall, in Penna., 1682.
Eighth in descent from Robert Pyle, in Penna., 1684.
Eighth in descent from Samuel Sellers, in Penna., 1682.
Seventh in descent from William Garrett, in Penna., 1684.
Seventh in descent from Samuel Levis, in Penna., 1684.
Seventh in descent from Robert Lloyd, in Penna., 1683.
Seventh in descent from Henry Oborn, in Penna., 1684.
Seventh in descent from Robert Taylor, in Penna., 1683.
Sixth in descent from David Ogden, in Penna., 1682.
Sixth in descent from John Pancoast, in West Jersey, before 1695.
Sixth in descent from John Worrall, in Penna., 1682.

𝕷𝖎𝖌𝖌𝖊𝖙

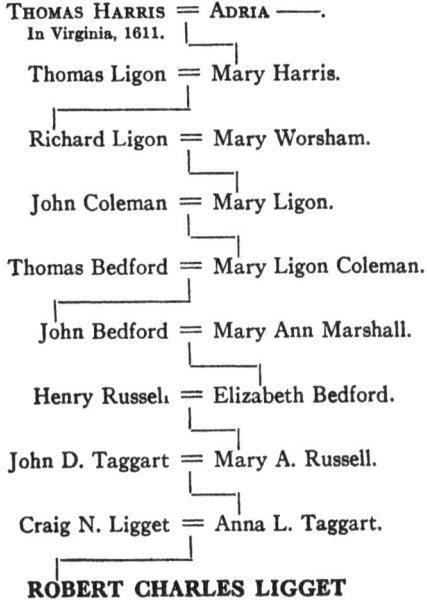

THOMAS HARRIS = ADRIA ——.
In Virginia, 1611.

Thomas Ligon = Mary Harris.

Richard Ligon = Mary Worsham.

John Coleman = Mary Ligon.

Thomas Bedford = Mary Ligon Coleman.

John Bedford = Mary Ann Marshall.

Henry Russell = Elizabeth Bedford.

John D. Taggart = Mary A. Russell.

Craig N. Ligget = Anna L. Taggart.

ROBERT CHARLES LIGGET

𝕷𝖑𝖔𝖞𝖉

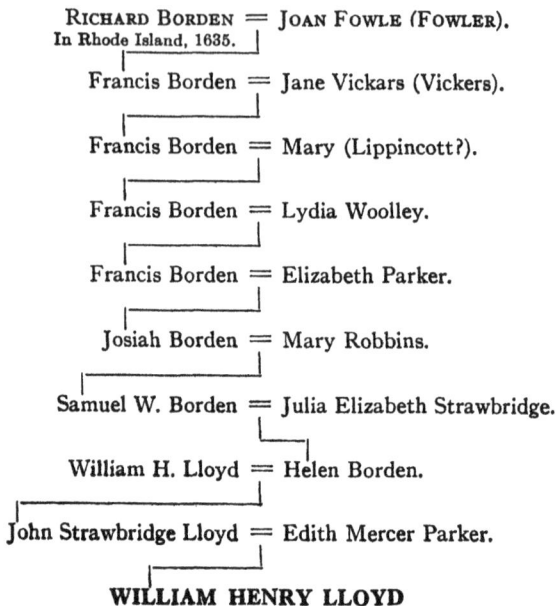

RICHARD BORDEN = JOAN FOWLE (FOWLER).
In Rhode Island, 1635.

Francis Borden = Jane Vickars (Vickers).

Francis Borden = Mary (Lippincott?).

Francis Borden = Lydia Woolley.

Francis Borden = Elizabeth Parker.

Josiah Borden = Mary Robbins.

Samuel W. Borden = Julia Elizabeth Strawbridge.

William H. Lloyd = Helen Borden.

John Strawbridge Lloyd = Edith Mercer Parker.

WILLIAM HENRY LLOYD

𝕷𝖔𝖙𝖙

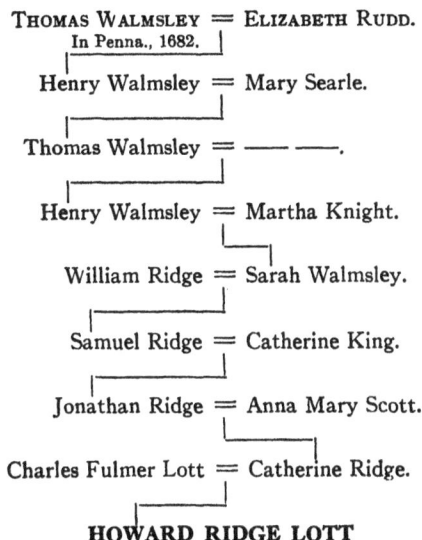

THOMAS WALMSLEY = ELIZABETH RUDD.
In Penna., 1682.

Henry Walmsley = Mary Searle.

Thomas Walmsley = —— ——.

Henry Walmsley = Martha Knight.

William Ridge = Sarah Walmsley.

Samuel Ridge = Catherine King.

Jonathan Ridge = Anna Mary Scott.

Charles Fulmer Lott = Catherine Ridge.

HOWARD RIDGE LOTT

𝕷𝖚𝖊𝖉𝖊𝖗𝖘

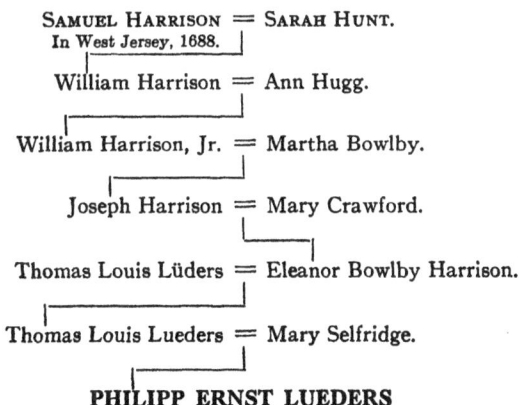

SAMUEL HARRISON = SARAH HUNT.
In West Jersey, 1688.

William Harrison = Ann Hugg.

William Harrison, Jr. = Martha Bowlby.

Joseph Harrison = Mary Crawford.

Thomas Louis Lüders = Eleanor Bowlby Harrison.

Thomas Louis Lueders = Mary Selfridge.

PHILIPP ERNST LUEDERS

SUPPLEMENTALS

Seventh in descent from Francis Collins, in West Jersey, 1677.
Seventh in descent from John Hillman, in West Jersey, 1697.
Seventh in descent from John Hugg, in West Jersey, 1683.

Lutz

WILLIAM FLEMING = MARY MOORE.
In Penna., 1698.

John Fleming = Sara Chatham.

John Flemming = Abigail Cowan.

Lazarus Lowrey = Mary Flemming.

John Holliday = Mary Fleming Lowrey.

Solomon Filler = Sara Holliday.

John Lutz = Emily C. Filler.

REV. WILLIAM FILLER LUTZ

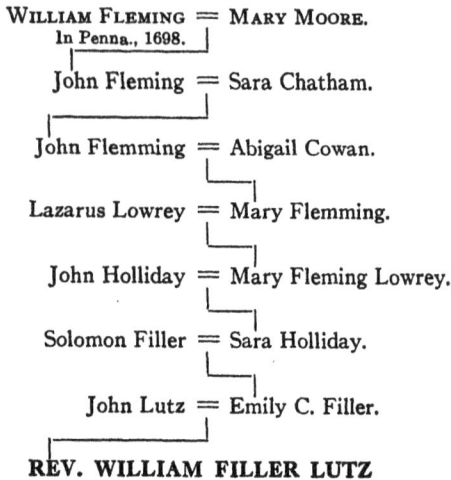

SUPPLEMENTALS

Ninth in descent from Thomas Green, in Penna., 1686.
Eighth in descent from Richard Moore, in Penna., 1686.
Seventh in descent from Neil Campbell, in East Jersey, 1685.

HENRY WOODWARD = MARY (GODFREY) BROWN.
In South Carolina, 1666.

Richard Woodward = Sarah Stanyarne.

Rev. William Hutson = Mary (Woodward) Chardon.

Arthur Peronneau = Mary Hutson.

William Hayne = Elizabeth Peronneau.

Hext McCall = Susan Branford Hayne.

Luther M. McBee = Susan Branford McCall.

Alexander McBee = Anna Bolyn Crosswell.

REV. CROSSWELL McBEE

JOHANNES DE PEYSTER = CORNELIA LUBBERTS.
In New Netherland, 1649.

Johannes de Peyster = Anna Bancker.

Matthew Clarkson = Cornelia de Peyster.

Matthew Clarkson = Mary Boude.

Robert Ralston = Sarah Clarkson.

John Syng Dorsey, M.D. = Maria Ralston.

Robert Ralston Dorsey, M.D. = Anna Yerger.

Frederick George McKean = Caroline Dorsey.

FREDERICK GEORGE McKEAN

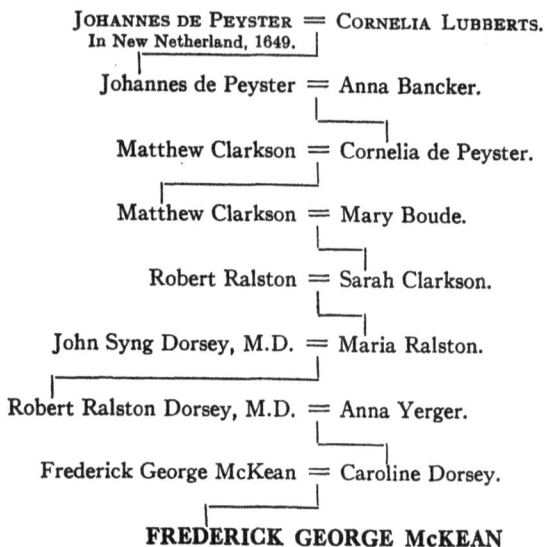

SUPPLEMENTAL

Eighth in descent from Michael Newbould, in West Jersey, 1681.

𝕸𝖆𝖓𝖘𝖋𝖎𝖊𝖑𝖉

RICHARD MANSFIELD = GILLIAN DRAKE.
In Conn., 1639.

Moses Mansfield = Mercy Glover.

Jonathan Mansfield = Sarah Alling.

Nathan Mansfield = Deborah Dayton.

Nathan Mansfield = Anna Tomlinson.

Jared Mansfield = Eunice (Jennings) Lum.

Stephen Mansfield = Eliza Craig.

John Clark Mansfield = Catherine Hoctor.

JOHN CLARK MANSFIELD

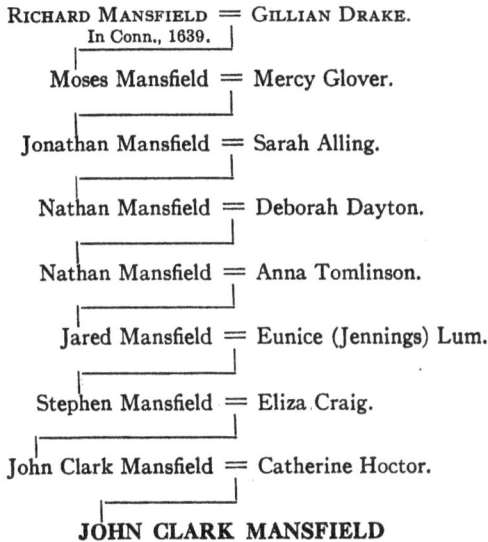

SUPPLEMENTALS

Eleventh in descent from Rev. Peter Bulkeley, in Mass., 1635.
Eleventh in descent from Rev. John Jones, in Mass., 1635.
Tenth in descent from Francis Bell, in Conn., 1638.
Tenth in descent from Francis Browne, in Conn., 1637.
Tenth in descent from Robert Coe, in Mass., 1634.
Tenth in descent from Ralph Dayton, in Conn., 1639.
Tenth in descent from Matthew Mitchell, in Mass., 1635.
Tenth in descent from Thomas Nash, in Conn., 1638.
Tenth in descent from Robert Seeley, in Mass., 1630.
Tenth in descent from Giles Smith, in Conn., 1639.
Tenth in descent from William Tuttle, in Mass., 1635.
Tenth in descent from Thomas Wheeler, in Mass., 1635.
Ninth in descent from Roger Alling, in Conn., 1638.
Ninth in descent from James Bennett, in Mass., before 1637.
Ninth in descent from Henry Glover, in Conn., 1643.
Ninth in descent from George Godwin, in Conn., 1652.
Ninth in descent from Richard Harvey, in Conn., 1644.
Ninth in descent from John Holly, in Conn., 1647.
Ninth in descent from Henry Jackson, in Mass., 1635.
Ninth in descent from William Odell, in Mass., 1639.
Ninth in descent from Thomas Sanford, in Mass., 1634.

Ninth in descent from Christopher Todd, in Conn., 1639.
Ninth in descent from Henry Tomlinson, in Conn., 1652.
Ninth in descent from Benjamin Turney, in Mass., 1631.
Eighth in descent from Paul Engle, in Penna., 1698.
Eighth in descent from John Hide, in Conn., 1668.
Eighth in descent from Joshua Jennings, in Conn., 1647.
Eighth in descent from William Tomlinson, in Conn., 1677.
Eighth in descent from Cornelius Tyson, in Penna., 1684.
Seventh in descent from Johnathan Fanton, in Conn., before 1693.

Elected
1939

ﬃﬧﬧﬧﬦﬦ Maris

No.
603

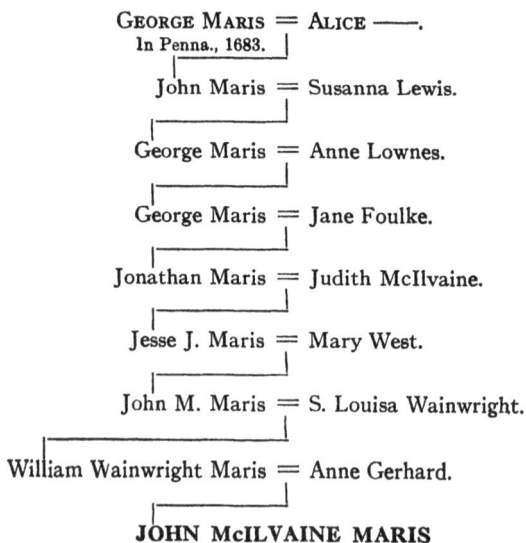

GEORGE MARIS = ALICE ——.
In Penna., 1683.

John Maris = Susanna Lewis.

George Maris = Anne Lownes.

George Maris = Jane Foulke.

Jonathan Maris = Judith McIlvaine.

Jesse J. Maris = Mary West.

John M. Maris = S. Louisa Wainwright.

William Wainwright Maris = Anne Gerhard.

JOHN McILVAINE MARIS

𝔐𝔞𝔰𝔰𝔢𝔭

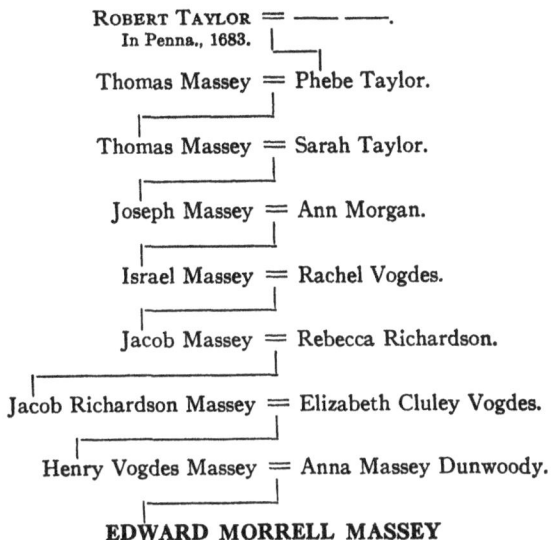

ROBERT TAYLOR = ——— ———.
In Penna., 1683.

Thomas Massey = Phebe Taylor.

Thomas Massey = Sarah Taylor.

Joseph Massey = Ann Morgan.

Israel Massey = Rachel Vogdes.

Jacob Massey = Rebecca Richardson.

Jacob Richardson Massey = Elizabeth Cluley Vogdes.

Henry Vogdes Massey = Anna Massey Dunwoody.

EDWARD MORRELL MASSEY

𝔐𝔞𝔰𝔰𝔢𝔭

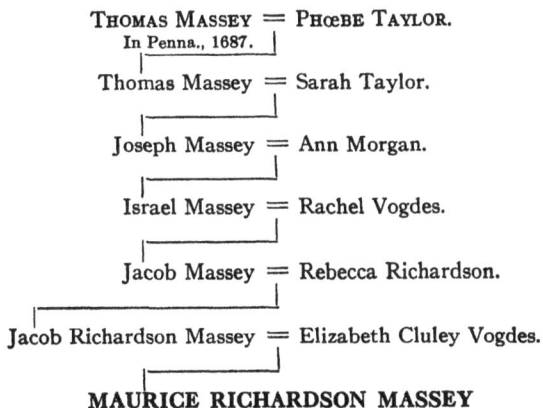

THOMAS MASSEY = PHŒBE TAYLOR.
In Penna., 1687.

Thomas Massey = Sarah Taylor.

Joseph Massey = Ann Morgan.

Israel Massey = Rachel Vogdes.

Jacob Massey = Rebecca Richardson.

Jacob Richardson Massey = Elizabeth Cluley Vogdes.

MAURICE RICHARDSON MASSEY

SUPPLEMENTALS

Seventh in descent from Robert Taylor, in Penna., 1683.
Sixth in descent from John Bevan, in Penna., 1683.
Sixth in descent from Samuel Richardson, in Penna., 1686.

𝔐𝔞𝔰𝔰𝔢𝔭

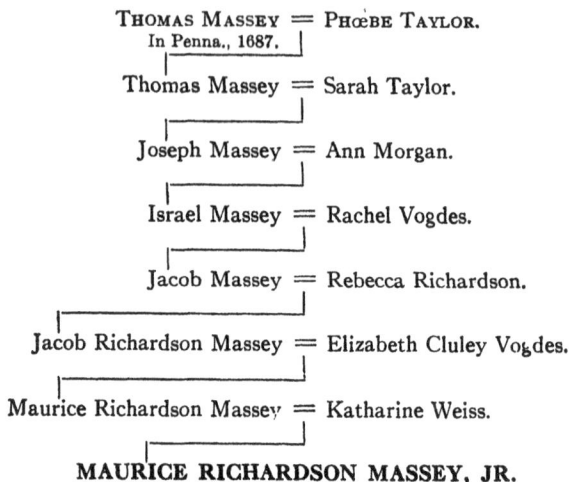

THOMAS MASSEY = PHŒBE TAYLOR.
In Penna., 1687.

Thomas Massey = Sarah Taylor.

Joseph Massey = Ann Morgan.

Israel Massey = Rachel Vogdes.

Jacob Massey = Rebecca Richardson.

Jacob Richardson Massey = Elizabeth Cluley Vogdes.

Maurice Richardson Massey = Katharine Weiss.

MAURICE RICHARDSON MASSEY, JR.

𝔐𝔞𝔱𝔱𝔥𝔢𝔴𝔰

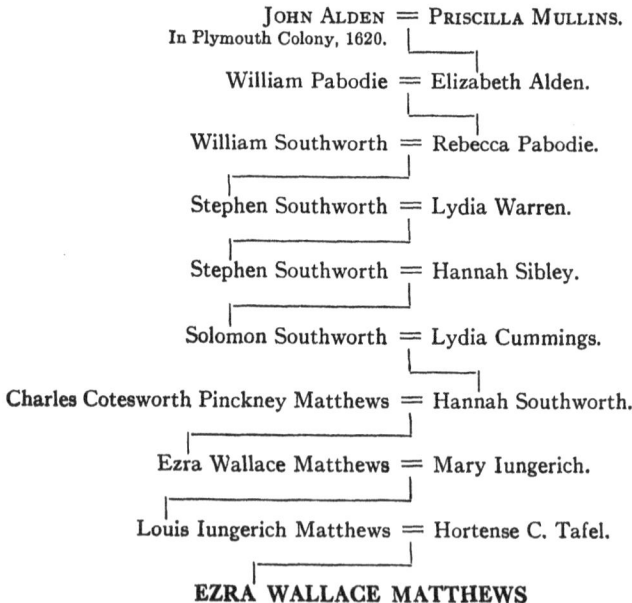

JOHN ALDEN = PRISCILLA MULLINS.
In Plymouth Colony, 1620.

William Pabodie = Elizabeth Alden.

William Southworth = Rebecca Pabodie.

Stephen Southworth = Lydia Warren.

Stephen Southworth = Hannah Sibley.

Solomon Southworth = Lydia Cummings.

Charles Cotesworth Pinckney Matthews = Hannah Southworth.

Ezra Wallace Matthews = Mary Iungerich.

Louis Iungerich Matthews = Hortense C. Tafel.

EZRA WALLACE MATTHEWS

𝔐𝔞𝔱𝔱𝔥𝔢𝔴𝔰

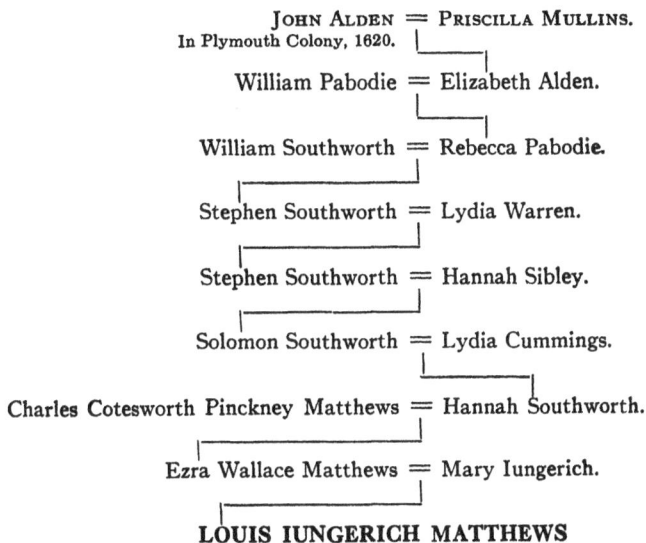

JOHN ALDEN = PRISCILLA MULLINS.
In Plymouth Colony, 1620.

William Pabodie = Elizabeth Alden.

William Southworth = Rebecca Pabodie.

Stephen Southworth = Lydia Warren.

Stephen Southworth = Hannah Sibley.

Solomon Southworth = Lydia Cummings.

Charles Cotesworth Pinckney Matthews = Hannah Southworth.

Ezra Wallace Matthews = Mary Iungerich.

LOUIS IUNGERICH MATTHEWS

CHRISTOPHER LEAMING = ESTHER BURNETT.
In Long Island, circa 1671.

Thomas Leaming = Hannah Whilldin.

Jacob Hughes = Priscilla (Leaming) Stites.

Jacob Hughes = Ann Lawrence.

John Bennett = Mary Hughes.

Isaac Printz Merritt = Louisa Stevens Bennett.

Alexis Grasson Merritt = Susannah Dale.

Bascom Worthing Melvin = Amanda Louisa Merritt.

FRANK WORTHINGTON MELVIN

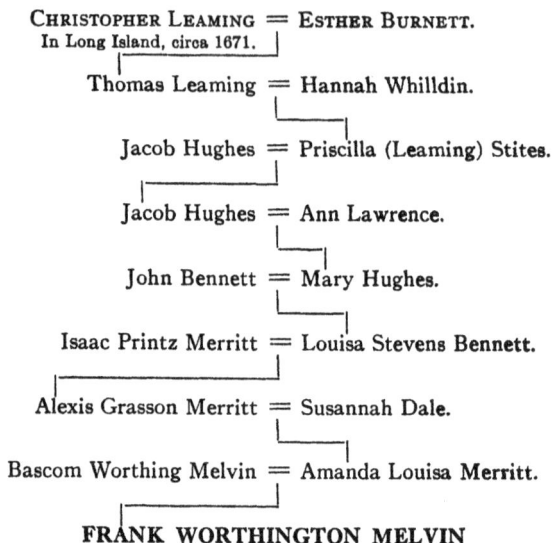

SUPPLEMENTALS

Eleventh in descent from John Tilley, in Plymouth Colony, 1620.
Tenth in descent from Thomas Falland, in Plymouth Colony, 1640.
Tenth in descent from Sven Gonderson, in New Sweden, before 1664.
Tenth in descent from John Howland, in Plymouth Colony, 1620.
Tenth in descent from Gabriel Wheldon (Whilldin), in Plymouth Colony,
    1638.
Ninth in descent from Thomas Burnett, in Long Island, before 1643.
Ninth in descent from Peter Larssen Cock, in New Sweden, 1641.
Ninth in descent from Yelverton Crowell, in Plymouth Colony, 1643.
Ninth in descent from John Gorham, in Plymouth Colony, 1643.
Ninth in descent from James Matthews, in Plymouth Colony, 1634.
Eighth in descent from Humphrey Hughes, in Long Island, 1659.
Eighth in descent from Andrew Wheeler, in Upland, now Penna., before
    1677.

Middleton

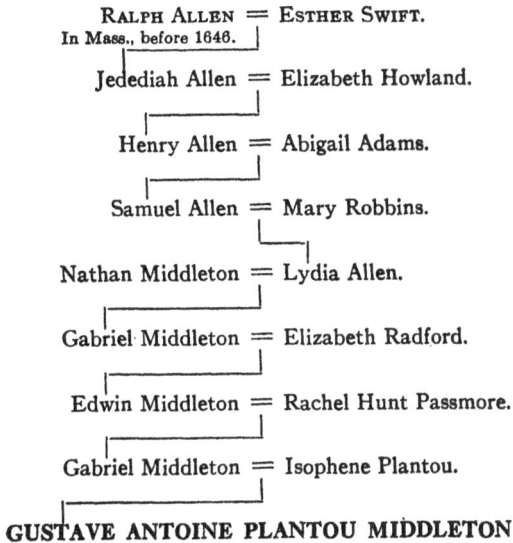

RALPH ALLEN = ESTHER SWIFT.
In Mass., before 1646.

Jedediah Allen = Elizabeth Howland.

Henry Allen = Abigail Adams.

Samuel Allen = Mary Robbins.

Nathan Middleton = Lydia Allen.

Gabriel Middleton = Elizabeth Radford.

Edwin Middleton = Rachel Hunt Passmore.

Gabriel Middleton = Isophene Plantou.

GUSTAVE ANTOINE PLANTOU MIDDLETON

Miller

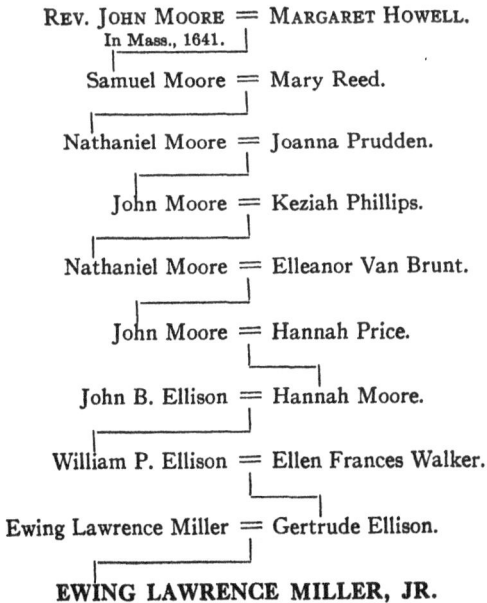

REV. JOHN MOORE = MARGARET HOWELL.
In Mass., 1641.

Samuel Moore = Mary Reed.

Nathaniel Moore = Joanna Prudden.

John Moore = Keziah Phillips.

Nathaniel Moore = Elleanor Van Brunt.

John Moore = Hannah Price.

John B. Ellison = Hannah Moore.

William P. Ellison = Ellen Frances Walker.

Ewing Lawrence Miller = Gertrude Ellison.

EWING LAWRENCE MILLER, JR.

Mills

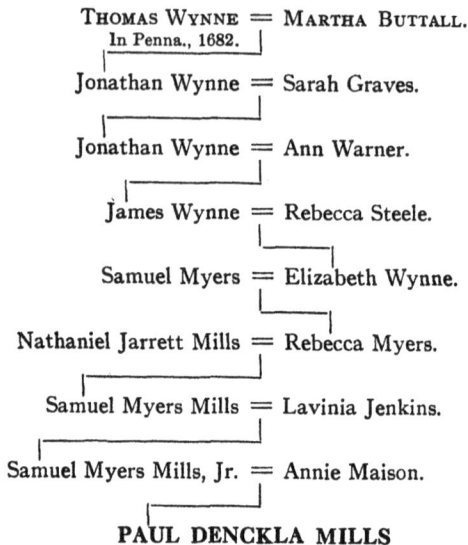

THOMAS WYNNE = MARTHA BUTTALL.
In Penna., 1682.

Jonathan Wynne = Sarah Graves.

Jonathan Wynne = Ann Warner.

James Wynne = Rebecca Steele.

Samuel Myers = Elizabeth Wynne.

Nathaniel Jarrett Mills = Rebecca Myers.

Samuel Myers Mills = Lavinia Jenkins.

Samuel Myers Mills, Jr. = Annie Maison.

PAUL DENCKLA MILLS

Milne

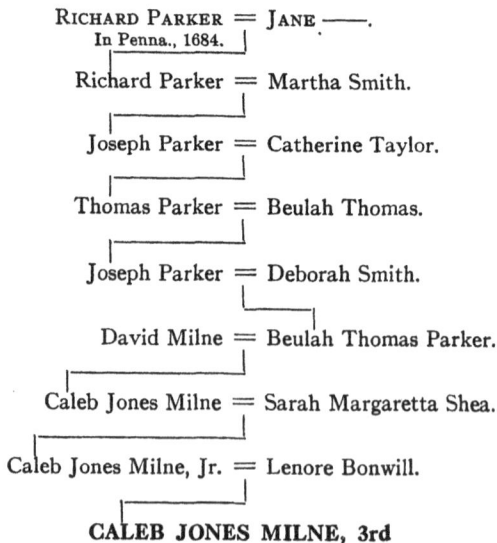

RICHARD PARKER = JANE ——.
In Penna., 1684.

Richard Parker = Martha Smith.

Joseph Parker = Catherine Taylor.

Thomas Parker = Beulah Thomas.

Joseph Parker = Deborah Smith.

David Milne = Beulah Thomas Parker.

Caleb Jones Milne = Sarah Margaretta Shea.

Caleb Jones Milne, Jr. = Lenore Bonwill.

CALEB JONES MILNE, 3rd

SUPPLEMENTALS

Tenth in descent from George Allen, in Mass., 1636.
Tenth in descent from Ellis Barron, in Mass., 1640.
Tenth in descent from Ralph Smith, in Mass., 1635.
Tenth in descent from William Swift, in Mass., 1634.
Tenth in descent from Nathaniel Sylvester, in Long Island, 1652.
Ninth in descent from Phesant Eastwick, in Mass., 1670.
Ninth in descent from John Hallowell, in Penna., 1683.
Ninth in descent from William Hearn, in Penna., 1685.
Ninth in descent from Thomas Heathers, on the Delaware, 1679.
Ninth in descent from Henry Howland, in Mass., 1633.
Ninth in descent from Henry Lewis, in Penna., 1682.
Ninth in descent from James Lloyd, in Mass., 1673.
Ninth in descent from Mary Newland, in Mass., 1637.
Ninth in descent from Robert Taylor, in Penna., 1683.
Eighth in descent from Thomas Clark, in West Jersey, 1685.
Eighth in descent from Margaret Duhurst, in West Jersey, 1692.
Eighth in descent from Robert Edmonds, in Penna., now Del., 1685.
Eighth in descent from Martha Hugh, in Penna., 1684.
Eighth in descent from Walter Newberry, in Rhode Island, 1674.
Eighth in descent from John Smith, in Penna., 1684.
Seventh in descent from Garret Sipple, in Virginia, 1674.

Elected
1914

𝔐𝔦𝔩𝔫𝔢

No.
292

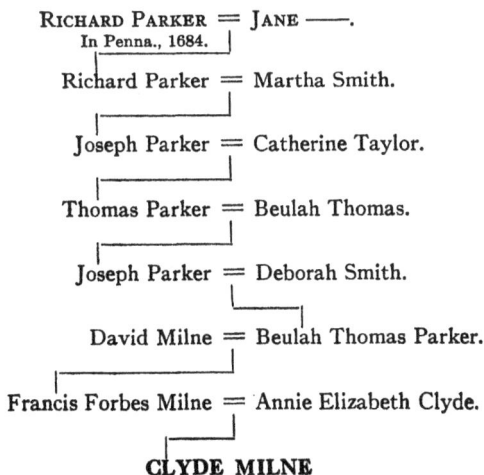

RICHARD PARKER = JANE ——.
In Penna., 1684.

Richard Parker = Martha Smith.

Joseph Parker = Catherine Taylor.

Thomas Parker = Beulah Thomas.

Joseph Parker = Deborah Smith.

David Milne = Beulah Thomas Parker.

Francis Forbes Milne = Annie Elizabeth Clyde.

CLYDE MILNE

175

𝔐ilne

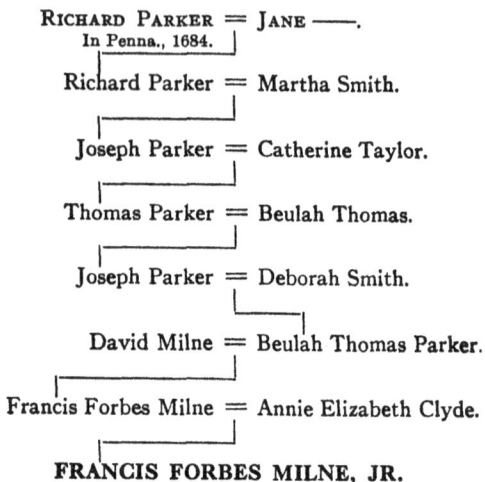

RICHARD PARKER = JANE ——.
In Penna., 1684.

Richard Parker = Martha Smith.

Joseph Parker = Catherine Taylor.

Thomas Parker = Beulah Thomas.

Joseph Parker = Deborah Smith.

David Milne = Beulah Thomas Parker.

Francis Forbes Milne = Annie Elizabeth Clyde.

FRANCIS FORBES MILNE, JR.

𝔐ilne

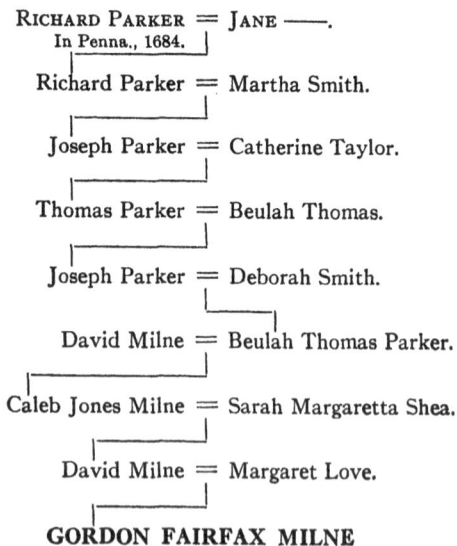

RICHARD PARKER = JANE ——.
In Penna., 1684.

Richard Parker = Martha Smith.

Joseph Parker = Catherine Taylor.

Thomas Parker = Beulah Thomas.

Joseph Parker = Deborah Smith.

David Milne = Beulah Thomas Parker.

Caleb Jones Milne = Sarah Margaretta Shea.

David Milne = Margaret Love.

GORDON FAIRFAX MILNE

RICHARD PARKER = JANE ——.
In Penna., 1684.

Richard Parker = Martha Smith.

Joseph Parker = Catherine Taylor.

Thomas Parker = Beulah Thomas.

Joseph Parker = Deborah Smith.

David Milne = Beulah Thomas Parker.

Caleb Jones Milne = Sarah Margaretta Shea.

Caleb Jones Milne, Jr. = Lenore Bonwill.

WARREN MILNE

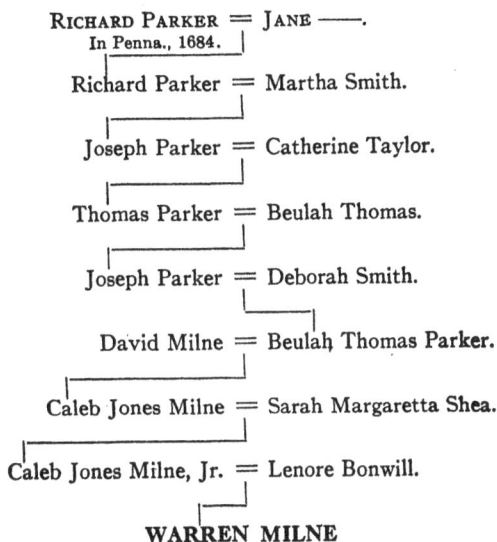

SUPPLEMENTALS

Tenth in descent from George Allen, in Mass., 1636.
Tenth in descent from Ellis Barron, in Mass., 1640.
Tenth in descent from Ralph Smith, in Mass., 1635.
Tenth in descent from William Swift, in Mass., 1634.
Tenth in descent from Nathaniel Sylvester, in Long Island, 1652.
Ninth in descent from Phesant Eastwick, in Mass., 1670.
Ninth in descent from John Hallowell, in Penna., 1683.
Ninth in descent from William Hearn, in Penna., 1685.
Ninth in descent from Thomas Heathers, on the Delaware, 1679.
Ninth in descent from Henry Howland, in Mass., 1633.
Ninth in descent from Henry Lewis, in Penna., 1682.
Ninth in descent from James Lloyd, in Mass., 1673.
Ninth in descent from Mary Newland, in Mass., 1637.
Ninth in descent from Robert Taylor, in Penna., 1683.
Eighth in descent from Thomas Clark, in West Jersey, 1685.
Eighth in descent from Margaret Duhurst, in West Jersey, 1692.
Eighth in descent from Robert Edmonds, in Penna., now Del., 1685.
Eighth in descent from Martha Hugh, in Penna., 1684.
Eighth in descent from Walter Newberry, in Rhode Island, 1674.
Eighth in descent from John Smith, in Penna., 1684.
Seventh in descent from Garret Sipple, in Virginia, 1674.

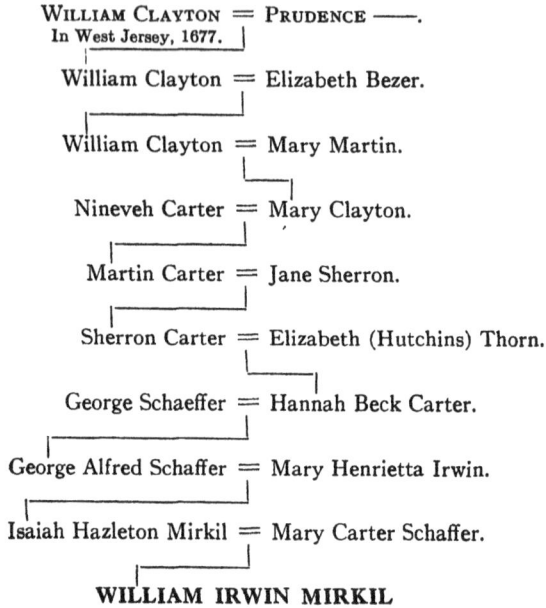

WILLIAM CLAYTON = PRUDENCE ——.
In West Jersey, 1677.

William Clayton = Elizabeth Bezer.

William Clayton = Mary Martin.

Nineveh Carter = Mary Clayton.

Martin Carter = Jane Sherron.

Sherron Carter = Elizabeth (Hutchins) Thorn.

George Schaeffer = Hannah Beck Carter.

George Alfred Schaffer = Mary Henrietta Irwin.

Isaiah Hazleton Mirkil = Mary Carter Schaffer.

WILLIAM IRWIN MIRKIL

Montgomery

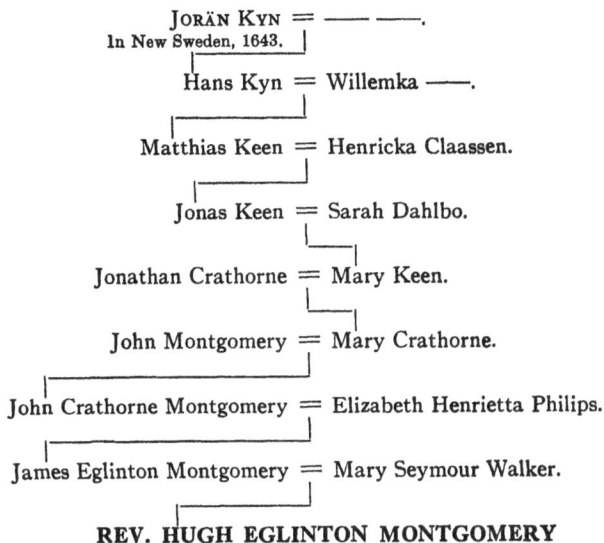

JORÄN KYN = —— ——.
In New Sweden, 1643.

Hans Kyn = Willemka ——.

Matthias Keen = Henricka Claassen.

Jonas Keen = Sarah Dahlbo.

Jonathan Crathorne = Mary Keen.

John Montgomery = Mary Crathorne.

John Crathorne Montgomery = Elizabeth Henrietta Philips.

James Eglinton Montgomery = Mary Seymour Walker.

REV. HUGH EGLINTON MONTGOMERY

Moore

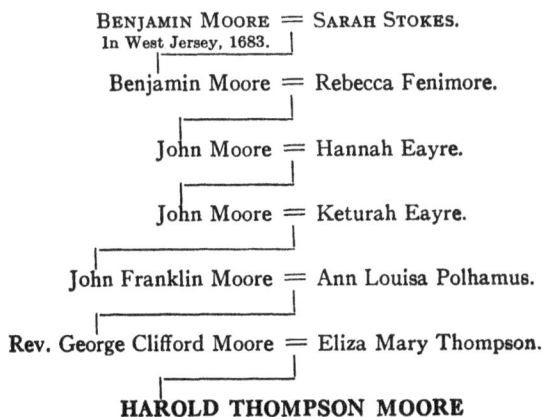

BENJAMIN MOORE = SARAH STOKES.
In West Jersey, 1683.

Benjamin Moore = Rebecca Fenimore.

John Moore = Hannah Eayre.

John Moore = Keturah Eayre.

John Franklin Moore = Ann Louisa Polhamus.

Rev. George Clifford Moore = Eliza Mary Thompson.

HAROLD THOMPSON MOORE

𝔐𝔬𝔯𝔤𝔞𝔫

WILLIAM CLAYTON = PRUDENCE ———.
In West Jersey, 1677.

James Brown = Honour Clayton.

William Brown = Esther (Baker) Yardley.

John Churchman = Margaret Brown.

George Churchman = Hannah James.

Edward Churchman = Rebecca Peirce.

Caleb Churchman = Martha Shelley.

Henry Lawrence Churchman = Sarah Reed.

George Morgan = Mary Francis Reed Churchman.

RALPH MORGAN

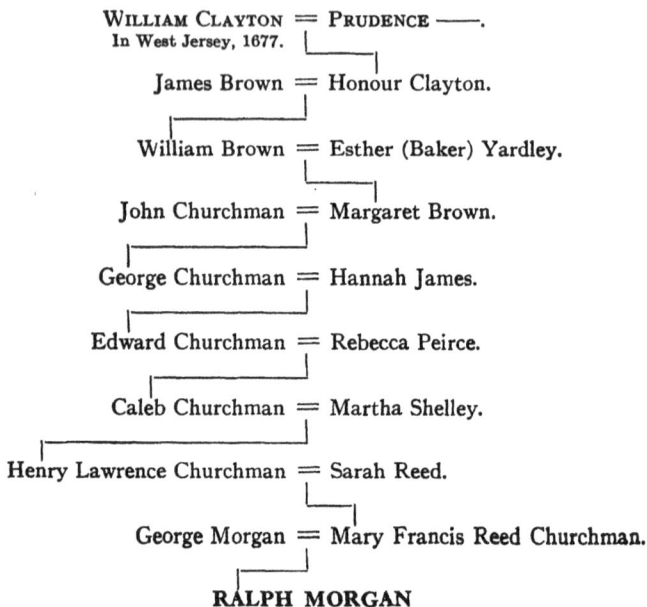

SUPPLEMENTAL

Sixth in descent from Joshua Morgan, in Penna., 1691.

Morris

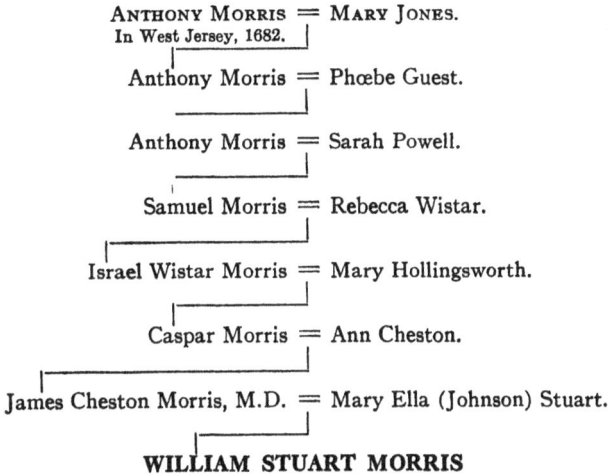

ANTHONY MORRIS = MARY JONES.
In West Jersey, 1682.

Anthony Morris = Phœbe Guest.

Anthony Morris = Sarah Powell.

Samuel Morris = Rebecca Wistar.

Israel Wistar Morris = Mary Hollingsworth.

Caspar Morris = Ann Cheston.

James Cheston Morris, M.D. = Mary Ella (Johnson) Stuart.

WILLIAM STUART MORRIS

Morrison

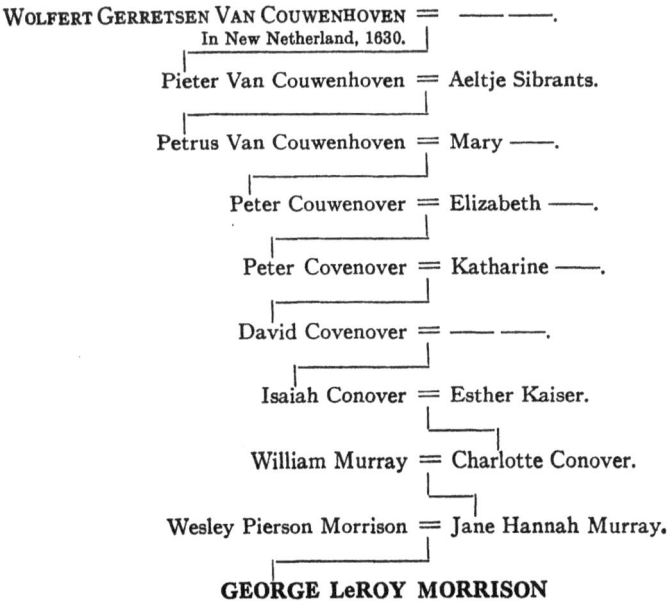

WOLFERT GERRETSEN VAN COUWENHOVEN = —— ——.
In New Netherland, 1630.

Pieter Van Couwenhoven = Aeltje Sibrants.

Petrus Van Couwenhoven = Mary ——.

Peter Couwenover = Elizabeth ——.

Peter Covenover = Katharine ——.

David Covenover = —— ——.

Isaiah Conover = Esther Kaiser.

William Murray = Charlotte Conover.

Wesley Pierson Morrison = Jane Hannah Murray.

GEORGE LeROY MORRISON

Mustin

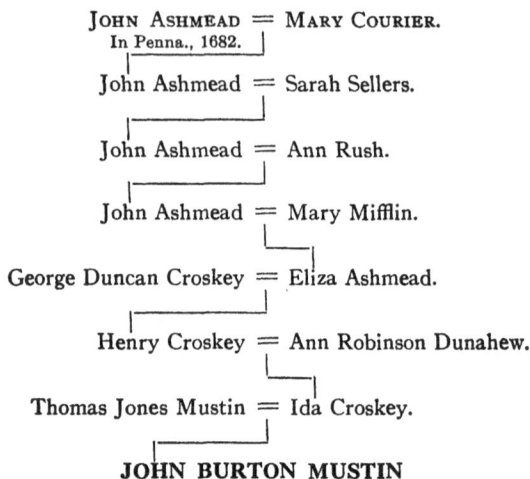

JOHN ASHMEAD = MARY COURIER.
In Penna., 1682.

John Ashmead = Sarah Sellers.

John Ashmead = Ann Rush.

John Ashmead = Mary Mifflin.

George Duncan Croskey = Eliza Ashmead.

Henry Croskey = Ann Robinson Dunahew.

Thomas Jones Mustin = Ida Croskey.

JOHN BURTON MUSTIN

Newhall

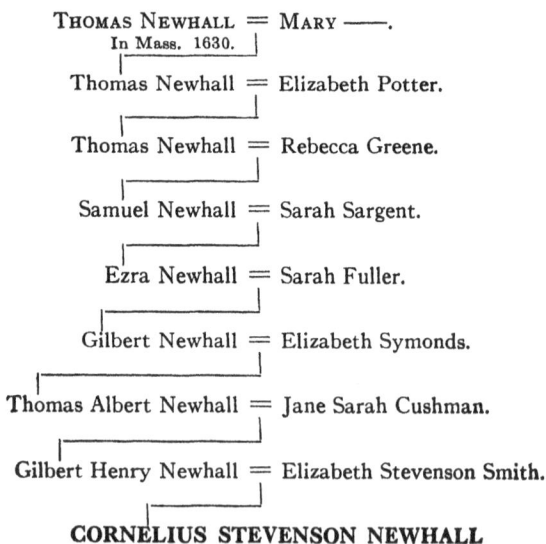

THOMAS NEWHALL = MARY ——.
In Mass. 1630.

Thomas Newhall = Elizabeth Potter.

Thomas Newhall = Rebecca Greene.

Samuel Newhall = Sarah Sargent.

Ezra Newhall = Sarah Fuller.

Gilbert Newhall = Elizabeth Symonds.

Thomas Albert Newhall = Jane Sarah Cushman.

Gilbert Henry Newhall = Elizabeth Stevenson Smith.

CORNELIUS STEVENSON NEWHALL

𝕹𝖊𝖜𝖓𝖆𝖒

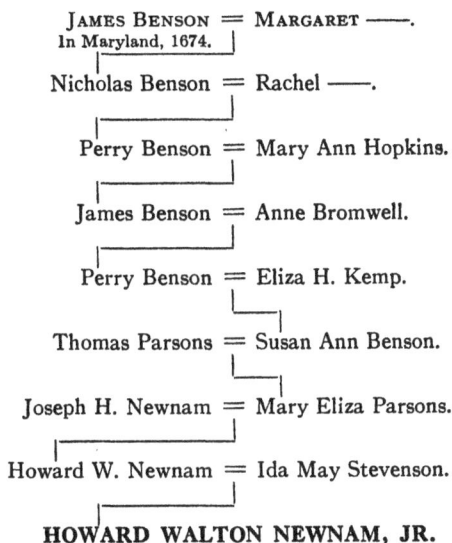

JAMES BENSON = MARGARET ——.
In Maryland, 1674.

Nicholas Benson = Rachel ——.

Perry Benson = Mary Ann Hopkins.

James Benson = Anne Bromwell.

Perry Benson = Eliza H. Kemp.

Thomas Parsons = Susan Ann Benson.

Joseph H. Newnam = Mary Eliza Parsons.

Howard W. Newnam = Ida May Stevenson.

HOWARD WALTON NEWNAM, JR.

𝕹𝖔𝖗𝖗𝖎𝖘

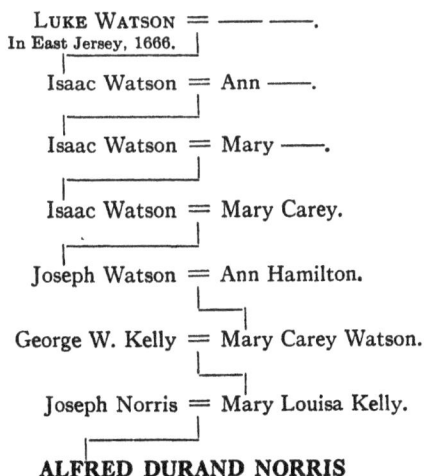

LUKE WATSON = —— ——.
In East Jersey, 1666.

Isaac Watson = Ann ——.

Isaac Watson = Mary ——.

Isaac Watson = Mary Carey.

Joseph Watson = Ann Hamilton.

George W. Kelly = Mary Carey Watson.

Joseph Norris = Mary Louisa Kelly.

ALFRED DURAND NORRIS

Norris

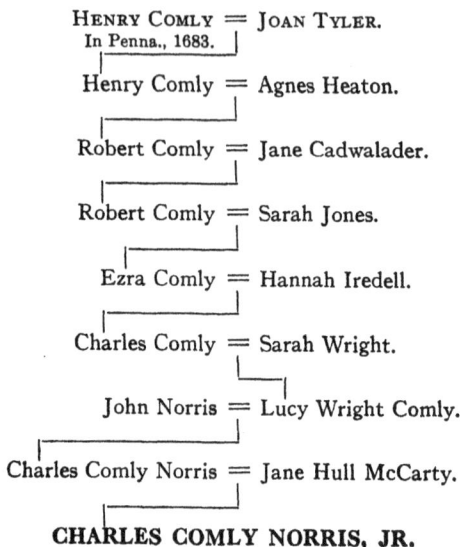

HENRY COMLY = JOAN TYLER.
In Penna., 1683.

Henry Comly = Agnes Heaton.

Robert Comly = Jane Cadwalader.

Robert Comly = Sarah Jones.

Ezra Comly = Hannah Iredell.

Charles Comly = Sarah Wright.

John Norris = Lucy Wright Comly.

Charles Comly Norris = Jane Hull McCarty.

CHARLES COMLY NORRIS, JR.

North

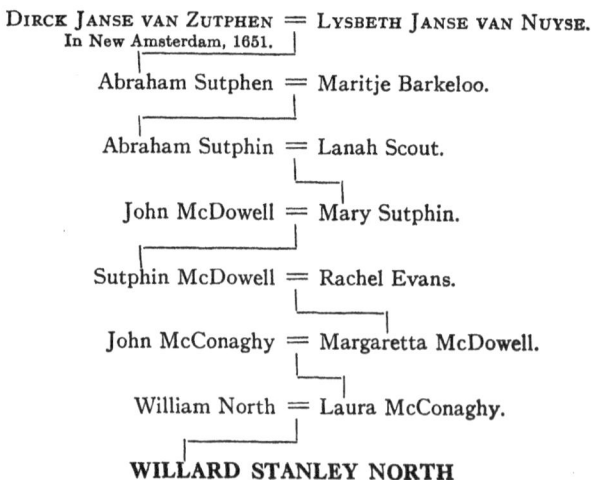

DIRCK JANSE VAN ZUTPHEN = LYSBETH JANSE VAN NUYSE.
In New Amsterdam, 1651.

Abraham Sutphen = Maritje Barkeloo.

Abraham Sutphin = Lanah Scout.

John McDowell = Mary Sutphin.

Sutphin McDowell = Rachel Evans.

John McConaghy = Margaretta McDowell.

William North = Laura McConaghy.

WILLARD STANLEY NORTH

⚙gden

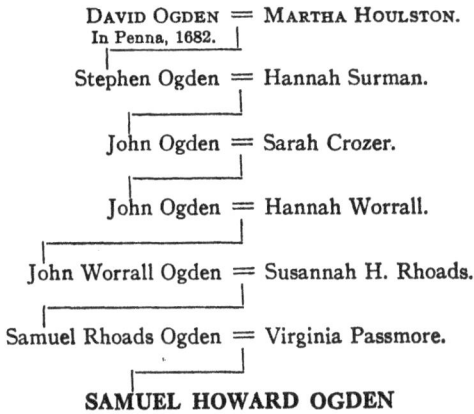

DAVID OGDEN = MARTHA HOULSTON.
In Penna, 1682.

Stephen Ogden = Hannah Surman.

John Ogden = Sarah Crozer.

John Ogden = Hannah Worrall.

John Worrall Ogden = Susannah H. Rhoads.

Samuel Rhoads Ogden = Virginia Passmore.

SAMUEL HOWARD OGDEN

JOHN PALMER = MARY SOUTHERY.
In Penna., 1683.

John Palmer = Martha Yearsley.

Moses Palmer = Abigail Newlin.

John Palmer = Hannah Martin.

John Palmer = Beulah Walter.

Charles Palmer = Deborah Pitman.

Lewis Palmer = Hannah Hancock Pancoast.

CHARLES PALMER

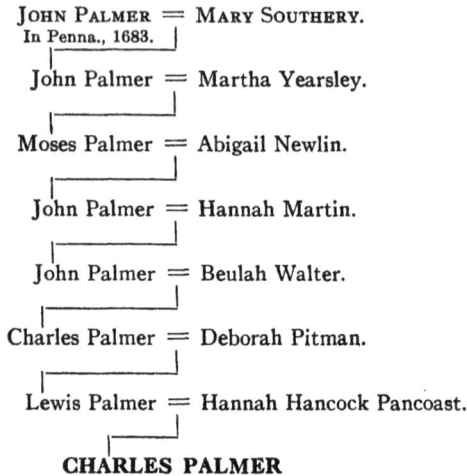

SUPPLEMENTALS

Eighth in descent from Nicholas Newlin, in Penna., 1683.
Eighth in descent from Robert Southery, in Penna., 1682.
Seventh in descent from John Martin, in Penna., 1682.
Seventh in descent from John Pancoast, in West Jersey, 1680.
Seventh in descent from Andrew Thompson, in West Jersey, 1677.
Sixth in descent from Godwin Walter, in Penna., 1685.

FRANS JANSEN BLOETGOET = LYSBETH JANS.
In New Amsterdam, 1659.

John Bloodgood = Mary ——.

William Bloodgood = Mary Gach.

Aaron Bloodgood = Abigail Carman.

Aaron Bloodgood = Mary Robinson Chandler.

Joseph Brooks Bloodgood = Sarah Ann Gardiner Baird.

Alvin Afflick Parker = Annie Catharine Bloodgood.

ALVIN MERCER PARKER

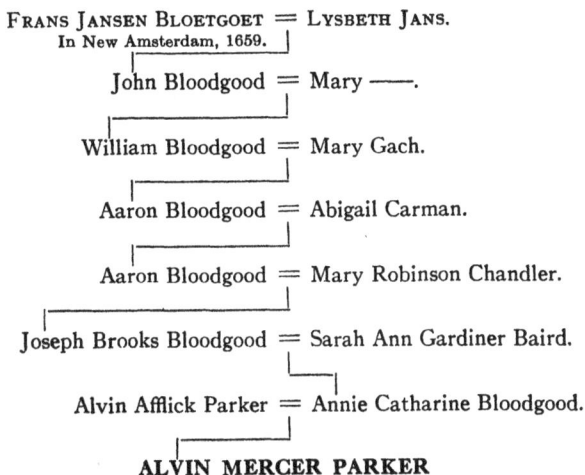

SUPPLEMENTALS

Tenth in descent from Thomas Blossom, in Plymouth Colony, 1629.
Ninth in descent from John Carman, in Mass., 1631.
Ninth in descent from Edward Fitz Randolph, in Plymouth Colony, 1636.
Ninth in descent from Rev. Joseph Hull, in Plymouth Colony, 1635.
Ninth in descent from James Hurst, in Plymouth Colony, 1632.
Eighth in descent from Anthony Annable, in Plymouth Colony, 1623.
Eighth in descent from Edward Bangs, in Plymouth Colony, 1623.
Eighth in descent from Henry Cobb, in Plymouth Colony, 1631.
Eighth in descent from John Crowell, in Plymouth Colony, 1639.
Eighth in descent from John Derby, in Plymouth Colony, 1637.
Eighth in descent from Andrew Hallett, in Plymouth Colony, 1637.
Eighth in descent from Richard Knowles, in Plymouth Colony, 1638.
Eighth in descent from Bernard Lombard, in Plymouth Colony, 1630.
Eighth in descent from Matthew Moores, in Mass., 1659.
Eighth in descent from Thomas Tobey, in Plymouth Colony, 1650.
Seventh in descent from Thomas Dexter, in Mass., 1630.
Seventh in descent from John Holley, in Conn., 1647.
Seventh in descent from Robert Parker, in Plymouth Colony, 1656.
Seventh in descent from Richard Webb, in Conn., before 1662.
Sixth in descent from Thomas Gach, in New York, before 1693.

187

ROBERT PARKER = PATIENCE COBB.
In Plymouth Colony, 1656.

Benjamin Parker = Rebecca Lombard.

Jacob Parker = Rebecca Tobey.

Jabez Parker = Sarah Hallett.

Ebenezer Parker = Mercy Holley.

Alvin Hallett Parker = Jane Dalzell Mercer.

Alvin Afflick Parker = Annie Catharine Bloodgood.

JOSEPH BROOKS BLOODGOOD PARKER

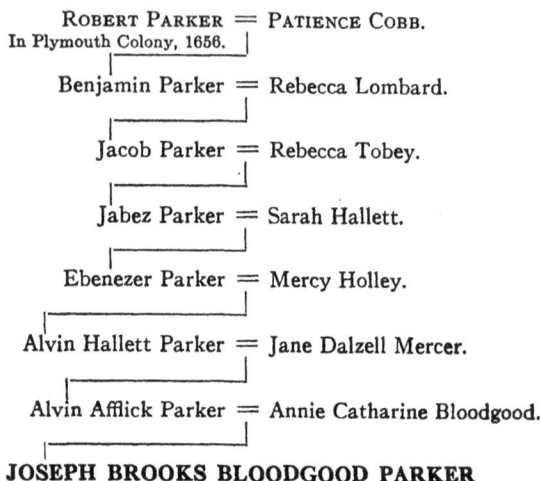

SUPPLEMENTALS

Tenth in descent from Thomas Blossom, in Plymouth Colony, 1629.
Ninth in descent from John Carman, in Mass., 1631.
Ninth in descent from Edward Fitz Randolph, in Plymouth Colony, 1636.
Ninth in descent from Rev. Joseph Hull, in Plymouth Colony, 1635.
Ninth in descent from James Hurst, in Plymouth Colony, 1632.
Eighth in descent from Anthony Annable, in Plymouth Colony, 1623.
Eighth in descent from Edward Bangs, in Plymouth Colony, 1623.
Eighth in descent from Henry Cobb, in Plymouth Colony, 1631.
Eighth in descent from John Crowell, in Plymouth Colony, 1639.
Eighth in descent from John Derby, in Plymouth Colony, 1637.
Eighth in descent from Andrew Hallett, in Plymouth Colony, 1637.
Eighth in descent from Richard Knowles, in Plymouth Colony, 1638.
Eighth in descent from Bernard Lombard, in Plymouth Colony, 1630.
Eighth in descent from Matthew Moores, in Mass., 1659.
Eighth in descent from Thomas Tobey, in Plymouth Colony, 1650.
Seventh in descent from Frans Jansen Bloetgoet, in New Amsterdam, 1659.
Seventh in descent from Thomas Dexter, in Mass., 1630.
Seventh in descent from John Holley, in Conn., 1647.
Seventh in descent from Richard Webb, in Conn., before 1662.
Sixth in descent from Thomas Gach, in New York, before 1693.

Patterson

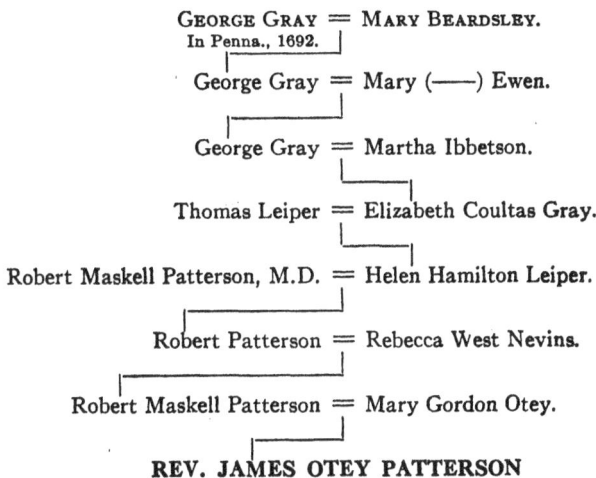

GEORGE GRAY = MARY BEARDSLEY.
In Penna., 1692.

George Gray = Mary (——) Ewen.

George Gray = Martha Ibbetson.

Thomas Leiper = Elizabeth Coultas Gray.

Robert Maskell Patterson, M.D. = Helen Hamilton Leiper.

Robert Patterson = Rebecca West Nevins.

Robert Maskell Patterson = Mary Gordon Otey.

REV. JAMES OTEY PATTERSON

Pearson

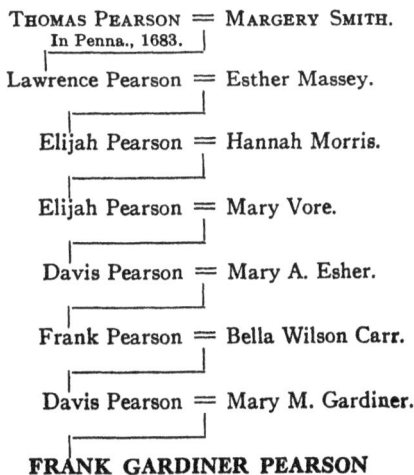

THOMAS PEARSON = MARGERY SMITH.
In Penna., 1683.

Lawrence Pearson = Esther Massey.

Elijah Pearson = Hannah Morris.

Elijah Pearson = Mary Vore.

Davis Pearson = Mary A. Esher.

Frank Pearson = Bella Wilson Carr.

Davis Pearson = Mary M. Gardiner.

FRANK GARDINER PEARSON

𝔓enrose

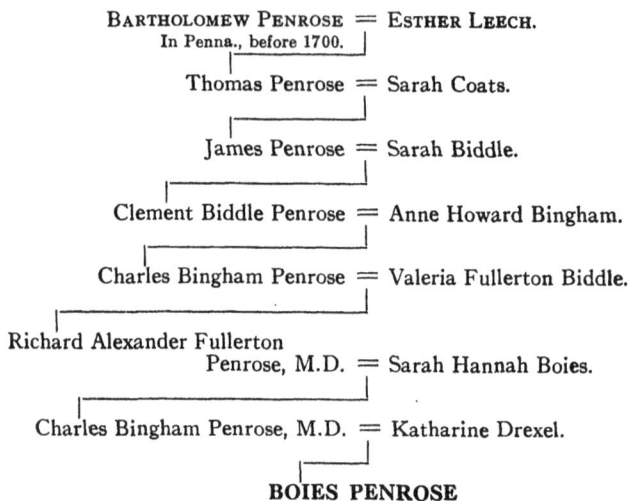

BARTHOLOMEW PENROSE = ESTHER LEECH.
In Penna., before 1700.

Thomas Penrose = Sarah Coats.

James Penrose = Sarah Biddle.

Clement Biddle Penrose = Anne Howard Bingham.

Charles Bingham Penrose = Valeria Fullerton Biddle.

Richard Alexander Fullerton
Penrose, M.D. = Sarah Hannah Boies.

Charles Bingham Penrose, M.D. = Katharine Drexel.

BOIES PENROSE

𝔓erry

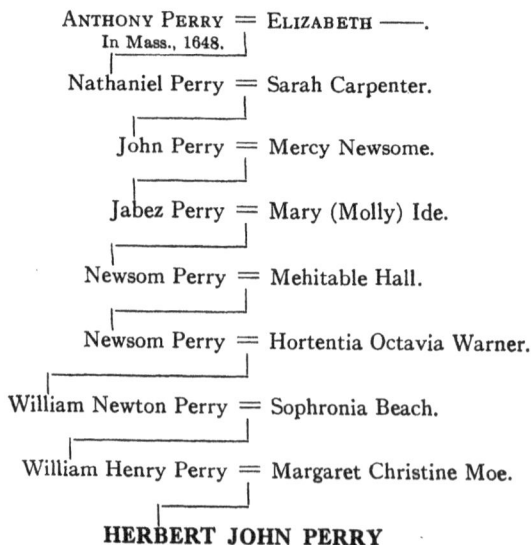

ANTHONY PERRY = ELIZABETH ——.
In Mass., 1648.

Nathaniel Perry = Sarah Carpenter.

John Perry = Mercy Newsome.

Jabez Perry = Mary (Molly) Ide.

Newsom Perry = Mehitable Hall.

Newsom Perry = Hortentia Octavia Warner.

William Newton Perry = Sophronia Beach.

William Henry Perry = Margaret Christine Moe.

HERBERT JOHN PERRY

JOHN KNOWLES = ——— ———.
In Virginia, 1665. |
|_____|
William Giles = Bethinia Knowles.
|_____|
Thomas Harden = Mary Giles.
|_____|
Nicholas Perkins = Bethinia Harden.
|_____
Nicholas Perkins = Leah Pryor.
|_____|
Nicholas Scales = Betsey Perkins.
|_____|
George Paris Plowman = Agatha Tennessee Scales.
|_____
Thomas Scales Plowman = Anne Martha Montgomery.
|_____
CLAUDE MONTGOMERY PLOWMAN

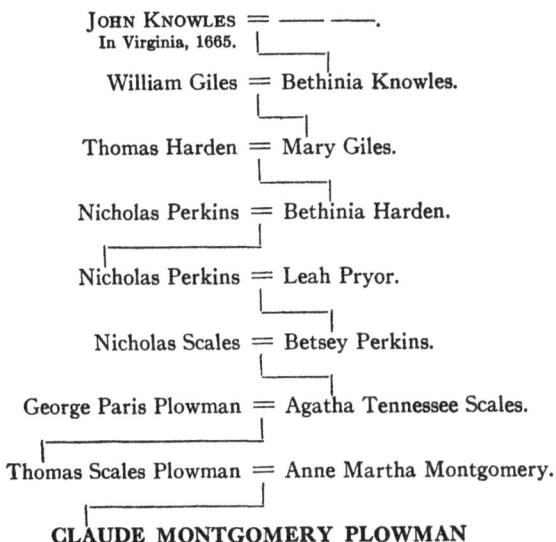

SUPPLEMENTALS

Seventh in descent from William Giles, in Virginia, 1683.
Seventh in descent from Thomas Harden, in Virginia, 1650.

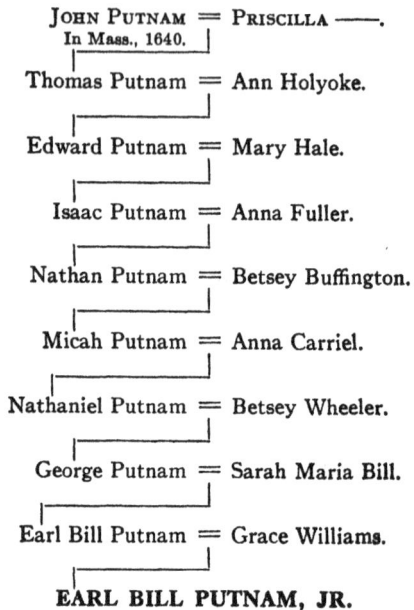

JOHN PUTNAM = PRISCILLA ——.
In Mass., 1640.

Thomas Putnam = Ann Holyoke.

Edward Putnam = Mary Hale.

Isaac Putnam = Anna Fuller.

Nathan Putnam = Betsey Buffington.

Micah Putnam = Anna Carriel.

Nathaniel Putnam = Betsey Wheeler.

George Putnam = Sarah Maria Bill.

Earl Bill Putnam = Grace Williams.

EARL BILL PUTNAM, JR.

Rambo

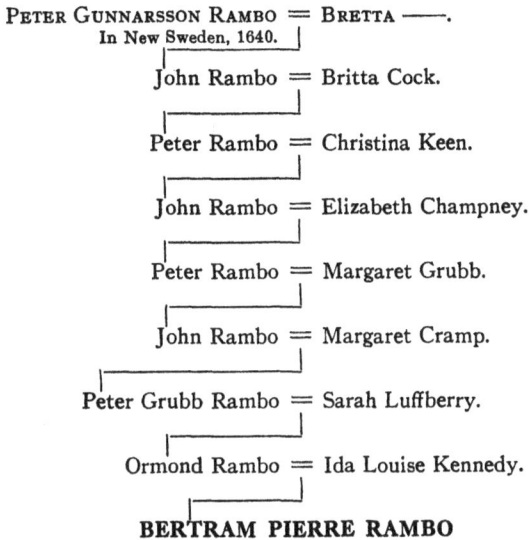

PETER GUNNARSSON RAMBO = BRETTA ———.
In New Sweden, 1640.

John Rambo = Britta Cock.

Peter Rambo = Christina Keen.

John Rambo = Elizabeth Champney.

Peter Rambo = Margaret Grubb.

John Rambo = Margaret Cramp.

Peter Grubb Rambo = Sarah Luffberry.

Ormond Rambo = Ida Louise Kennedy.

BERTRAM PIERRE RAMBO

Randolph

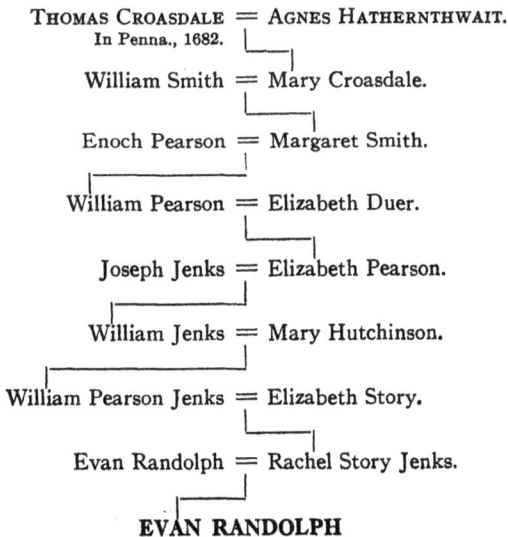

THOMAS CROASDALE = AGNES HATHERNTHWAIT.
In Penna., 1682.

William Smith = Mary Croasdale.

Enoch Pearson = Margaret Smith.

William Pearson = Elizabeth Duer.

Joseph Jenks = Elizabeth Pearson.

William Jenks = Mary Hutchinson.

William Pearson Jenks = Elizabeth Story.

Evan Randolph = Rachel Story Jenks.

EVAN RANDOLPH

Rankin

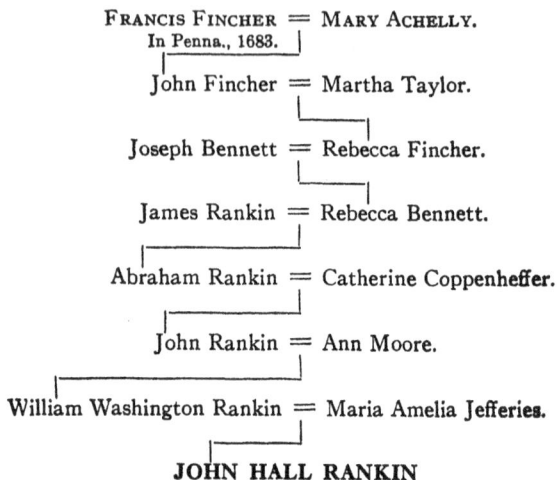

FRANCIS FINCHER = MARY ACHELLY.
In Penna., 1683.

John Fincher = Martha Taylor.

Joseph Bennett = Rebecca Fincher.

James Rankin = Rebecca Bennett.

Abraham Rankin = Catherine Coppenheffer.

John Rankin = Ann Moore.

William Washington Rankin = Maria Amelia Jefferies.

JOHN HALL RANKIN

Reckefus

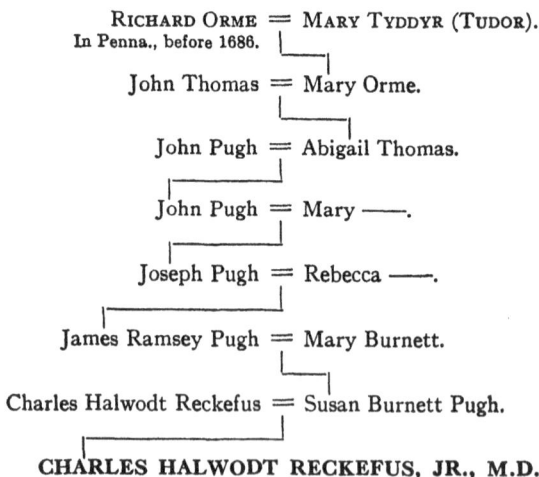

RICHARD ORME = MARY TYDDYR (TUDOR).
In Penna., before 1686.

John Thomas = Mary Orme.

John Pugh = Abigail Thomas.

John Pugh = Mary ——.

Joseph Pugh = Rebecca ——.

James Ramsey Pugh = Mary Burnett.

Charles Halwodt Reckefus = Susan Burnett Pugh.

CHARLES HALWODT RECKEFUS, JR., M.D.

SUPPLEMENTALS

Seventh in descent from Joseph Gilpin, in Penna., 1695.
Seventh in descent from William Thomas, in Penna., circa 1690.
Sixth in descent from David Pugh, in Penna., before 1691.

JOHN HAND = ALICE GRANSDEN.
In Long Island, 1644.

Benjamin Hand = Elizabeth Whittier.

Abraham Hand = Elizabeth Corson.

Jeremiah Hand = Deborah (Garrison) Hand.

Downs Edmunds = Experience Hand.

Ephraim Kent = Rachel (Edmunds) Foster.

John Bancroft, 3d = Deborah Kent.

Michael Rhoades Tallman = Hetty Merial Bancroft.

David LeRoy Reeves = Katharine Cornell Tallman.

JOHN WOOLSON REEVES, 2nd

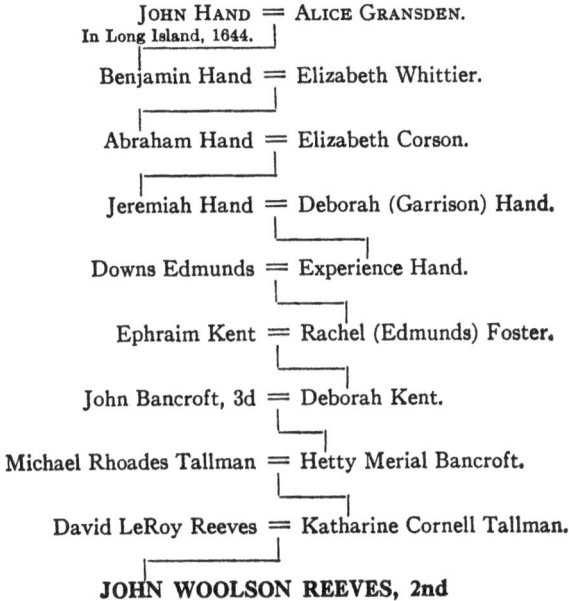

SUPPLEMENTAL

Eighth in descent from Thomas Hand, in Long Island, 1646.

ROWLAND ELLIS = MARGARET,
In Penna., 1686. |____dau. of Robert ap Owen.

John Evans = Eleanor (Ellen) Ellis.

John Hubbs = Jane Evans.

Amos Lewis = Rachel Hubbs.

Jesse Lukens = Eleanor Lewis.

Amos Lewis Lukens = Aseneth Conrad.

Israel Reifsnyder = Ellen Lukens.

Howard Reifsnyder = Hannah Gillam.

HENRY GILLAM REIFSNYDER

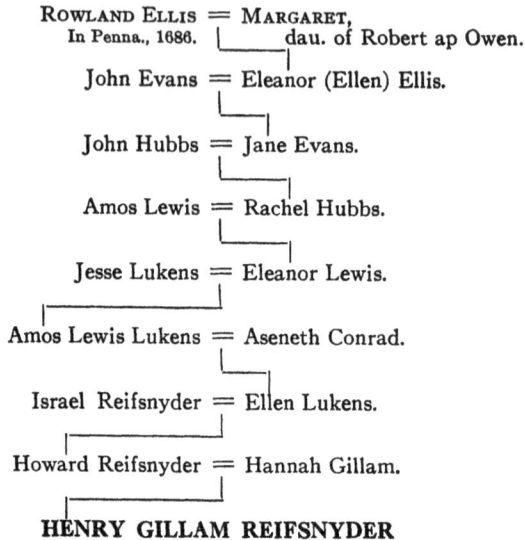

SUPPLEMENTALS

Ninth in descent from William Paxson, in Penna., before 1683.
Eighth in descent from Everard Bolton, in Penna., 1683.
Eighth in descent from Robert Cadwallader, in Penna., 1699.
Eighth in descent from William Coulston, in Penna., 1690.
Eighth in descent from Cadwallader Evans, in Penna., 1698.
Eighth in descent from John Hallowell, in Penna., 1683.
Eighth in descent from Adam Harker, in Penna., 1699.
Eighth in descent from Sarah Howell, in Penna., 1689.
Eighth in descent from Thones Kunders, in Penna., 1683.
Eighth in descent from Jan Lucken, in Penna., 1683.
Eighth in descent from John Michener, in Penna., 1686.
Eighth in descent from Robert Naylor, in Penna., 1683.
Eighth in descent from Reynier Tyson, in Penna., 1683.
Eighth in descent from Thomas Walmsley, in Penna., 1682.
Eighth in descent from William Walton, in Penna., before 1689.
Seventh in descent from Elizabeth Edwards, in Penna., 1689.
Seventh in descent from Thomas Lloyd, in Penna., 1683.
Seventh in descent from Mary Potts, in Penna., 1698.
Seventh in descent from John Roberts, in Penna., 1698.

𝕽𝖎𝖈𝖍

WILLIAM BRADFORD = ALICE (CARPENTER) SOUTHWORTH.
In Plymouth Colony, 1620.

William Bradford = Alice Richards.

Samuel Steele = Mercy Bradford.

John Webster = Abiel Steele.

Aaron Webster = Lydia ——.

Aaron Webster = Phoebe Winston.

Sheldon Rich = Laurena Webster.

George Shipman Rich = Lydia Ann O'Neal McVey.

William Shipman Rich = Susan Blanche Slager.

THADDEUS RICH

𝕽𝖚𝖊

ELLIS COOK = MARTHA COOPER.
In Long Island, 1644.

Abiel (Abial) Cook = Frances ——.

Abiel Cook = —— ——.

Abiel Cook = Parthenia Leonard.

Abiel Cook = Mary Thompson.

Joseph Stephens = Hannah Cook.

John Hanna = Clementine Lloyd Stephens.

John Rego Rue, Jr. = Mary Hill Hanna.

HOWARD STEPHENS RUE

Rue

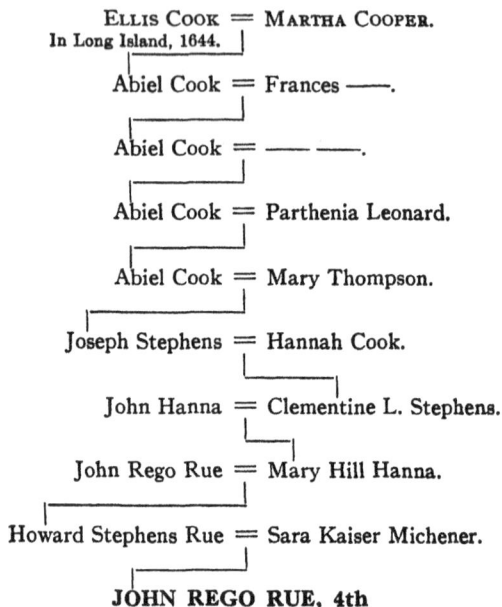

ELLIS COOK = MARTHA COOPER.
In Long Island, 1644.

Abiel Cook = Frances ——.

Abiel Cook = —— ——.

Abiel Cook = Parthenia Leonard.

Abiel Cook = Mary Thompson.

Joseph Stephens = Hannah Cook.

John Hanna = Clementine L. Stephens.

John Rego Rue = Mary Hill Hanna.

Howard Stephens Rue = Sara Kaiser Michener.

JOHN REGO RUE, 4th

Rue

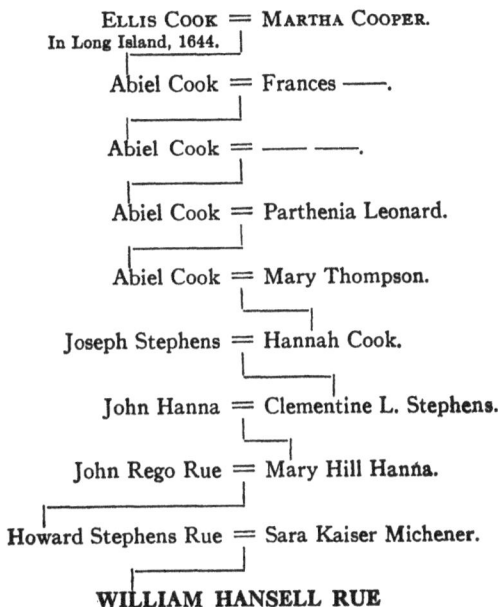

ELLIS COOK = MARTHA COOPER.
In Long Island, 1644.

Abiel Cook = Frances ——.

Abiel Cook = —— ——.

Abiel Cook = Parthenia Leonard.

Abiel Cook = Mary Thompson.

Joseph Stephens = Hannah Cook.

John Hanna = Clementine L. Stephens.

John Rego Rue = Mary Hill Hanna.

Howard Stephens Rue = Sara Kaiser Michener.

WILLIAM HANSELL RUE

Rulon=Miller

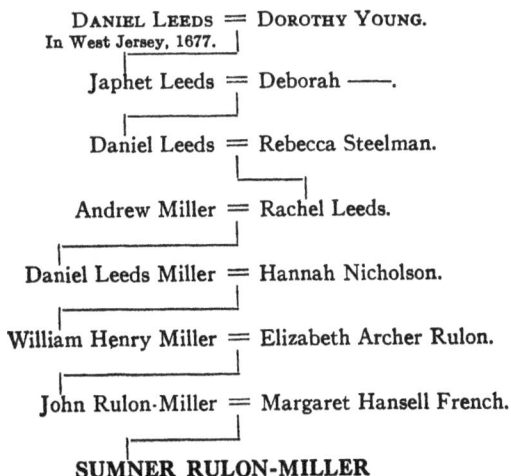

DANIEL LEEDS = DOROTHY YOUNG.
In West Jersey, 1677.

Japhet Leeds = Deborah ——.

Daniel Leeds = Rebecca Steelman.

Andrew Miller = Rachel Leeds.

Daniel Leeds Miller = Hannah Nicholson.

William Henry Miller = Elizabeth Archer Rulon.

John Rulon-Miller = Margaret Hansell French.

SUMNER RULON-MILLER

Runk

JEREMIAS VAN RENSSELAER = MARIA VAN CORTLANDT.
In Rensselaerwyck, 1658.

Hendrick Van Rensselaer = Catharina Van Brugh.

Johannes Ten Broeck = Catryna Van Rensselaer.

John Ten Broeck = Patience Williamson.

Peter Ten Broeck = Anne Chamberlain.

John Runk = Emma Ten Broeck.

Peter Ten Broeck Runk = Fanny Barcroft.

William Mentz Runk = Elizabeth Cogswell Hill.

Louis Barcroft Runk = Mary Amelia Rankin.

JOHN TEN BROECK RUNK

JEREMIAS VAN RENSSELAER = MARIA VAN CORTLANDT.
In Rensselaerwyck, 1658.

Hendrick Van Rensselaer = Catharina Van Brugh.

Johannes Ten Broeck = Catryna Van Rensselaer.

John Ten Broeck = Patience Williamson.

Peter Ten Broeck = Anne Chamberlain.

John Runk = Emma Ten Broeck.

Peter Ten Broeck Runk = Fanny Barcroft.

William Mentz Runk = Elizabeth Cogswell Hill.

LOUIS BARCROFT RUNK

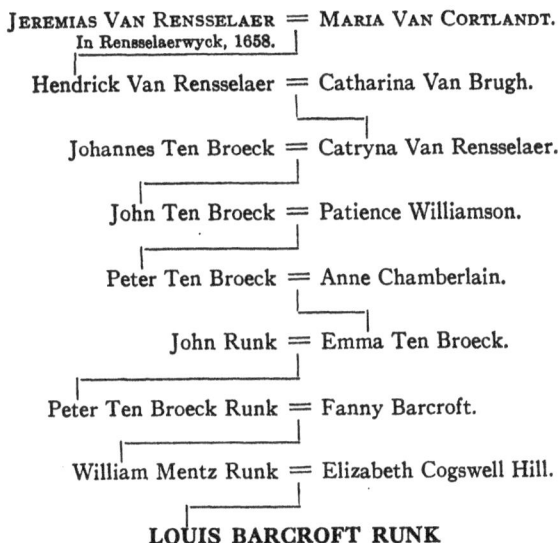

SUPPLEMENTALS

Ninth in descent from Oloff Stevenson Van Cortlandt, in New York, 1645.
Eighth in descent from Peter Hill, in Mass., 1633.
Eighth in descent from Johannes Pietersen Van Brugh, in New York, 1652.
Seventh in descent from Dirk Wesselse TenBroeck, in New York, 1662.
Seventh in descent from John Wheelwright, in Mass., 1664.
Sixth in descent from Thomas Wallingford, in Mass., 1697.

Rutter

THOMAS RUTTER = REBECCA STAPLES.
In Penna., 1685.

Thomas Rutter = Mary Catherine Gheslin.

Thomas Rutter = Martha Potts.

David Rutter = Mary Ann Potts.

Charles Rutter = Mary Anna Ives.

William Ives Rutter = Sarah May Hobart.

WILLIAM IVES RUTTER, JR.

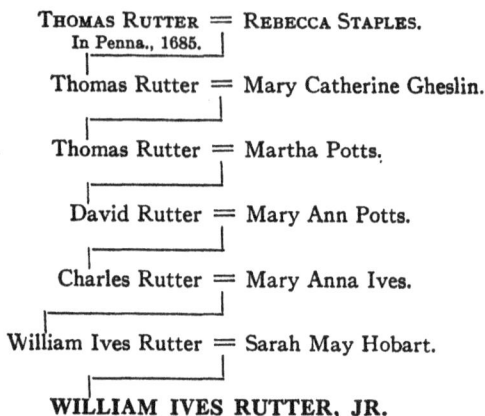

SUPPLEMENTALS

Ninth in descent from Peter Larssen Cock, in New Sweden, 1641.
Eighth in descent from John Albro, in Mass., 1634.
Eighth in descent from John Anthony, in Rhode Island, circa 1640.
Eighth in descent from Daniel Axtell, in South Carolina, before 1671.
Eighth in descent from Edmund Hobart, in Mass., 1633.
Seventh in descent from Grimston Boude, in Penna., prior to 1699.
Seventh in descent from James Claypoole, in Penna., 1683.
Seventh in descent from Pieter Keurlis, in Penna., 1683.
Seventh in descent from John Moore, in South Carolina, 1682.
Sixth in descent from Cesar Ghiselin, in Penna., 1693.
Sixth in descent from Thomas Potts, in Penna., 1690.

§argent

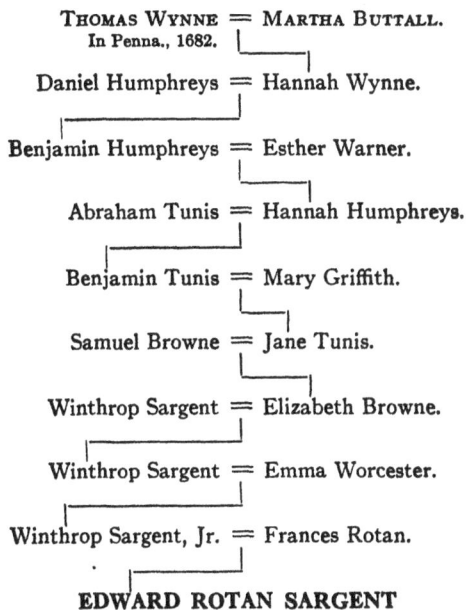

THOMAS WYNNE = MARTHA BUTTALL.
In Penna., 1682.

Daniel Humphreys = Hannah Wynne.

Benjamin Humphreys = Esther Warner.

Abraham Tunis = Hannah Humphreys.

Benjamin Tunis = Mary Griffith.

Samuel Browne = Jane Tunis.

Winthrop Sargent = Elizabeth Browne.

Winthrop Sargent = Emma Worcester.

Winthrop Sargent, Jr. = Frances Rotan.

EDWARD ROTAN SARGENT

𝕾argent

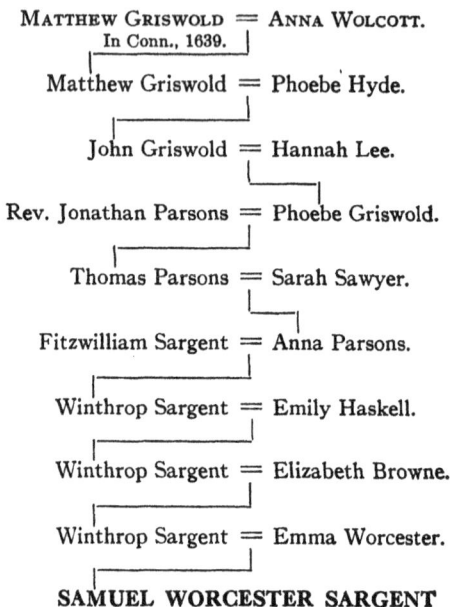

MATTHEW GRISWOLD = ANNA WOLCOTT.
In Conn., 1639.

Matthew Griswold = Phoebe Hyde.

John Griswold = Hannah Lee.

Rev. Jonathan Parsons = Phoebe Griswold.

Thomas Parsons = Sarah Sawyer.

Fitzwilliam Sargent = Anna Parsons.

Winthrop Sargent = Emily Haskell.

Winthrop Sargent = Elizabeth Browne.

Winthrop Sargent = Emma Worcester.

SAMUEL WORCESTER SARGENT

𝕾argent

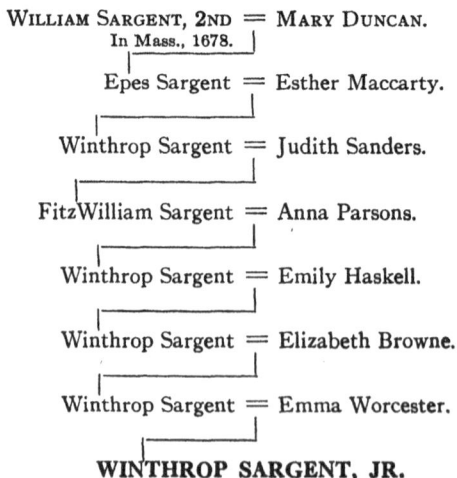

WILLIAM SARGENT, 2ND = MARY DUNCAN.
In Mass., 1678.

Epes Sargent = Esther Maccarty.

Winthrop Sargent = Judith Sanders.

FitzWilliam Sargent = Anna Parsons.

Winthrop Sargent = Emily Haskell.

Winthrop Sargent = Elizabeth Browne.

Winthrop Sargent = Emma Worcester.

WINTHROP SARGENT, JR.

SUPPLEMENTALS

Tenth in descent from John Cutting, in Mass., before 1636.
Tenth in descent from John Greenoway (Greenway), in Mass., 1630.
Tenth in descent from William Hyde, in Conn., 1636.
Tenth in descent from Richard Ingersoll, in Mass., 1629.
Tenth in descent from Robert Kinsman, in Mass., 1633/4.
Tenth in descent from John Tuttle, in Mass., 1635.
Tenth in descent from Henry Wolcott, in Mass., 1630.
Ninth in descent from William Adams, in Mass., 1635.
Ninth in descent from Christopher Batt, in Mass., 1639.
Ninth in descent from Edward Carleton, in Mass., 1639.
Ninth in descent from Samuel Chapin, in Mass., 1638.
Ninth in descent from John Cheney, in Mass., before 1637.
Ninth in descent from Balthazar de Wolfe, in Conn., 1656.
Ninth in descent from Thomas Dickinson, in Mass., 1639.
Ninth in descent from Nathaniel Duncan, in Mass., 1630.
Ninth in descent from William Fellows, in Mass., 1639.
Ninth in descent from George Fraile, in Mass., 1635.
Ninth in descent from George Giddings, in Mass., 1635.
Ninth in descent from William Goodhue, in Mass., 1635.
Ninth in descent from Matthew Griswold, in Conn., 1639.
Ninth in descent from Edward Haraden, in Mass., 1651.
Ninth in descent from Robert Haseltine, in Mass., 1639.
Ninth in descent from Joseph Jewett, in Mass., 1639.
Ninth in descent from Richard Kimball, in Mass., 1635.
Ninth in descent from Thomas Lynde, in Mass., 1634.
Ninth in descent from Thomas Marshfield, in Conn., 1637.
Ninth in descent from Thomas Millet, in Mass., 1635.
Ninth in descent from Nicholas Noyes, in Mass., 1634.
Ninth in descent from Christopher Osgood, in Mass., 1633/4.
Ninth in descent from Francis Parrot, in Mass., 1640.
Ninth in descent from Daniel Ringe, in Mass., 1648.
Ninth in descent from Abraham Robinson, in Mass., 1645.
Ninth in descent from John Sanders, in Mass., 1635.
Ninth in descent from Thomas Skelling (Skilling), in Mass., 1640.
Ninth in descent from William Taylor, in Mass., 1653.
Ninth in descent from Walter Tybbot, in Mass., 1640/41.
Ninth in descent from Richard Vore, in Conn., 1630.
Ninth in descent from John Whipple, in Mass., 1640.
Ninth in descent from Rev. William Worcester, in Mass., 1638/9.
Eighth in descent from Edmund Angier, in Mass., 1636.
Eighth in descent from Thomas Bray, in Mass., 1642.
Eighth in descent from John Curney, in Mass., before 1671.
Eighth in descent from Richard Dodge, in Mass., 1638.
Eighth in descent from Mary Epes, in Mass., before 1659.
Eighth in descent from William Haskell, in Mass., 1636.
Eighth in descent from William John or Jones, in Penna., 1683.

Eighth in descent from Arendt Klincken, in Penna., 1687.
Eighth in descent from Thomas Lee, in Conn., 1641.
Eighth in descent from Michael Newbold, in West Jersey, 1681.
Eighth in descent from Benjamin Parsons, in Mass., 1636.
Eighth in descent from Robert Pierpoint, in Mass., 1648.
Eighth in descent from Thomas Riggs,in Mass., 1658.
Eighth in descent from William Sawyer, in Mass., 1643.
Eighth in descent from Thomas Scattergood, in West Jersey, 1685.
Eighth in descent from William Titcomb, in Mass., 1634.
Eighth in descent from William Warner, in Penna., before 1678.
Eighth in descent from Thomas Wynne, in Penna., 1682.
Seventh in descent from Thomas Brian, in West Jersey, 1688.
Seventh in descent from Daniel Humphreys, in Penna., 1682.
Seventh in descent from Florence Maccarty, in Mass., 1686.
Seventh in descent from Richard Stockton, in Long Island, 1656.
Seventh in descent from Abraham Tunis, in Penna., 1683.
Seventh in descent from William Wood, in West Jersey, before 1680.

Elected
1940

Sargent

No.
615

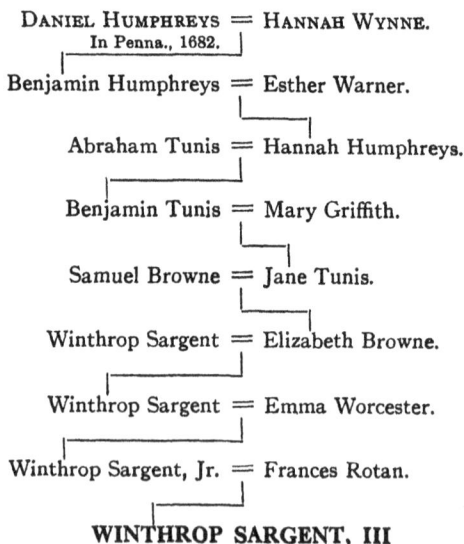

DANIEL HUMPHREYS = HANNAH WYNNE.
In Penna., 1682.

Benjamin Humphreys = Esther Warner.

Abraham Tunis = Hannah Humphreys.

Benjamin Tunis = Mary Griffith.

Samuel Browne = Jane Tunis.

Winthrop Sargent = Elizabeth Browne.

Winthrop Sargent = Emma Worcester.

Winthrop Sargent, Jr. = Frances Rotan.

WINTHROP SARGENT, III

206

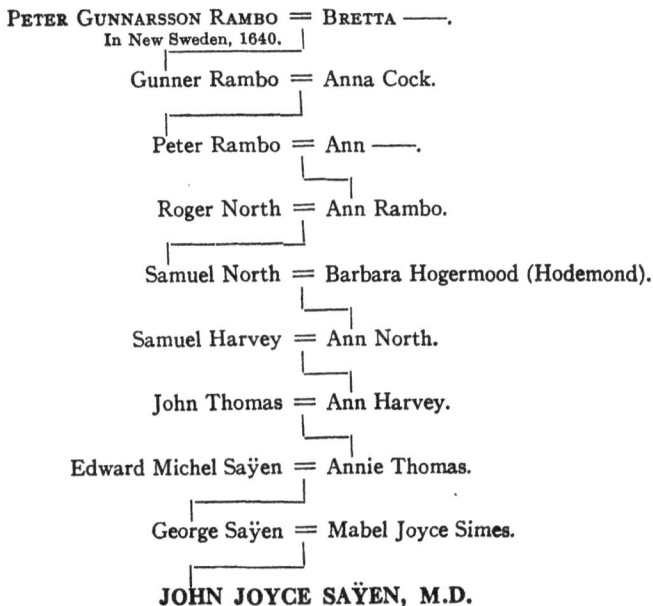

PETER GUNNARSSON RAMBO = BRETTA ——.
In New Sweden, 1640.

Gunner Rambo = Anna Cock.

Peter Rambo = Ann ——.

Roger North = Ann Rambo.

Samuel North = Barbara Hogermood (Hodemond).

Samuel Harvey = Ann North.

John Thomas = Ann Harvey.

Edward Michel Saÿen = Annie Thomas.

George Saÿen = Mabel Joyce Simes.

JOHN JOYCE SAŸEN, M.D.

ROBERT SHEILD = ELIZABETH BRAY.
In Virginia, before 1646.

Robert Sheild = Elizabeth (Davis?).

Robert Sheild = Mary Dunn.

Robert Sheild = Sarah (——) Barber.

Robert Sheild = Rebecca Hyde.

Robert Sheild = Martha Hansford.

Samuel Sheild = Maria Drummond.

Henry Samuel Kendall = Penelope Sheild.

George Boardman Seal = Maria Kendall.

HENRY KENDALL SEAL

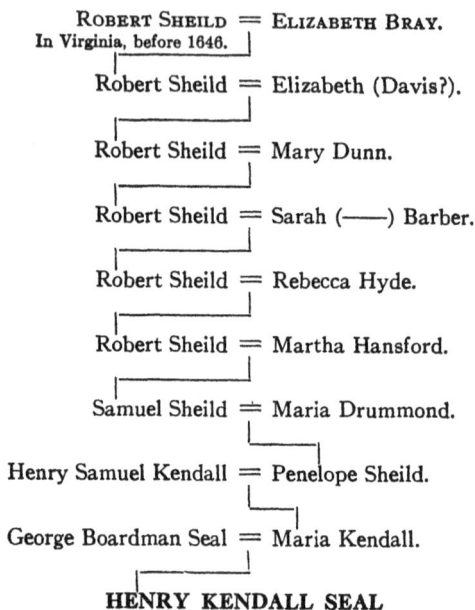

SUPPLEMENTAL

Tenth in descent from William Bradford, in Plymouth Colony, 1620.

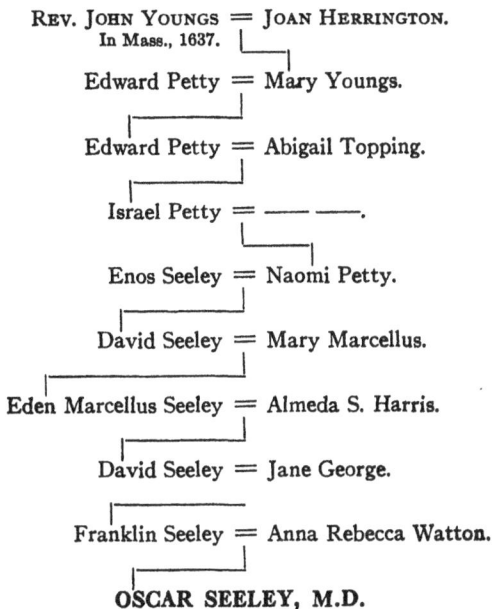

REV. JOHN YOUNGS = JOAN HERRINGTON.
In Mass., 1637.

Edward Petty = Mary Youngs.

Edward Petty = Abigail Topping.

Israel Petty = —— ——.

Enos Seeley = Naomi Petty.

David Seeley = Mary Marcellus.

Eden Marcellus Seeley = Almeda S. Harris.

David Seeley = Jane George.

Franklin Seeley = Anna Rebecca Watton.

OSCAR SEELEY, M.D.

THOMAS SELDEN = HESTER WAKEMAN.
In Conn., 1639.

Joseph Selden = Rebecca Church.

Samuel Selden = Deborah Dudley.

Samuel Selden = Elizabeth Ely.

George Selden = Olive West.

George Selden = Louise Sophie Shattuck.

George Shattuck Selden = Elizabeth Wright Clark.

EDWIN VAN DEUSEN SELDEN

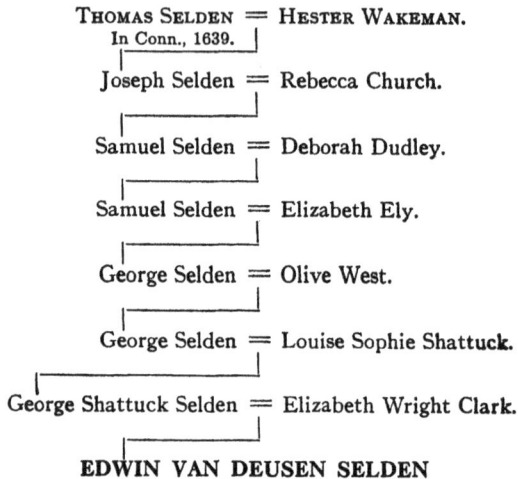

SUPPLEMENTALS

Tenth in descent from Christopher Avery, in Mass., 1646.
Tenth in descent from John Sackett, in Mass., 1631.
Ninth in descent from Ellis Barron, in Mass., 1640.
Ninth in descent from Chad Brown, in Rhode Island, 1638.
Ninth in descent from William Browne, in Conn., 1645.
Ninth in descent from William Chadbourne, in Mass., 1631.
Ninth in descent from John Clark, in Mass., 1632.
Ninth in descent from William Learned, in Mass., 1632.
Ninth in descent from Walter Palmer, in Mass., 1629.
Ninth in descent from William Palmer, in Mass., 1636.
Ninth in descent from Stephen Tracy, in Plymouth Colony, 1623.
Eighth in descent from Thomas Barnes, in Conn., 1643.
Eighth in descent from Richard Church, in Conn., 1637.
Eighth in descent from George Clark, in Conn., 1639.
Eighth in descent from William Curtiss, in Mass., 1632.
Eighth in descent from Balthazar de Wolf, in Conn., 1664.
Eighth in descent from William Dudley, in Conn., 1639.
Eighth in descent from Thomas Farrar, in Mass., 1639.
Eighth in descent from Zaccheus Gould, in Mass., 1639.
Eighth in descent from John Hall, in Conn., 1639.
Eighth in descent from Agnes Hitcheson, in Conn., 1684.
Eighth in descent from Thomas Jones, in Conn., 1639.
Eighth in descent from Philip Leeke, in Conn., 1644.
Eighth in descent from Rev. John Lothrop, in Plymouth Colony, 1634.

Eighth in descent from Thomas Lothrop, in Mass.,1637.
Eighth in descent from Reinold Marvin, in Conn., 1639.
Eighth in descent from Nathaniel Merriman, in Conn., 1651.
Eighth in descent from Thomas Miner, in Mass., 1632.
Eighth in descent from Edward Parker, in Conn., 1644.
Eighth in descent from George Partridge, in Plymouth Colony, 1636.
Eighth in descent from William Peck, in Conn., 1638.
Eighth in descent from William Pratt, in Conn., before 1642.
Eighth in descent from Stephen Randall, in Mass., 1653.
Eighth in descent from Hugh Roe, in Mass., 1642.
Eighth in descent from William Shattuck, in Mass., 1642.
Eighth in descent from John Sherman, in Mass., 1634.
Eighth in descent from Thomas Spencer, in Mass., 1630.
Eighth in descent from Richard Sperry, in Conn., 1643.
Eighth in descent from Francis West, in Plymouth Colony, 1639.
Eighth in descent from Edward Winship, in Mass., 1635.
Eighth in descent from William Woodin, in Conn., 1643.
Seventh in descent from Richard Ely, in Mass., 1664.
Seventh in descent from Daniel Goodwin, in Mass., 1662.
Seventh in descent from Thomas Lee, in Conn., 1641.
Seventh in descent from John Redington, in Mass., 1645.
Sixth in descent from Philip Hubbard, in Mass., before 1692.

Elected
1929

$\mathfrak{Selden}$

No.
455

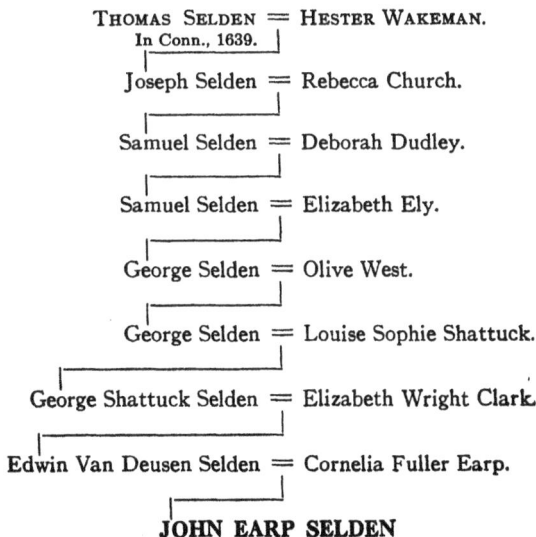

THOMAS SELDEN = HESTER WAKEMAN.
In Conn., 1639.

Joseph Selden = Rebecca Church.

Samuel Selden = Deborah Dudley.

Samuel Selden = Elizabeth Ely.

George Selden = Olive West.

George Selden = Louise Sophie Shattuck.

George Shattuck Selden = Elizabeth Wright Clark.

Edwin Van Deusen Selden = Cornelia Fuller Earp.

JOHN EARP SELDEN

211

WILLIAM WARNER = ANN DYDE.
In Penna., before 1681.

John Warner = Ann Campden.

John Warner = Mary Kirk.

William Roberts = Elizabeth Warner.

John Roberts = Sarah ——.

Walter Amos = Ann Roberts.

Hugh McClellan = Sophia Roberts Amos.

Joseph Martin Merrill = Amanda Rittenhouse McClellan.

John Bachman Shelley = Alveretta McClellan Merrill.

HOWARD MERRILL SHELLEY

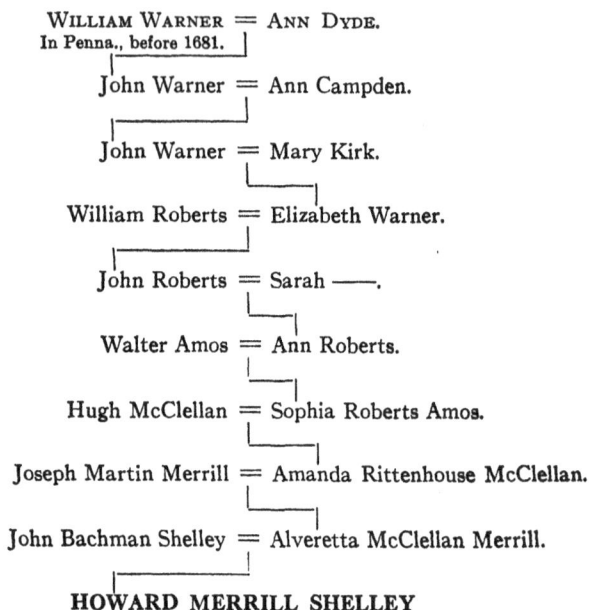

SUPPLEMENTALS

Tenth in descent from Joseph Andrews, in Mass., 1635.
Ninth in descent from Peter Ellet, in Penna., 1686.
Ninth in descent from Rev. Joseph Hull, in Plymouth Colony, 1635.
Ninth in descent from John Kirk, in Penna., 1687.
Ninth in descent from Jeffrey Manning, in East Jersey, 1670.
Eighth in descent from Rene Piat, (alias LeFleur), in East Jersey, 1678.
Eighth in descent from Richard Walter, in Penna., 1690.
Seventh in descent from William Roberts, in Penna., 1697.

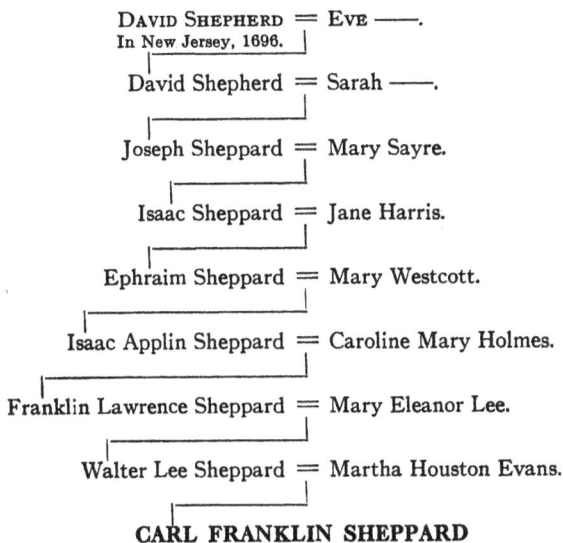

Elected
1935

𝔖𝔥𝔢𝔭𝔭𝔞𝔯𝔡

No.
568

DAVID SHEPHERD = EVE ——.
In New Jersey, 1696.

David Shepherd = Sarah ——.

Joseph Sheppard = Mary Sayre.

Isaac Sheppard = Jane Harris.

Ephraim Sheppard = Mary Westcott.

Isaac Applin Sheppard = Caroline Mary Holmes.

Franklin Lawrence Sheppard = Mary Eleanor Lee.

Walter Lee Sheppard = Martha Houston Evans.

CARL FRANKLIN SHEPPARD

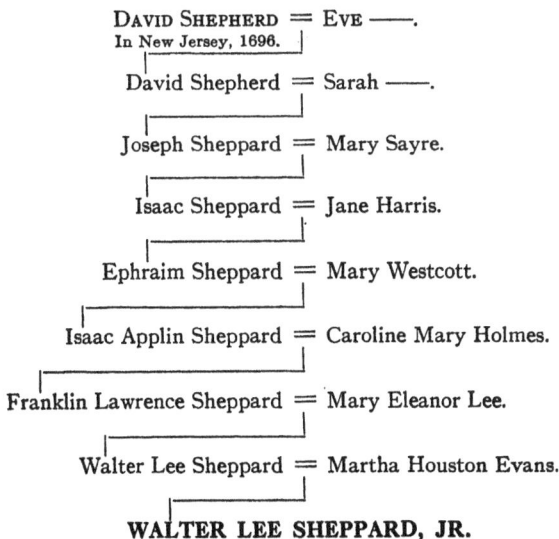

Elected
1933

𝔖𝔥𝔢𝔭𝔭𝔞𝔯𝔡

No.
566

DAVID SHEPHERD = EVE ——.
In New Jersey, 1696.

David Shepherd = Sarah ——.

Joseph Sheppard = Mary Sayre.

Isaac Sheppard = Jane Harris.

Ephraim Sheppard = Mary Westcott.

Isaac Applin Sheppard = Caroline Mary Holmes.

Franklin Lawrence Sheppard = Mary Eleanor Lee.

Walter Lee Sheppard = Martha Houston Evans.

WALTER LEE SHEPPARD, JR.

213

Sherron

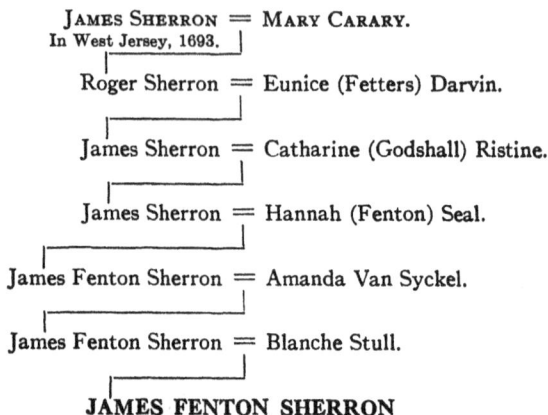

JAMES SHERRON = MARY CARARY.
In West Jersey, 1693.

Roger Sherron = Eunice (Fetters) Darvin.

James Sherron = Catharine (Godshall) Ristine.

James Sherron = Hannah (Fenton) Seal.

James Fenton Sherron = Amanda Van Syckel.

James Fenton Sherron = Blanche Stull.

JAMES FENTON SHERRON

Shewbrooks

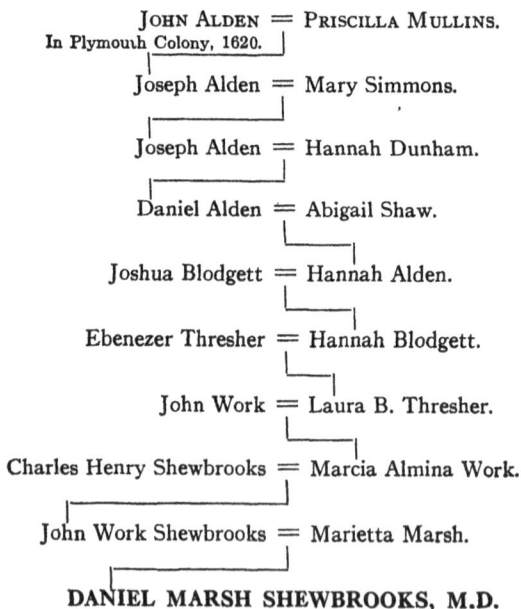

JOHN ALDEN = PRISCILLA MULLINS.
In Plymouth Colony, 1620.

Joseph Alden = Mary Simmons.

Joseph Alden = Hannah Dunham.

Daniel Alden = Abigail Shaw.

Joshua Blodgett = Hannah Alden.

Ebenezer Thresher = Hannah Blodgett.

John Work = Laura B. Thresher.

Charles Henry Shewbrooks = Marcia Almina Work.

John Work Shewbrooks = Marietta Marsh.

DANIEL MARSH SHEWBROOKS, M.D.

𝔖𝔥𝔬𝔢𝔪𝔞𝔨𝔢𝔯

GEORGE SHOEMAKER = SARAH WALL.
In Penna., 1686.

Abraham Shoemaker = Amelia Levering.

Benjamin Shoemaker = Mary Comly.

Robert Shoemaker = Martha Leech.

Richard M. Shoemaker = Amelia (Hallowell) Bird.

Benjamin H. Shoemaker = Susan Brinton Trump.

Benjamin H. Shoemaker = Edith Hacker.

BENJAMIN HALLOWELL SHOEMAKER, 3rd

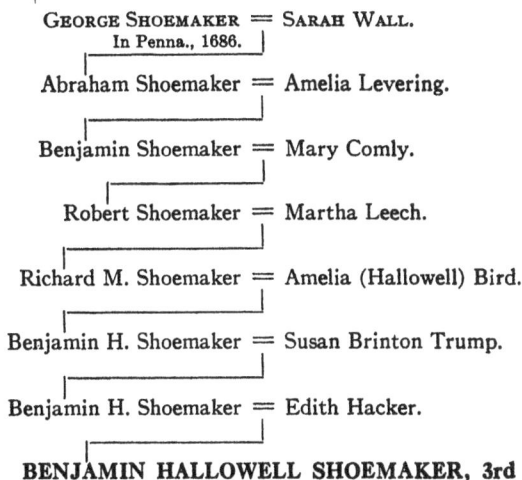

SUPPLEMENTAL

Eighth in descent from Sarah Shoemaker, in Penna., 1686.

𝕾𝖍𝖔𝖊𝖒𝖆𝖐𝖊𝖗

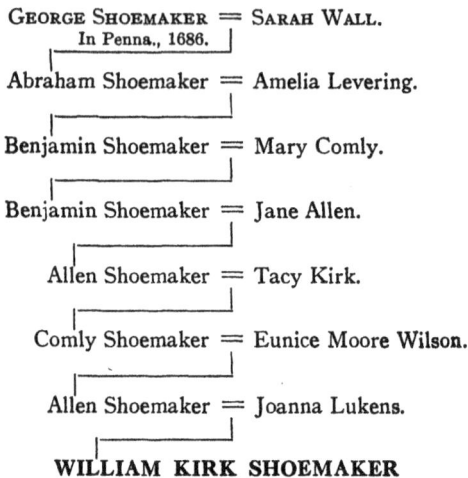

GEORGE SHOEMAKER = SARAH WALL.
In Penna., 1686.

Abraham Shoemaker = Amelia Levering.

Benjamin Shoemaker = Mary Comly.

Benjamin Shoemaker = Jane Allen.

Allen Shoemaker = Tacy Kirk.

Comly Shoemaker = Eunice Moore Wilson.

Allen Shoemaker = Joanna Lukens.

WILLIAM KIRK SHOEMAKER

SUPPLEMENTAL

Eighth in descent from Sarah Shoemaker, in Penna., 1686.

𝕾𝖍𝖗𝖞𝖔𝖈𝖐

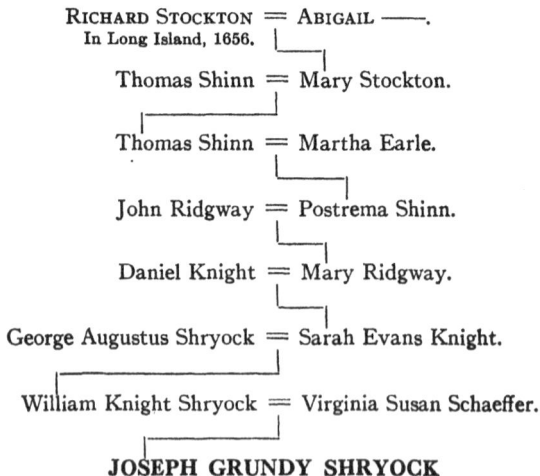

RICHARD STOCKTON = ABIGAIL ——.
In Long Island, 1656.

Thomas Shinn = Mary Stockton.

Thomas Shinn = Martha Earle.

John Ridgway = Postrema Shinn.

Daniel Knight = Mary Ridgway.

George Augustus Shryock = Sarah Evans Knight.

William Knight Shryock = Virginia Susan Schaeffer.

JOSEPH GRUNDY SHRYOCK

SUPPLEMENTALS

Ninth in descent from Peter Wright, in Plymouth Colony, 1638.
Eighth in descent from Samuel Andrews, in Long Island, 1661.
Eighth in descent from Pierre Cresson, in New Sweden, 1657.
Eighth in descent from Ralph Earle, in Rhode Island, 1638.
Eighth in descent from Sarah Ong, in West Jersey, 1694.
Seventh in descent from James Cock, in Long Island, 1655.
Seventh in descent from Nicolas De la Plaine, in New Amsterdam, 1658.
Seventh in descent from Richard Ridgway, in West Jersey, 1679.
Seventh in descent from John Shinn, in West Jersey, 1678.
Sixth in descent from Joseph Phipps, in Penna., 1682.

Elected   𝖘𝖎𝖈𝖐𝖊𝖑   No.
1929   446

JACOB LEENDERTSEN VANDERGRIFT = REBECCA FREDERICKSE LUBBERTSE.
In New Amsterdam, 1644.

Johannes Vandergrift = Neeltje (Volkers) Cortelyou.

Fulkert Vandegrift = Elizabeth Van Sandt.

Fulkart Vandegrift = Elisabeth ——.

Benjamin Vandegrift = Elizabeth ——.

Charles Vandegrift = Anna H. Croasdale.

Sylvester Jackson = Amanda Vandegrift.

William Tillton Sickel = Josephine Bonaparte Jackson.

HOWARD SYLVESTER JACKSON SICKEL

217

$mith

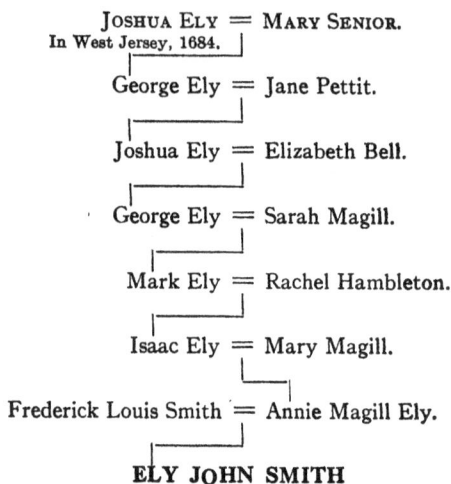

JOSHUA ELY = MARY SENIOR.
In West Jersey, 1684.

George Ely = Jane Pettit.

Joshua Ely = Elizabeth Bell.

George Ely = Sarah Magill.

Mark Ely = Rachel Hambleton.

Isaac Ely = Mary Magill.

Frederick Louis Smith = Annie Magill Ely.

ELY JOHN SMITH

$mith

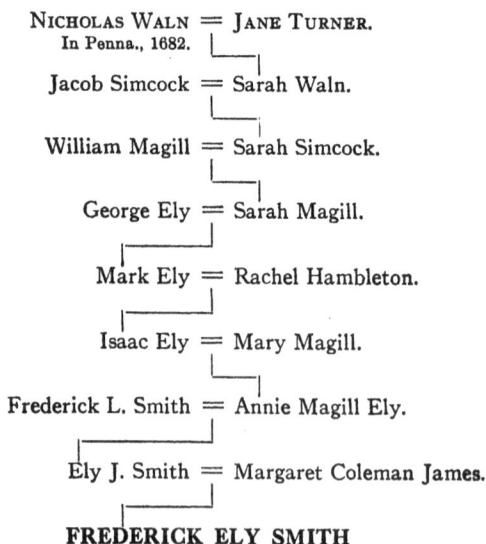

NICHOLAS WALN = JANE TURNER.
In Penna., 1682.

Jacob Simcock = Sarah Waln.

William Magill = Sarah Simcock.

George Ely = Sarah Magill.

Mark Ely = Rachel Hambleton.

Isaac Ely = Mary Magill.

Frederick L. Smith = Annie Magill Ely.

Ely J. Smith = Margaret Coleman James.

FREDERICK ELY SMITH

$\mathfrak{Smith}$

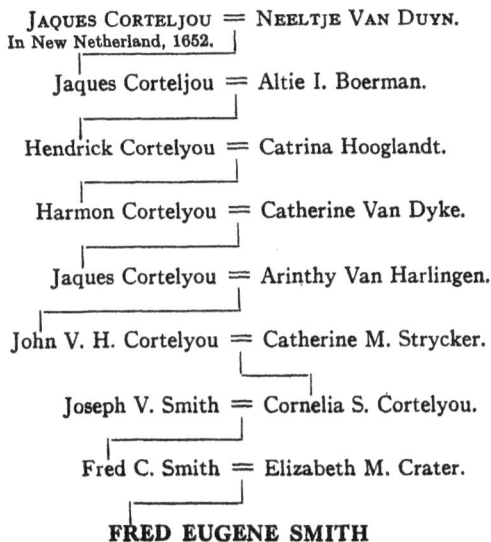

JAQUES CORTELJOU = NEELTJE VAN DUYN.
In New Netherland, 1652.

Jaques Corteljou = Altie I. Boerman.

Hendrick Cortelyou = Catrina Hooglandt.

Harmon Cortelyou = Catherine Van Dyke.

Jaques Cortelyou = Arinthy Van Harlingen.

John V. H. Cortelyou = Catherine M. Strycker.

Joseph V. Smith = Cornelia S. Cortelyou.

Fred C. Smith = Elizabeth M. Crater.

FRED EUGENE SMITH

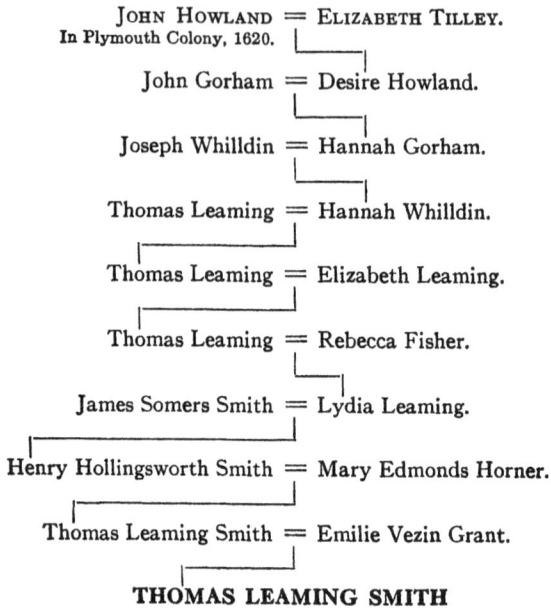

JOHN HOWLAND = ELIZABETH TILLEY.
In Plymouth Colony, 1620.

John Gorham = Desire Howland.

Joseph Whilldin = Hannah Gorham.

Thomas Leaming = Hannah Whilldin.

Thomas Leaming = Elizabeth Leaming.

Thomas Leaming = Rebecca Fisher.

James Somers Smith = Lydia Leaming.

Henry Hollingsworth Smith = Mary Edmonds Horner.

Thomas Leaming Smith = Emilie Vezin Grant.

THOMAS LEAMING SMITH

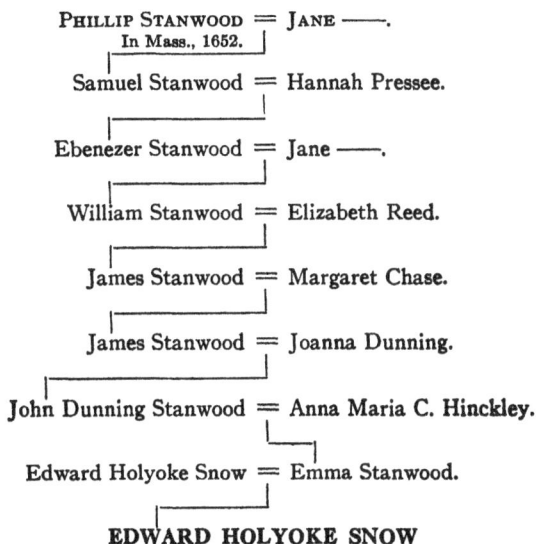

PHILLIP STANWOOD = JANE ——.
In Mass., 1652.

Samuel Stanwood = Hannah Pressee.

Ebenezer Stanwood = Jane ——.

William Stanwood = Elizabeth Reed.

James Stanwood = Margaret Chase.

James Stanwood = Joanna Dunning.

John Dunning Stanwood = Anna Maria C. Hinckley.

Edward Holyoke Snow = Emma Stanwood.

EDWARD HOLYOKE SNOW

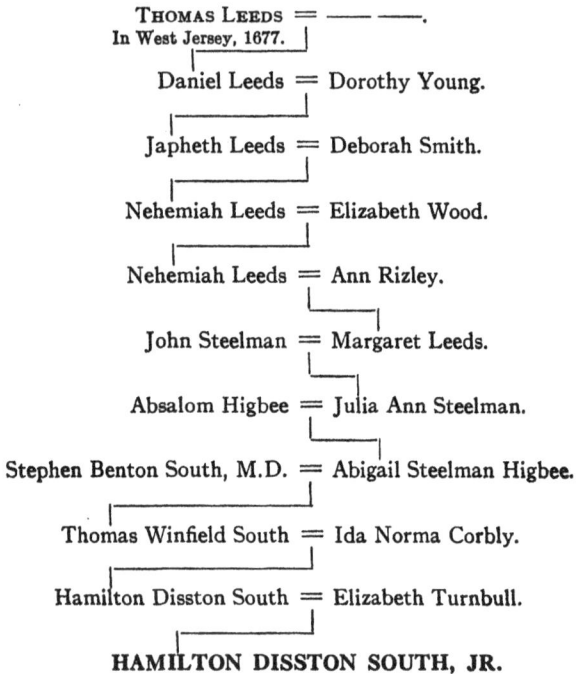

THOMAS LEEDS = —— ——.
In West Jersey, 1677.

Daniel Leeds = Dorothy Young.

Japheth Leeds = Deborah Smith.

Nehemiah Leeds = Elizabeth Wood.

Nehemiah Leeds = Ann Rizley.

John Steelman = Margaret Leeds.

Absalom Higbee = Julia Ann Steelman.

Stephen Benton South, M.D. = Abigail Steelman Higbee.

Thomas Winfield South = Ida Norma Corbly.

Hamilton Disston South = Elizabeth Turnbull.

HAMILTON DISSTON SOUTH, JR.

$\mathfrak{Steere}$

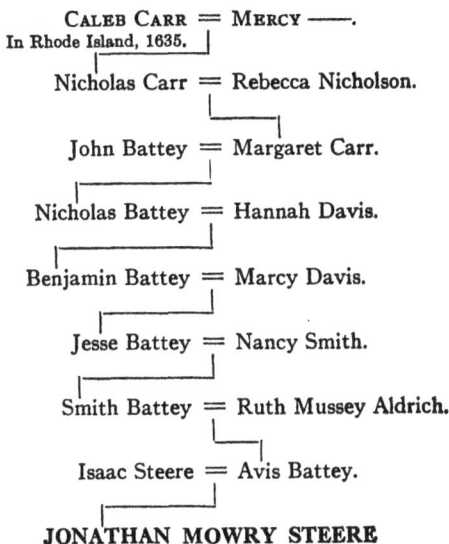

CALEB CARR = MERCY ——.
In Rhode Island, 1635.

Nicholas Carr = Rebecca Nicholson.

John Battey = Margaret Carr.

Nicholas Battey = Hannah Davis.

Benjamin Battey = Marcy Davis.

Jesse Battey = Nancy Smith.

Smith Battey = Ruth Mussey Aldrich.

Isaac Steere = Avis Battey.

JONATHAN MOWRY STEERE

$\mathfrak{Stewart}$

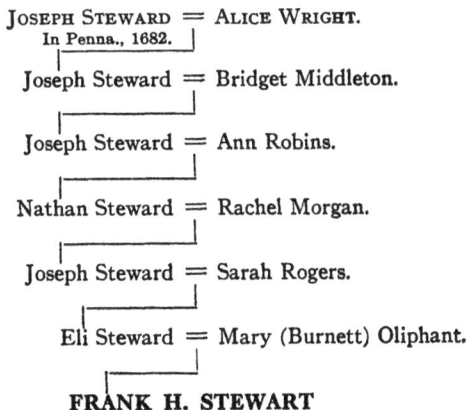

JOSEPH STEWARD = ALICE WRIGHT.
In Penna., 1682.

Joseph Steward = Bridget Middleton.

Joseph Steward = Ann Robins.

Nathan Steward = Rachel Morgan.

Joseph Steward = Sarah Rogers.

Eli Steward = Mary (Burnett) Oliphant.

FRANK H. STEWART

𝔖𝔱𝔬𝔠𝔨𝔴𝔢𝔩𝔩

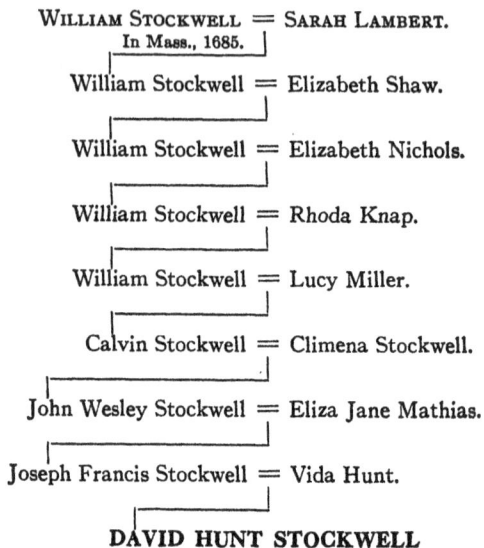

WILLIAM STOCKWELL = SARAH LAMBERT.
In Mass., 1685.

William Stockwell = Elizabeth Shaw.

William Stockwell = Elizabeth Nichols.

William Stockwell = Rhoda Knap.

William Stockwell = Lucy Miller.

Calvin Stockwell = Climena Stockwell.

John Wesley Stockwell = Eliza Jane Mathias.

Joseph Francis Stockwell = Vida Hunt.

DAVID HUNT STOCKWELL

𝕾trassburger

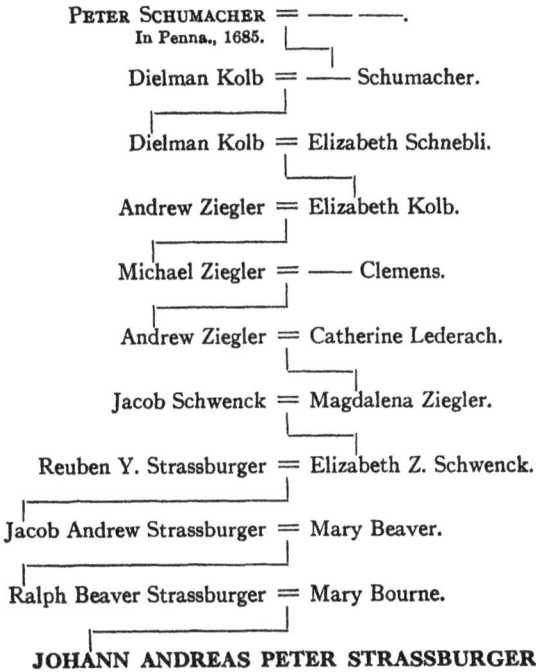

PETER SCHUMACHER = —— ——.
In Penna., 1685.

Dielman Kolb = —— Schumacher.

Dielman Kolb = Elizabeth Schnebli.

Andrew Ziegler = Elizabeth Kolb.

Michael Ziegler = —— Clemens.

Andrew Ziegler = Catherine Lederach.

Jacob Schwenck = Magdalena Ziegler.

Reuben Y. Strassburger = Elizabeth Z. Schwenck.

Jacob Andrew Strassburger = Mary Beaver.

Ralph Beaver Strassburger = Mary Bourne.

JOHANN ANDREAS PETER STRASSBURGER

PETER SCHUMACHER = —— ——.
In Penna., 1685.

Dielman Kolb = —— Schumacher.

Dielman Kolb = Elizabeth Schnebli.

Andrew Ziegler = Elizabeth Kolb.

Michael Ziegler = —— Clemens.

Andrew Ziegler = Catherine Lederach.

Jacob Schwenk = Magdalena Ziegler.

Reuben Young Strassburger = Elizabeth Ziegler Schwenk.

Jacob Andrew Strassburger = Mary Beaver.

RALPH BEAVER STRASSBURGER

ANTHONY STURGIS = ANN ——.
In Penna., 1681.

Cornelius Sturgis = Elizabeth ——.

John Sturgis = Mary Evans.

Thomas Sturgis = Catherine Roberts.

Nathan Sturgis = Catherine Phillips.

Nathan Sturgis = Maria Kennedy.

Phillips Sturgis = Angelina Rodenboh.

Samuel Sturgis = Julia Vautier.

SAMUEL BOOTH STURGIS, M. D.

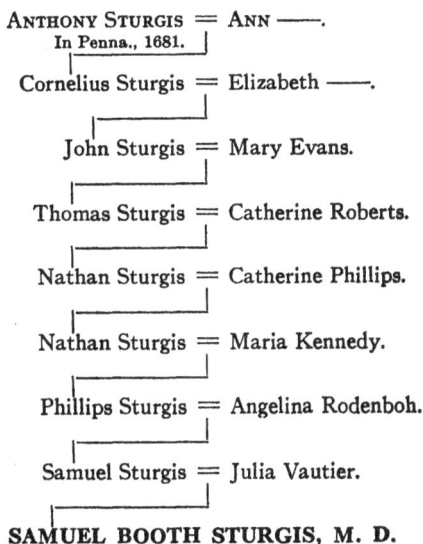

SUPPLEMENTALS

Ninth in descent from Mathias Bankson, in New Sweden, 1654.
Ninth in descent from Sven Skute, in New Sweden, 1643.
Eighth in descent from Mathew Holgate, in Penna., 1685.
Eighth in descent from Claus Johnson, in New Sweden, 1684.
Eighth in descent from Thomas Millard, in Penna., 1695/6.

THOMAS SHERIFF = MARTHA ———.
In Plymouth Colony, 1641.

Caleb Shreve = Sarah Areson.

Joshua Shreve = Jane ———.

James Shreve = Leah Davis.

Joshua Shreve = Rebecca Lamb.

Alexander Shreve = Mary Earl.

Joshua Shreve = Susanna Ridgway.

Richard Lott Ridgway Shreve = Margaret Webb.

William Ware Summers = Anna Richard Shreve.

WILLIAM GAMBLE SUMMERS

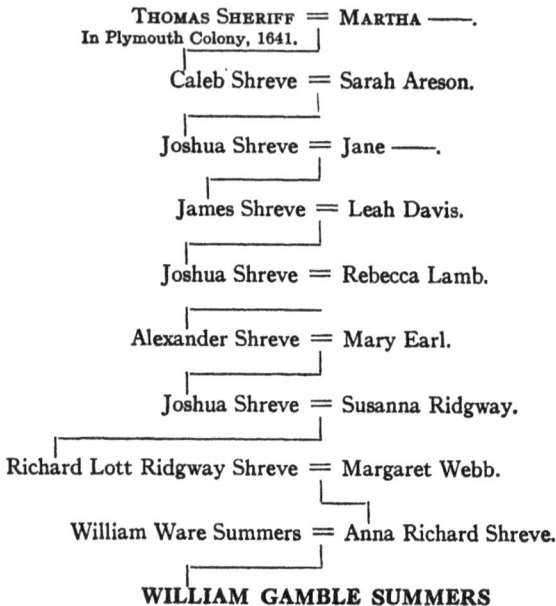

SUPPLEMENTAL

Ninth in descent from Ralph Earle, in Rhode Island, 1638.

𝔖utter

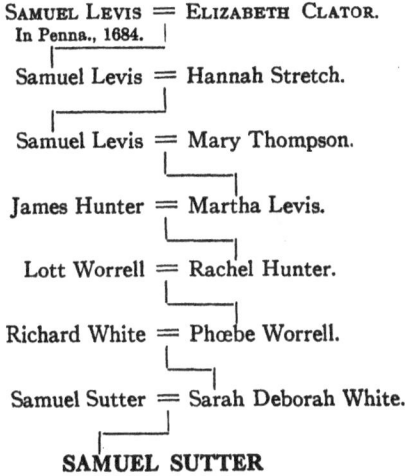

SAMUEL LEVIS = ELIZABETH CLATOR.
In Penna., 1684.

Samuel Levis = Hannah Stretch.

Samuel Levis = Mary Thompson.

James Hunter = Martha Levis.

Lott Worrell = Rachel Hunter.

Richard White = Phœbe Worrell.

Samuel Sutter = Sarah Deborah White.

SAMUEL SUTTER

𝔖utton

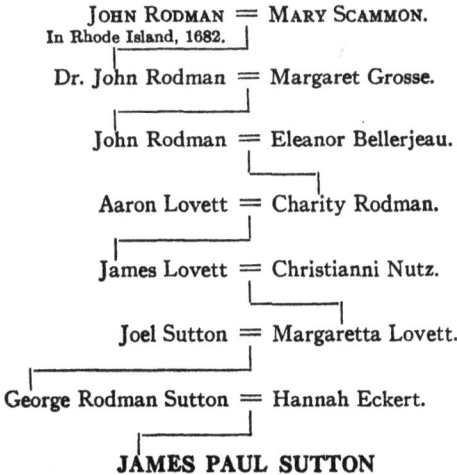

JOHN RODMAN = MARY SCAMMON.
In Rhode Island, 1682.

Dr. John Rodman = Margaret Grosse.

John Rodman = Eleanor Bellerjeau.

Aaron Lovett = Charity Rodman.

James Lovett = Christianni Nutz.

Joel Sutton = Margaretta Lovett.

George Rodman Sutton = Hannah Eckert.

JAMES PAUL SUTTON

Swing

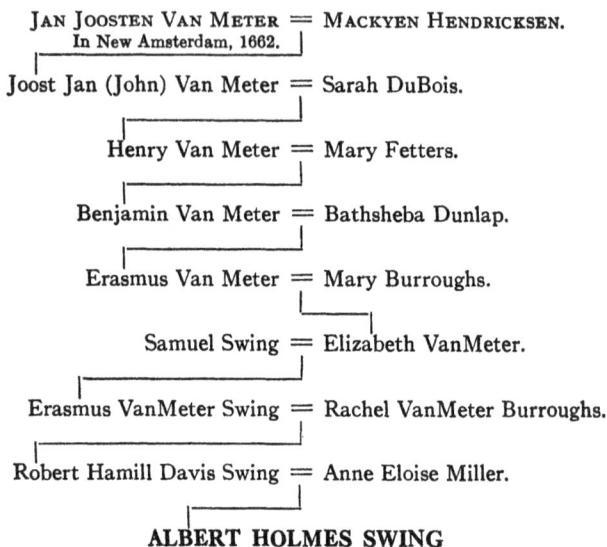

JAN JOOSTEN VAN METER = MACKYEN HENDRICKSEN.
In New Amsterdam, 1662.

Joost Jan (John) Van Meter = Sarah DuBois.

Henry Van Meter = Mary Fetters.

Benjamin Van Meter = Bathsheba Dunlap.

Erasmus Van Meter = Mary Burroughs.

Samuel Swing = Elizabeth VanMeter.

Erasmus VanMeter Swing = Rachel VanMeter Burroughs.

Robert Hamill Davis Swing = Anne Eloise Miller.

ALBERT HOLMES SWING

Swing

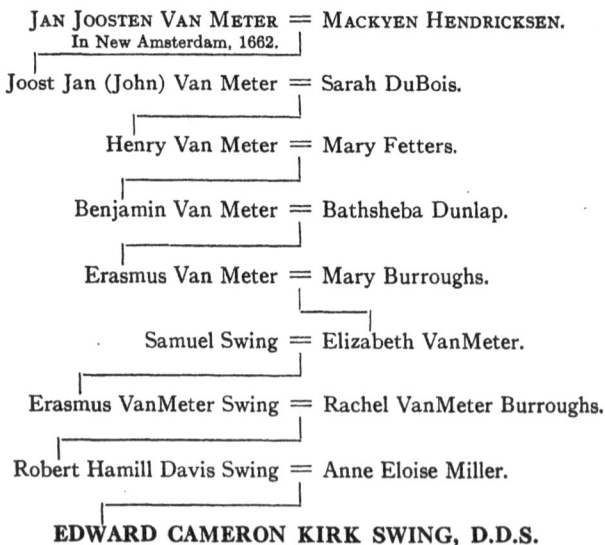

JAN JOOSTEN VAN METER = MACKYEN HENDRICKSEN.
In New Amsterdam, 1662.

Joost Jan (John) Van Meter = Sarah DuBois.

Henry Van Meter = Mary Fetters.

Benjamin Van Meter = Bathsheba Dunlap.

Erasmus Van Meter = Mary Burroughs.

Samuel Swing = Elizabeth VanMeter.

Erasmus VanMeter Swing = Rachel VanMeter Burroughs.

Robert Hamill Davis Swing = Anne Eloise Miller.

EDWARD CAMERON KIRK SWING, D.D.S.

JAN JOOSTEN VAN METER = MACKYEN HENDRICKSEN.
In New Amsterdam, 1662.

Joost Jan (John) Van Meter = Sarah DuBois.

Henry Van Meter = Mary Fetters.

Benjamin Van Meter = Bathsheba Dunlap.

Erasmus Van Meter = Mary Burroughs.

Samuel Swing = Elizabeth VanMeter.

Erasmus VanMeter Swing = Rachel VanMeter Burroughs.

Robert Hamill Davis Swing = Anne Eloise Miller.

JAMES TRUMAN SWING

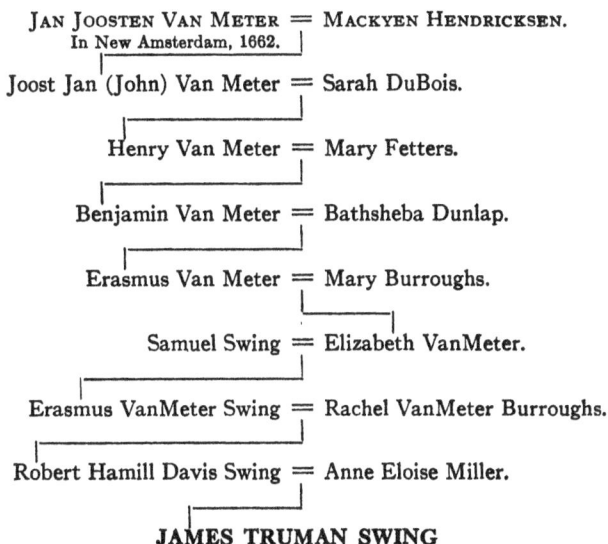

SUPPLEMENTAL

Eighth in descent from Louis DuBois, in New York, 1660.

JAN JOOSTEN VAN METER = MACKYEN HENDRICKSEN.
In New Amsterdam, 1662.

Joost Jan (John) Van Meter = Sarah DuBois.

Henry Van Meter = Mary Fetters.

Benjamin Van Meter = Bathsheba Dunlap.

Erasmus Van Meter = Mary Burroughs.

Samuel Swing = Elizabeth VanMeter.

Erasmus VanMeter Swing = Rachel VanMeter Burroughs.

Robert Hamill Davis Swing = Anne Eloise Miller.

ROBERT HAMILL DAVIS SWING, JR.

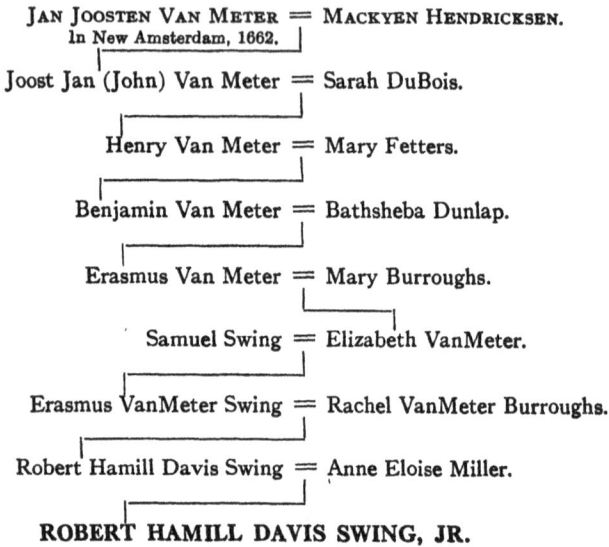

SUPPLEMENTAL

Eighth in descent from Louis DuBois, in New York, 1660.

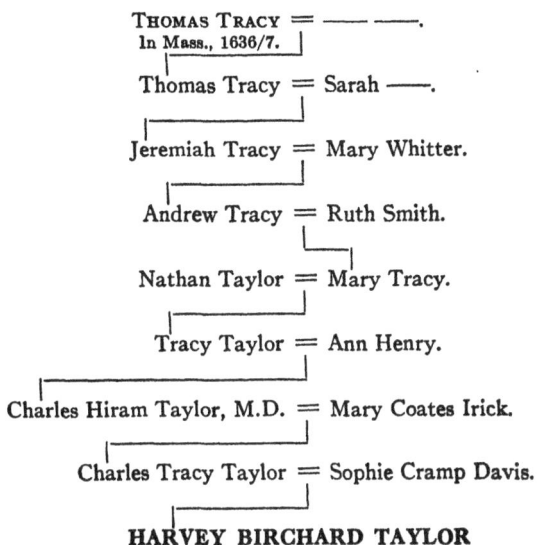

THOMAS TRACY = —— ——.
In Mass., 1636/7.

Thomas Tracy = Sarah ——.

Jeremiah Tracy = Mary Whitter.

Andrew Tracy = Ruth Smith.

Nathan Taylor = Mary Tracy.

Tracy Taylor = Ann Henry.

Charles Hiram Taylor, M.D. = Mary Coates Irick.

Charles Tracy Taylor = Sophie Cramp Davis.

HARVEY BIRCHARD TAYLOR

Taylor

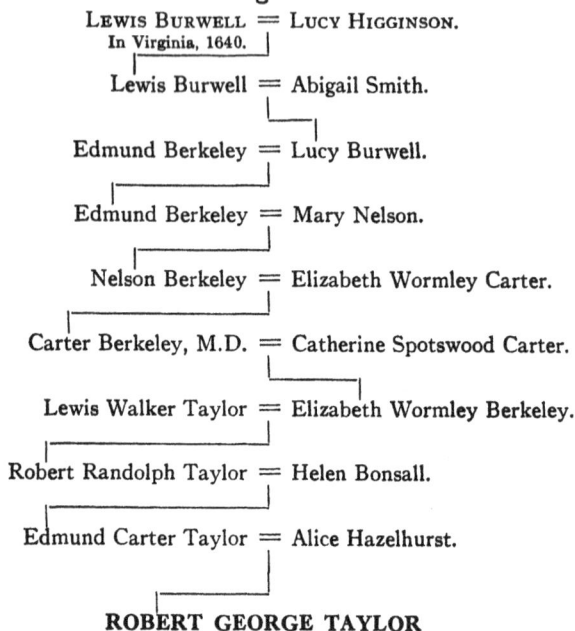

LEWIS BURWELL = LUCY HIGGINSON.
In Virginia, 1640.

Lewis Burwell = Abigail Smith.

Edmund Berkeley = Lucy Burwell.

Edmund Berkeley = Mary Nelson.

Nelson Berkeley = Elizabeth Wormley Carter.

Carter Berkeley, M.D. = Catherine Spotswood Carter.

Lewis Walker Taylor = Elizabeth Wormley Berkeley.

Robert Randolph Taylor = Helen Bonsall.

Edmund Carter Taylor = Alice Hazelhurst.

ROBERT GEORGE TAYLOR

Thomas

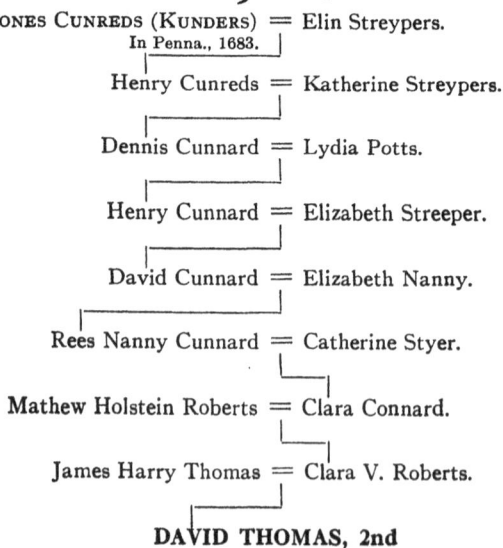

THONES CUNREDS (KUNDERS) = Elin Streypers.
In Penna., 1683.

Henry Cunreds = Katherine Streypers.

Dennis Cunnard = Lydia Potts.

Henry Cunnard = Elizabeth Streeper.

David Cunnard = Elizabeth Nanny.

Rees Nanny Cunnard = Catherine Styer.

Mathew Holstein Roberts = Clara Connard.

James Harry Thomas = Clara V. Roberts.

DAVID THOMAS, 2nd

Van Dyke

JAN TOMASSE VAN DYCK = TRYNTJE ACHIAS.
In Long Island, 1652.

Achias Janse Van Dyck = Jannetje Lambertsz.

Lambert Van Dyke = Marritje Hoogland.

Jacob Van Dyke = Hendrica Benham.

John Van Dyke = Mary Hall.

Jacob Van Dyke = Catherine Smith.

Frederick Smith Van Dyke = Margaret Crout.

Theodore Anthony Van Dyke = Josephine Miles.

THEODORE ANTHONY VAN DYKE, JR.

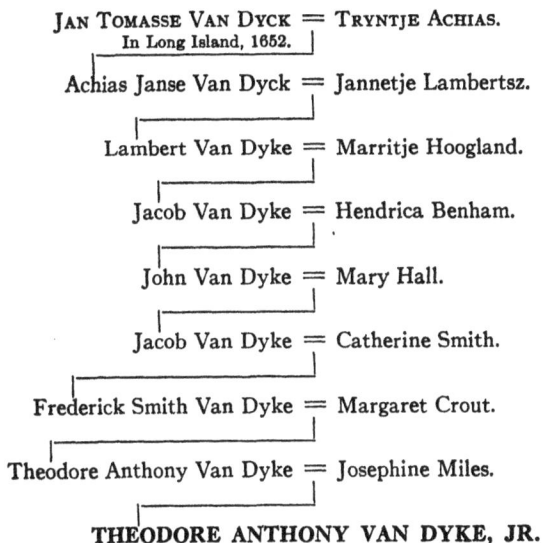

SUPPLEMENTALS

Ninth in descent from Jöran Kyn, in New Sweden, 1643.
Eighth in descent from Jan Claassen, in New Sweden, 1666.
Eighth in descent from Joseph Fisher, in Penna., 1683.
Eighth in descent from Jacob Hall, in Penna., 1684.
Eighth in descent from Cornelis Dierckse Hoogland, in New Netherland, 1638.
Eighth in descent from Adriaen Lambertsz, in Long Island, 1675.
Eighth in descent from Joris Jansen Rapalje, in New Netherland, 1623.
Eighth in descent from Thomas Rutter, in Penna., 1685.
Eighth in descent from John Swift, in Penna,, before 1684.
Seventh in descent from James Steelman, in West Jersey, 1693.

𝔚𝔞𝔩𝔨𝔢𝔯

PHILIP WALKER = JANE BUTTERWORTH.
In Mass., 1653.

Philip Walker = Sarah ———.

Nathaniel Walker = Ann Sweeting.

Enos Walker = Patience Peck.

Lewis Walker = Mary Potter.

William Walker = Abigail Ensign.

William Henry Walker = Jennett Allen Taber.

Edward Taber Walker = Fannie Louisa Supplee.

DANFORTH SUPPLEE WALKER

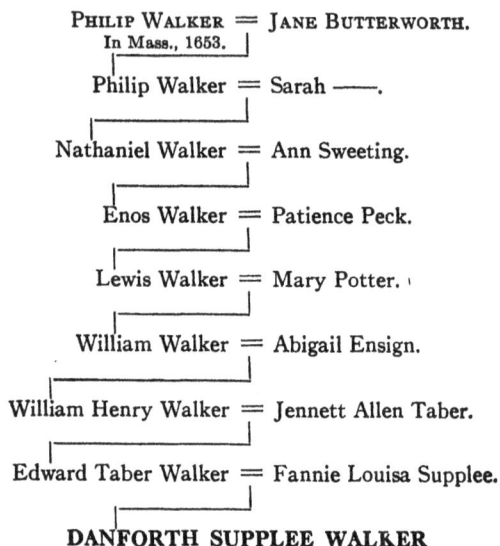

SUPPLEMENTALS

Eleventh in descent from George Morton, in Plymouth Colony, 1632.
Tenth in descent from William Phelps, in Mass., 1630.
Tenth in descent from William Spencer, in Mass., 1631.

𝔚alker

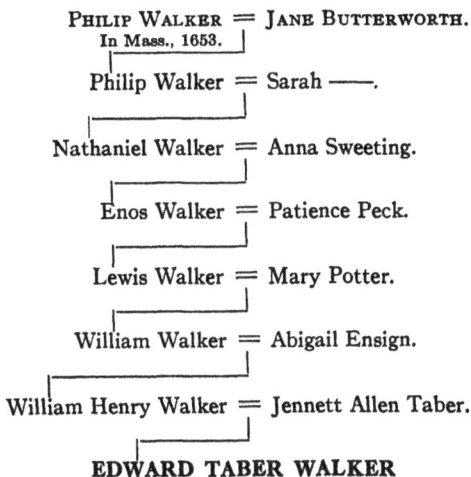

PHILIP WALKER = JANE BUTTERWORTH.
In Mass., 1653.

Philip Walker = Sarah ———.

Nathaniel Walker = Anna Sweeting.

Enos Walker = Patience Peck.

Lewis Walker = Mary Potter.

William Walker = Abigail Ensign.

William Henry Walker = Jennett Allen Taber.

EDWARD TABER WALKER

𝔚alton

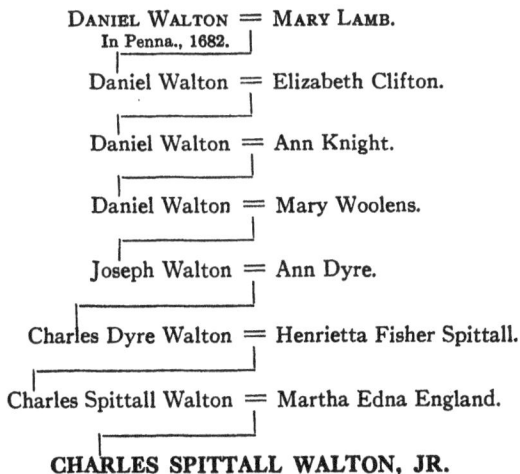

DANIEL WALTON = MARY LAMB.
In Penna., 1682.

Daniel Walton = Elizabeth Clifton.

Daniel Walton = Ann Knight.

Daniel Walton = Mary Woolens.

Joseph Walton = Ann Dyre.

Charles Dyre Walton = Henrietta Fisher Spittall.

Charles Spittall Walton = Martha Edna England.

CHARLES SPITTALL WALTON, JR.

Walton

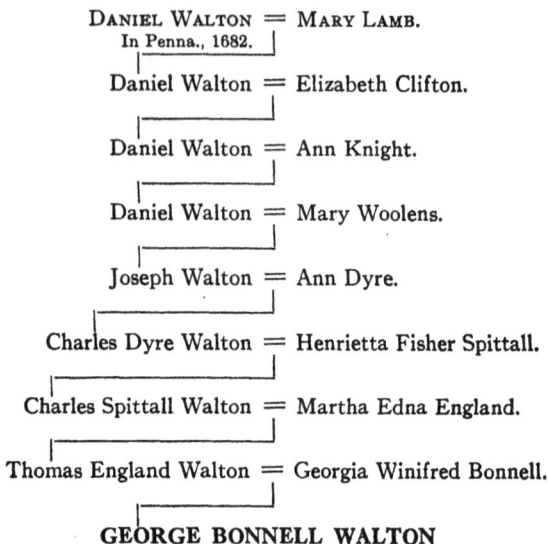

DANIEL WALTON = MARY LAMB.
In Penna., 1682.

Daniel Walton = Elizabeth Clifton.

Daniel Walton = Ann Knight.

Daniel Walton = Mary Woolens.

Joseph Walton = Ann Dyre.

Charles Dyre Walton = Henrietta Fisher Spittall.

Charles Spittall Walton = Martha Edna England.

Thomas England Walton = Georgia Winifred Bonnell.

GEORGE BONNELL WALTON

Walton

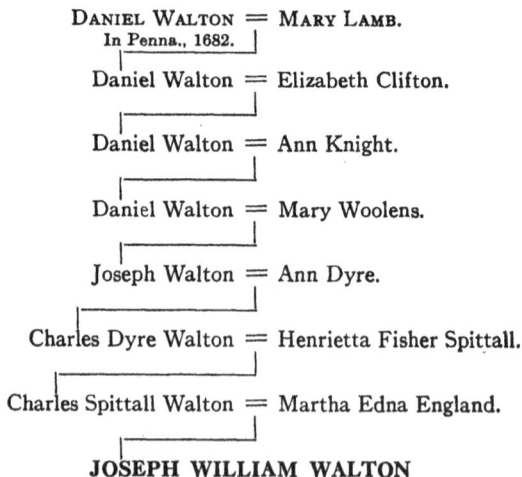

DANIEL WALTON = MARY LAMB.
In Penna., 1682.

Daniel Walton = Elizabeth Clifton.

Daniel Walton = Ann Knight.

Daniel Walton = Mary Woolens.

Joseph Walton = Ann Dyre.

Charles Dyre Walton = Henrietta Fisher Spittall.

Charles Spittall Walton = Martha Edna England.

JOSEPH WILLIAM WALTON

Walton

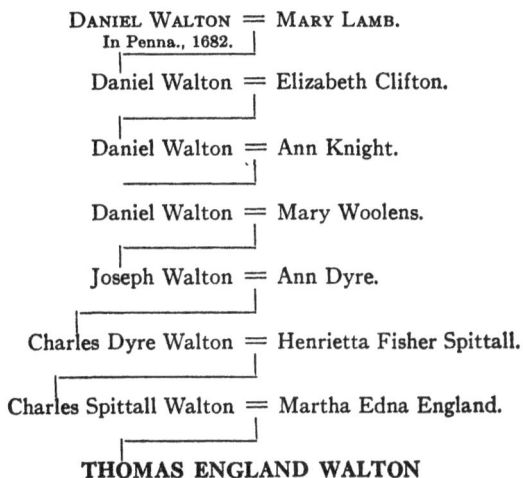

DANIEL WALTON = MARY LAMB.
In Penna., 1682.

Daniel Walton = Elizabeth Clifton.

Daniel Walton = Ann Knight.

Daniel Walton = Mary Woolens.

Joseph Walton = Ann Dyre.

Charles Dyre Walton = Henrietta Fisher Spittall.

Charles Spittall Walton = Martha Edna England.

THOMAS ENGLAND WALTON

Walton

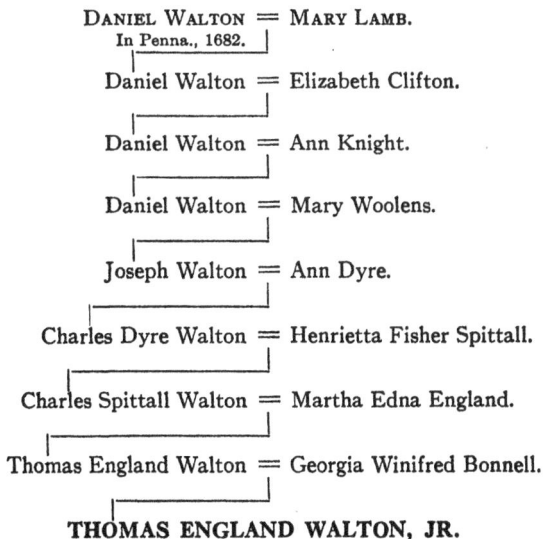

DANIEL WALTON = MARY LAMB.
In Penna., 1682.

Daniel Walton = Elizabeth Clifton.

Daniel Walton = Ann Knight.

Daniel Walton = Mary Woolens.

Joseph Walton = Ann Dyre.

Charles Dyre Walton = Henrietta Fisher Spittall.

Charles Spittall Walton = Martha Edna England.

Thomas England Walton = Georgia Winifred Bonnell.

THOMAS ENGLAND WALTON, JR.

𝖂𝖆𝖗𝖓𝖔𝖈𝖐

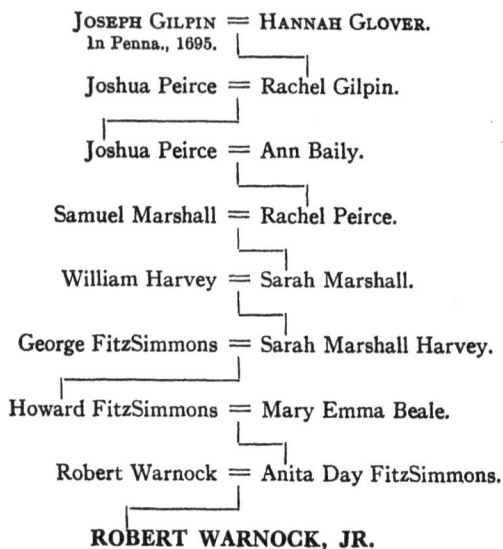

JOSEPH GILPIN = HANNAH GLOVER.
In Penna., 1695.

Joshua Peirce = Rachel Gilpin.

Joshua Peirce = Ann Baily.

Samuel Marshall = Rachel Peirce.

William Harvey = Sarah Marshall.

George FitzSimmons = Sarah Marshall Harvey.

Howard FitzSimmons = Mary Emma Beale.

Robert Warnock = Anita Day FitzSimmons.

ROBERT WARNOCK, JR.

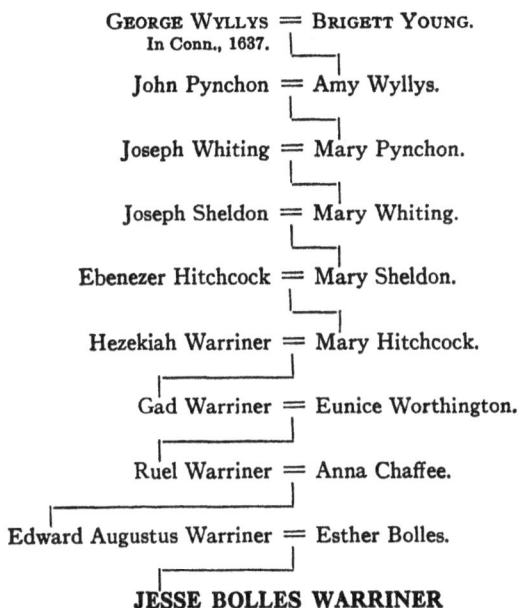

GEORGE WYLLYS = BRIGETT YOUNG.
In Conn., 1637.

John Pynchon = Amy Wyllys.

Joseph Whiting = Mary Pynchon.

Joseph Sheldon = Mary Whiting.

Ebenezer Hitchcock = Mary Sheldon.

Hezekiah Warriner = Mary Hitchcock.

Gad Warriner = Eunice Worthington.

Ruel Warriner = Anna Chaffee.

Edward Augustus Warriner = Esther Bolles.

JESSE BOLLES WARRINER

𝕬𝖆𝖙𝖐𝖎𝖓𝖘

THOMAS WATKINS = ELIZABETH ——.
In Mass., 1652.

John Watkins = Mary Russell.

John Watkins = Dorothy Pepperell.

Andrew Watkins = Jane Frost.

Benjamin Watkins = Ann Abraham.

Samuel Pote Watkins = Julia Ann Simmons.

Henry Hutchinson Watkins = Ann Massey.

Henry Hutchinson Watkins, Jr. = Josephine Joyce Moore.

JOSEPH MOORE WATKINS

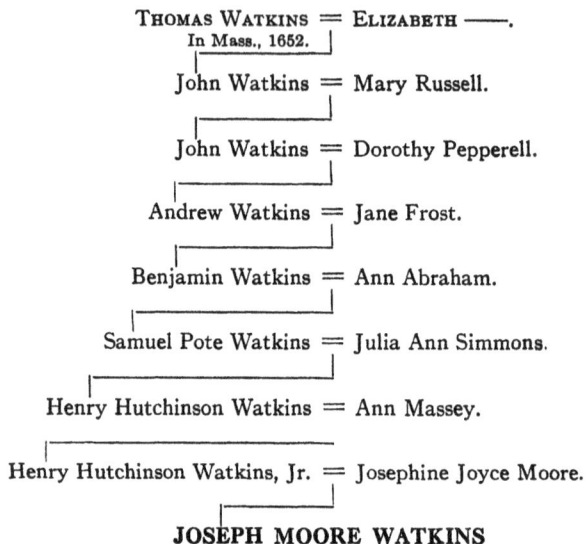

SUPPLEMENTALS

Eleventh in descent from William Mullins, in Plymouth Colony, 1620.
Tenth in descent from John Alden, in Plymouth Colony, 1620.
Tenth in descent from Richard Warren, in Plymouth Colony, 1620.
Ninth in descent from John Sanford, in Rhode Island, 1631.
Ninth in descent from Moses Simmons, in Plymouth Colony, 1621.

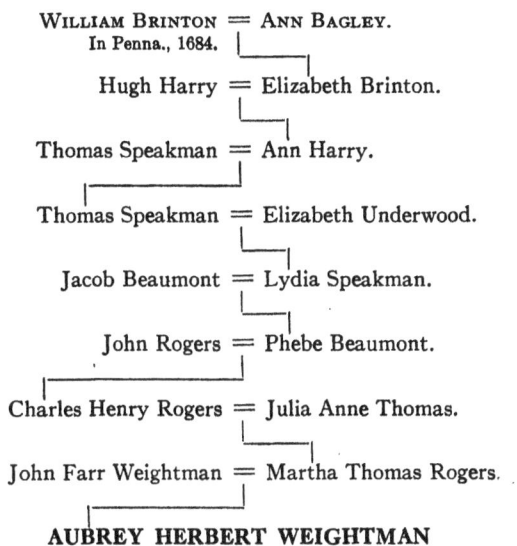

WILLIAM BRINTON = ANN BAGLEY.
In Penna., 1684.

Hugh Harry = Elizabeth Brinton.

Thomas Speakman = Ann Harry.

Thomas Speakman = Elizabeth Underwood.

Jacob Beaumont = Lydia Speakman.

John Rogers = Phebe Beaumont.

Charles Henry Rogers = Julia Anne Thomas.

John Farr Weightman = Martha Thomas Rogers.

AUBREY HERBERT WEIGHTMAN

JOHN BARTRAM = ELIZABETH ——.
In Penna., 1683.

William Bartram = Elizabeth Hunt.

John Bartram = Ann Mendenhall.

John Bartram = Eliza Howell.

James Howell Bartram, M.D. = Mary Ann Joyce.

John William Bartram = Williamina Amelia Middleton.

Oscar Franklin West = Caroline Gamber Bartram.

FRANCIS DARLEY WEST

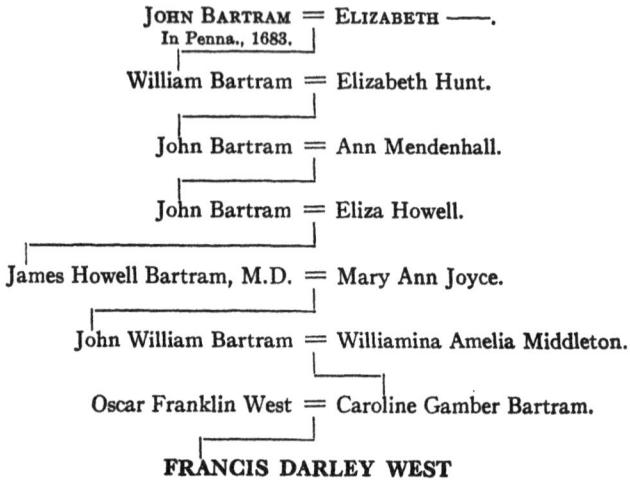

SUPPLEMENTALS

Eighth in descent from Jonathan Hayes, in Penna., 1684.
Eighth in descent from George Maris, in Penna., 1683.
Seventh in descent from John Howell, in Penna., 1687.
Seventh in descent from James Hunt, in Penna., 1684.
Seventh in descent from Robert Pennell, in Penna., 1686.
Seventh in descent from Randal Vernon, in Penna., 1682.
Sixth in descent from Benjamin Mendenhall, in Penna., 1685.

CHRISTOPHER WETHERILL = MARY HORNBY.
In New Jersey, 1683.

Thomas Wetherill = Anne Fearon.

Christopher Wetherill = Mary Stockton.

Samuel Wetherill = Sarah Yarnall.

Samuel Wetherill = Rachel Price.

William Wetherill, M.D. = Isabella Macomb.

William Henry Wetherill = Elizabeth Putnam Proctor.

REV. FRANCIS MACOMB WETHERILL

THOMAS WYNNE = MARTHA BUTTALL.
In Penna., 1682.

Jonathan Wynne = Sarah Greaves.

Thomas Wynne = Mary Warner.

Phineas Roberts = Ann Wynne.

Titus Roberts = Elizabeth Latch.

William White = Hannah Roberts.

Thomas Roberts White = Sarah Tomlin.

Richard Elmer White = Sarah Johnson.

Thomas Roberts White = Alice Griffith Sebold.

RICHARD KERR WHITE, M.D.

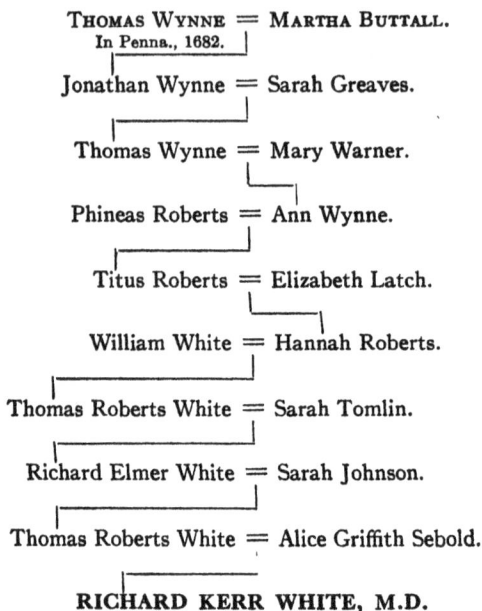

SUPPLEMENTALS

Tenth in descent from Thomas Howell, in West Jersey, 1683.
Ninth in descent from William Warner, in Penna., 1679.
Eighth in descent from John Roberts, in Penna. 1682.

𝖂𝖍𝖎𝖙𝖊

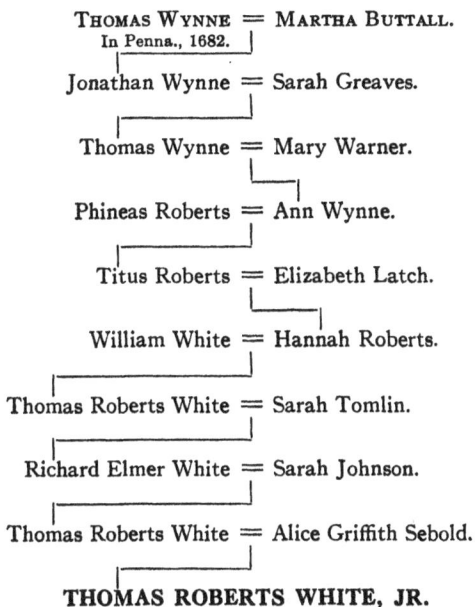

THOMAS WYNNE = MARTHA BUTTALL.
In Penna., 1682.

Jonathan Wynne = Sarah Greaves.

Thomas Wynne = Mary Warner.

Phineas Roberts = Ann Wynne.

Titus Roberts = Elizabeth Latch.

William White = Hannah Roberts.

Thomas Roberts White = Sarah Tomlin.

Richard Elmer White = Sarah Johnson.

Thomas Roberts White = Alice Griffith Sebold.

THOMAS ROBERTS WHITE, JR.

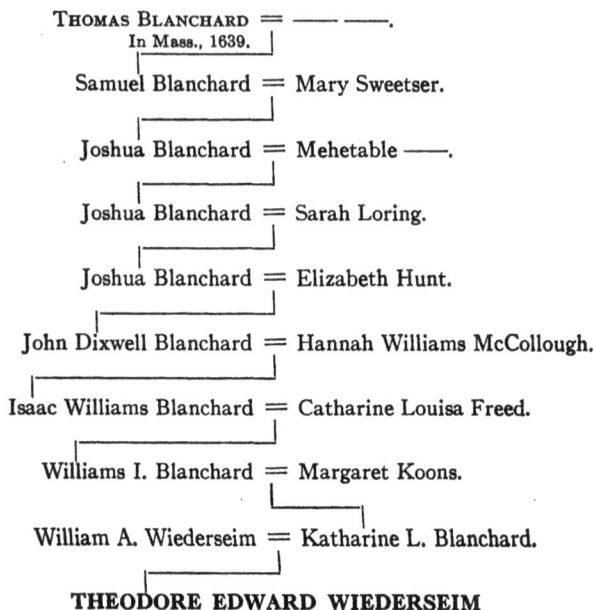

Thomas Blanchard = —— ——.
In Mass., 1639.

Samuel Blanchard = Mary Sweetser.

Joshua Blanchard = Mehetable ——.

Joshua Blanchard = Sarah Loring.

Joshua Blanchard = Elizabeth Hunt.

John Dixwell Blanchard = Hannah Williams McCollough.

Isaac Williams Blanchard = Catharine Louisa Freed.

Williams I. Blanchard = Margaret Koons.

William A. Wiederseim = Katharine L. Blanchard.

THEODORE EDWARD WIEDERSEIM

𝔚iener

JOHN LAWS = KATHARINE ——.
In Maryland, 1673.

William Laws = Sarah Beavens.

Bolitha Laws = Leah Sturgis.

Ezekiel Anderson = Elizabeth Laws.

Stephen Anderson = Nancy Davis.

Heinrich Wiener = Eliza Anderson.

Henry Wiener = Eugenia Duhring Mange.

Edward Wiener = Mary Katherine Loder.

ALEXANDER LODER WIENER

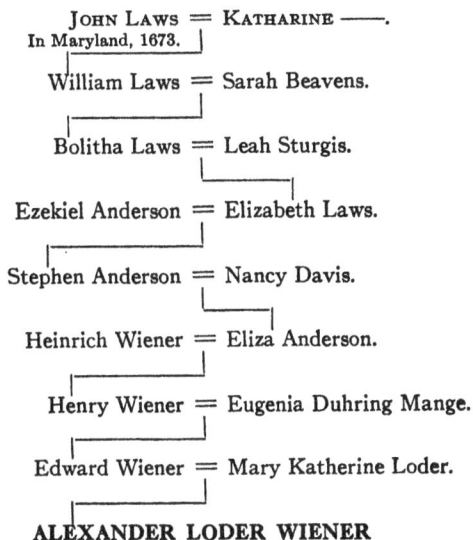

SUPPLEMENTALS

Ninth in descent from Ellen Cowgill, in Penna., 1682.
Ninth in descent from John Pancoast, in West Jersey, 1680.
Ninth in descent from Daniel Wills, in West Jersey, 1677.
Eighth in descent from Rowland Beavens, in Mass., 1660.
Eighth in descent from John Borton, in West Jersey, 1677.
Eighth in descent from Ralph Cowgill, in Penna., 1682.
Eighth in descent from John Davis, in Long Island, 1680.
Eighth in descent from David Sheppard, in West Jersey, before 1692.
Eighth in descent from John Sheppard, in West Jersey, before 1690.
Eighth in descent from Jonathan Sturgis, in Maryland, 1699.
Seventh in descent from Peter Long, in West Jersey, 1688.
Seventh in descent from Dickinson Sheppard, in West Jersey, 1694.
Seventh in descent from Richard Stites, in Long Island, 1653.

Wiener

JOHN LAWS = KATHARINE ——.
In Maryland, 1673.

William Laws = Sarah Beavens.

Bolitha Laws = Leah Sturgis.

Ezekiel Anderson = Elizabeth Laws.

Stephen Anderson = Nancy Davis.

Heinrich Wiener = Eliza Anderson.

Henry Wiener = Eugenia Duhring Mange.

EDWARD WIENER

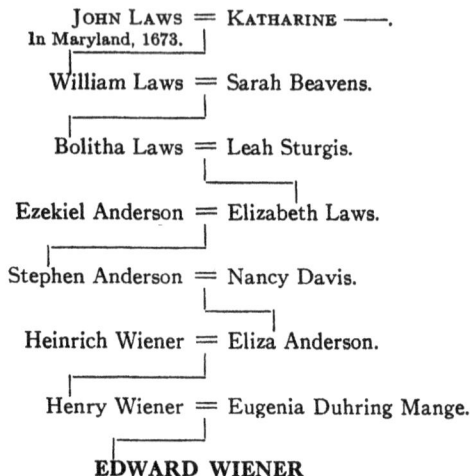

SUPPLEMENTALS

Eighth in descent from Ellen Cowgill, in Penna., 1682.
Eighth in descent from John Pancoast, in West Jersey, 1680.
Eighth in descent from Daniel Wills, in West Jersey, 1677.
Seventh in descent from Rowland Beavens, in Mass., 1660.
Seventh in descent from John Borton, in West Jersey, 1677.
Seventh in descent from Ralph Cowgill, in Penna., 1682.
Seventh in descent from John Davis, in Long Island, 1680.
Seventh in descent from Jonathan Sturgis, in Maryland, 1699.

JOHN LAWS = KATHARINE ———.
In Maryland, 1673.

William Laws = Sarah Beavens.

Bolitha Laws = Leah Sturgis.

Ezekiel Anderson = Elizabeth Laws.

Stephen Anderson = Nancy Davis.

Heinrich Wiener = Eliza Anderson.

Henry Wiener = Eugenia Duhring Mange.

Edward Wiener = Mary Katherine Loder.

EDWARD WIENER, 2d

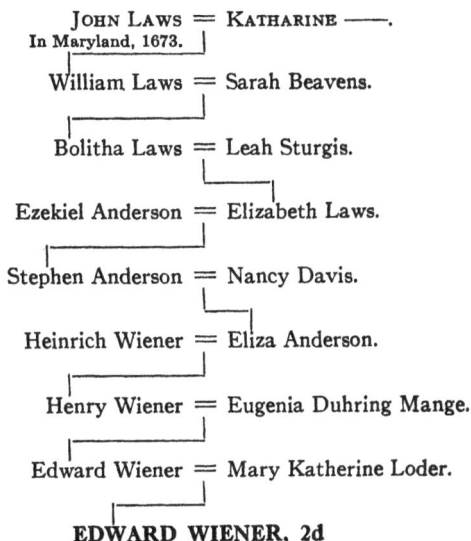

SUPPLEMENTALS

Ninth in descent from Ellen Cowgill, in Penna., 1682.
Ninth in descent from John Pancoast, in West Jersey, 1680.
Ninth in descent from Daniel Wills, in West Jersey, 1677.
Eighth in descent from Rowland Beavens, in Mass., 1660.
Eighth in descent from John Borton, in West Jersey, 1677.
Eighth in descent from Ralph Cowgill, in Penna., 1682.
Eighth in descent from John Davis, in Long Island, 1680.
Eighth in descent from David Sheppard, in West Jersey, before 1692.
Eighth in descent from John Sheppard, in West Jersey, before 1690.
Eighth in descent from Jonathan Sturgis, in Maryland, 1699.
Seventh in descent from Peter Long, in West Jersey, 1688.
Seventh in descent from Dickinson Sheppard, in West Jersey, 1694.
Seventh in descent from Richard Stites, in Long Island, 1653.

Wiener

JOHN LAWS = KATHARINE ——.
In Maryland, 1673.

William Laws = Sarah Beavens.

Bolitha Laws = Leah Sturgis.

Ezikiel Anderson = Elizabeth Laws.

Stephen Anderson = Nancy Davis.

Heinrich Wiener = Eliza Anderson.

Henry Wiener = Eugenia Duhring Mange.

HENRY WIENER, JR.

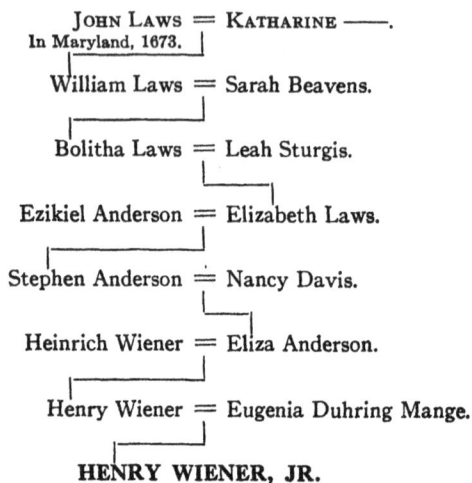

SUPPLEMENTALS

Eighth in descent from Ellen Cowgill, in Penna., 1682.
Eighth in descent from John Pancoast, in West Jersey, 1680.
Eighth in descent from Daniel Wills, in West Jersey, 1677.
Seventh in descent from Rowland Beavens, in Mass., 1660.
Seventh in descent from John Borton, in West Jersey, 1677.
Seventh in descent from Ralph Cowgill, in Penna., 1682.
Seventh in descent from John Davis, in Long Island, 1680.
Seventh in descent from Jonathan Sturgis, in Maryland, 1699.

𝔚illiams

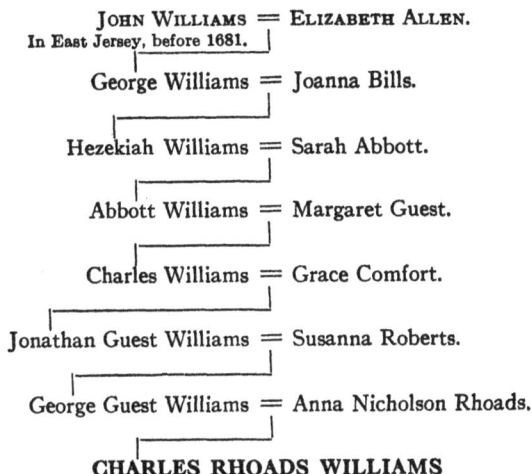

JOHN WILLIAMS = ELIZABETH ALLEN.
In East Jersey, before 1681.

George Williams = Joanna Bills.

Hezekiah Williams = Sarah Abbott.

Abbott Williams = Margaret Guest.

Charles Williams = Grace Comfort.

Jonathan Guest Williams = Susanna Roberts.

George Guest Williams = Anna Nicholson Rhoads.

CHARLES RHOADS WILLIAMS

𝔚ood

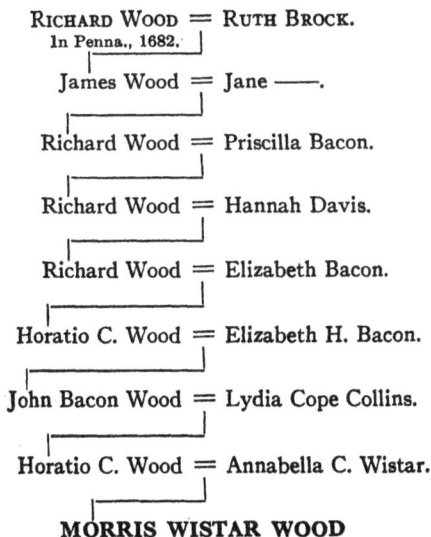

RICHARD WOOD = RUTH BROCK.
In Penna., 1682.

James Wood = Jane ——.

Richard Wood = Priscilla Bacon.

Richard Wood = Hannah Davis.

Richard Wood = Elizabeth Bacon.

Horatio C. Wood = Elizabeth H. Bacon.

John Bacon Wood = Lydia Cope Collins.

Horatio C. Wood = Annabella C. Wistar.

MORRIS WISTAR WOOD

𝔚urts

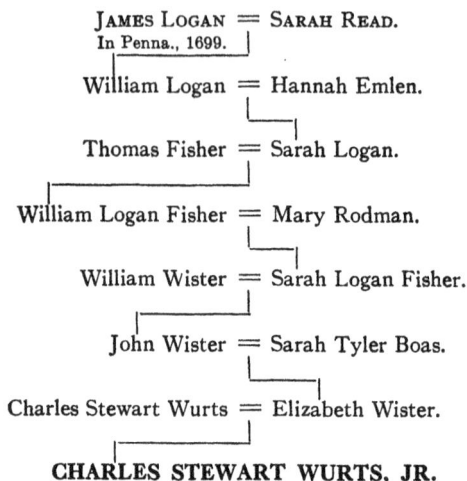

JAMES LOGAN = SARAH READ.
In Penna., 1699.

William Logan = Hannah Emlen.

Thomas Fisher = Sarah Logan.

William Logan Fisher = Mary Rodman.

William Wister = Sarah Logan Fisher.

John Wister = Sarah Tyler Boas.

Charles Stewart Wurts = Elizabeth Wister.

CHARLES STEWART WURTS, JR.

𝔚urts

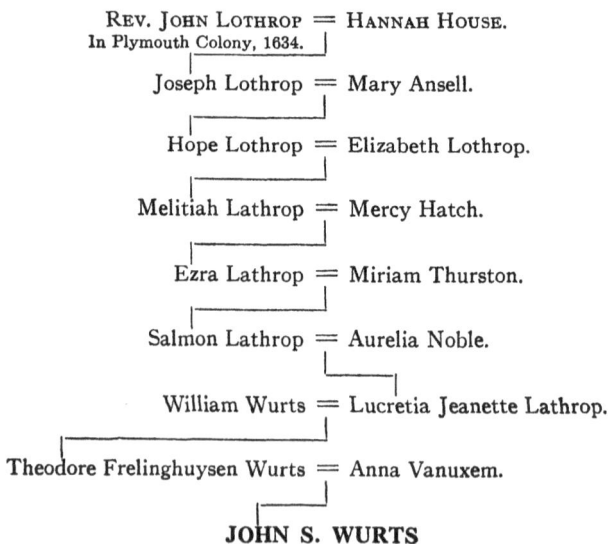

REV. JOHN LOTHROP = HANNAH HOUSE.
In Plymouth Colony, 1634.

Joseph Lothrop = Mary Ansell.

Hope Lothrop = Elizabeth Lothrop.

Melitiah Lathrop = Mercy Hatch.

Ezra Lathrop = Miriam Thurston.

Salmon Lathrop = Aurelia Noble.

William Wurts = Lucretia Jeanette Lathrop.

Theodore Frelinghuysen Wurts = Anna Vanuxem.

JOHN S. WURTS

SUPPLEMENTALS

Tenth in descent from John Drake, in Mass., 1630.

Tenth in descent from Anthony Fisher, in Mass., 1637.

Tenth in descent from Alice Gaylord, in Conn., 1657.

Tenth in descent from William Goodwin, in Mass., 1632.

Tenth in descent from John Moore, in Mass., 1630.

Tenth in descent from Samuel Morse, in Mass., 1635.

Tenth in descent from William Palmer, in Plymouth Colony, 1621.

Tenth in descent from Richard Treat, in Mass., before 1637.

Ninth in descent from James Allen, in Mass., 1637.

Ninth in descent from Richard Beckley, in Conn., 1639.

Ninth in descent from Matthew Beckwith, in Conn., 1639.

Ninth in descent from William Adriense Bennett, in New Amsterdam, 1636.

Ninth in descent from John Bishop, in Conn., 1639.

Ninth in descent from George Clark, in Conn., 1639.

Ninth in descent from Marten Cregier, in New Amsterdam, 1644.

Ninth in descent from John Crow, in Conn., 1637.

Ninth in descent from John Daggett, in Mass., 1630.

Ninth in descent from John Deming, in Conn., 1635.

Ninth in descent from John Dwight, in Mass., 1635.

Ninth in descent from John Eddy, in Mass., 1630.

Ninth in descent from Rev. Henry Flint, in Mass., 1635.

Ninth in descent from Ann Guild, in Mass., 1638.

Ninth in descent from Thomas Hatch, in Mass., 1634.

Ninth in descent from Margery Hoar, in Mass., circa 1639.

Ninth in descent from Thomas Judd, in Mass., 1634.

Ninth in descent from Hendrik Hendricksen Kip, in New Amsterdam, 1637.

Ninth in descent from William Learned, in Mass., 1632.

Ninth in descent from Joseph Loomis, in Conn., 1638.

Ninth in descent from Frederick Lubbertse, in New Amsterdam, 1625.

Ninth in descent from Reinold Marvin, in Conn., 1639.

Ninth in descent from Oliver Mellows, in Mass., 1634.

Ninth in descent from Andrew Newcomb, in Mass., circa 1640.

Ninth in descent from William Partridge, in Conn., 1644.

Ninth in descent from Henry Rowley, in Plymouth Colony, 1632.

Ninth in descent from William Sabin, in Mass., 1643.

Ninth in descent from Joanna Searl, in Mass., 1630.

Ninth in descent from Nicasius de Sille, in New Amsterdam, 1653.

Ninth in descent from Cornelis Barentsen Slecht, in New Netherland, 1658.

Ninth in descent from Mary Smith, in Conn., 1644.

Ninth in descent from John Thurston, in Mass., 1637.

Ninth in descent from Jan Tomasse Van Dyck, in Long Island, 1652.

Ninth in descent from Arthur Warren, in Mass., 1637.

Ninth in descent from William Warriner, in Mass., 1638.

Ninth in descent from Ralph Wheelock, in Mass., 1637.

Ninth in descent from Thomas Wight, in Mass., 1636.

Eighth in descent from Thomas Cadwell, in Conn., 1658.

Eighth in descent from Thomas Clark, in Conn., 1645.
Eighth in descent from Gerret Dircksen Croesen, in Long Island, 1661.
Eighth in descent from Thomas Farrar, in Mass., 1639.
Eighth in descent from Gerrit Fokker, in New York, 1668.
Eighth in descent from Jonathan Hatch, in Plymouth Colony, 1640.
Eighth in descent from John Higley, in Conn., 1666.
Eighth in descent from Henry Leonard, in Mass., 1645.
Eighth in descent from Thomas Lothrop, in Plymouth Colony, 1637.
Eighth in descent from Thomas Noble, in Mass., 1652.
Eighth in descent from Pieter de Nys, in New Amsterdam, 1660.
Eighth in descent from Thomas Pettit, in Mass., 1639.
Eighth in descent from John Throckmorton, in Mass., 1631.
Eighth in descent from Jacob Leendertsen Vandergrift, in New Amsterdam, 1644.
Eighth in descent from Gerret Stoffelsen (Van Sant), in New Amsterdam, 1651.
Eighth in descent from Heyndryck Reycke van Zutphen (Suydam), in New Amsterdam, 1663.
Eighth in descent from Jan Janszen (van Tubingen) Wanshaer, in New Amsterdam, 1649.
Eighth in descent from Cornelius Wynkoop, in New Amsterdam, 1638.
Seventh in descent from Andrew Heath, in Penna., 1682.

Elected
1940

𝔚𝔶𝔫𝔫

No.
638

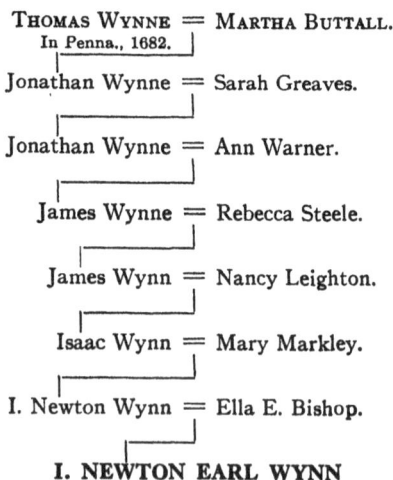

THOMAS WYNNE = MARTHA BUTTALL.
In Penna., 1682.

Jonathan Wynne = Sarah Greaves.

Jonathan Wynne = Ann Warner.

James Wynne = Rebecca Steele.

James Wynn = Nancy Leighton.

Isaac Wynn = Mary Markley.

I. Newton Wynn = Ella E. Bishop.

I. NEWTON EARL WYNN

Wynn

THOMAS WYNNE = MARTHA BUTTALL.
In Penna., 1682.

Jonathan Wynne = Sarah Greaves.

Jonathan Wynne = Ann Warner.

James Wynne = Rebecca Steele.

James Wynn = Nancy Leighton.

Isaac Wynn = Mary Markley.

James H. Wynn = Martha A. Knerr.

J. Maurice Wynn = Jennie Pratt.

JOHN SPARKS WYNN

Wynne

THOMAS WYNNE = MARTHA BUTTALL.
In Penna., 1682.

Jonathan Wynne = Sarah Greaves.

Thomas Wynne = Mary Warner.

Thomas Wynne = Margaret Coulton.

Thomas Wynne = Elizabeth Reese.

Samuel C. Wynne = Phoebe Sharp.

Joseph S. Wynne = Elizabeth Newlin Matlack.

Thomas Wynne = Elizabeth A. MacLean.

THOMAS ELLIOTT WYNNE

Index of Ancestors under whom
Claims are made

INDEX

Gach, Thomas, 187, 188.
Gardner, Thomas, 58.
Garnsey, Henry, 117.
Garrett, Thomas, 112.
    William, 159, 160.
Garwood, Thomas, 39, 118.
Gatchell, John, 50.
Gaylord, Alice, 255.
Ghiselin, Cesar, 202.
Gibbons, Henry, 88, 113.
Giddings, George, 205.
Giles, William, 191.
Gillam Benjamin, 50.
Gillingham, Yeamans, 114.
Gilpin, Joseph, 51, 194, 240.
Gladwin, Thomas, 42.
Glover, Henry, 167.
Goddard, William, 151.
Godwin, George, 167.
Goffe, Edward, 50.
Gonderson, Sven, 172.
Goodhue, William, 205.
Goodwin, Daniel, 211.
    William, 255.
Gorham, John, 58, 172.
Gould, Zaccheus, 210.
Graef, (see Op den Graef).
Grant, Thomas, 50.
Gray, George, 147, 188.
Grayson, John, 93.
Green, Thomas, 115, 164.
Greenoway, (Greenway), John, 205.
Griswold, Matthew, 204, 205.
Grubb, John, 88, 159, 160.
Guild, Ann, 255.
Gwin, Thomas, 51.

Haines, Richard, 85.
Hall, Jacob, 98, 99, 235.
    John, 210.
Hallett, Andrew, 187, 188.
Hallowell, John, 175, 177, 196.
Hance, John, 38, 39.
Hancock, Richard, 118.
Hand, John, 195.
    Thomas, 195.
Hankinson, Thomas, 119.

Hanson, Thomas, 39.
Haraden, Edward, 205.
Harden, Thomas, 191.
Harker, Adam, 196.
Harris, Thomas, 161.
Harrison, Burr, 93.
    Samuel, 89, 98, 99, 163.
Harvey, Richard, 167.
Haseltine, Robert, 205.
Haskell, William, 205.
Hatch, Jonathan, 256.
    Thomas, 58, 255.
Hathernthwaite, Agnes, 74, 114.
Hayes, Jonathan, 244.
Hayhurst, Cuthbert, 137.
Haynes, Walter, 50.
Hayward, William, 58.
Hazen, Edward, 51.
Heard, John, 74.
Hearn, William, 175, 177.
Heath, Andrew, 256.
Heathers, Thomas, 175, 177.
Heaton, Robert, 114.
Henshaw, Joshua, 33.
Herndon, William, 123.
Hewes, John, 58.
Hide, John, 168.
Highley, John, 256.
Hill, Peter, 201.
Hilliard, John, 85.
Hillman, John, 163.
Hinchman, John, 98, 99.
Hitchborn, Thomas, 51.
Hitcheson, Agnes, 210.
Hoar, Margery, 255.
Hobart, Edmund, 202.
Holgate, Mathew, 227.
Holley, John, 167, 187, 188.
Holme, Thomas, 125.
Holton, Joseph, 51.
Hoochlandt, (Hoogland) Cornelis
    Dierckse, 127, 235.
Hood, John, 130.
Hooper, Ann, 51.
Hoopes, Joshua, 73, 112, 130.
Hopkins, John, 33.
Hopper, John, 118, 131.

Levering, William, 114.
Levis, Samuel, 154, 159, 160, 229.
Lewis, George, 50.
    Henry, 175, 177.
    Ralph, 51.
    William, 157, 158, 159, 160.
Lincoln, Daniel, 51.
Linderman, John (Jan), 62.
Lippincott, Richard, 142.
Little, Thomas, 74.
Lloyd, James, 175, 177.
    Robert, 159, 160.
    Thomas, 97 (2), 196.
Logan, James, 254.
Loker, John, 51.
Lombard, Bernard, 187, 188.
Long, Peter, 249, 251.
Look, Thomas, 58.
Loomis, Joseph, 255.
Loring, Thomas, 50.
Lothrop, Rev. John, 210, 254.
    Thomas, 211, 256.
Lubbertse, Frederick, 255.
Lucas, Robert, 114.
Lucken, Jan, 86, 136, 196.
Lunt, Henry, 50.
Lynde, Thomas, 205.

Maccarty, Florence, 206.
Mackclaflin, Robert, 63.
McKnitt, John, 123.
Macy, Thomas, 59.
Manning, Jeffrey, 212.
    William, 151.
Mansfield, Richard, 167.
Maris, George, 77, 168, 244.
Marshfield, Thomas, 205.
Martin, John, 186.
    Richard, 51.
Marvin, Reinold, 211, 255.
Mason, Richard, 51.
Massey, Thomas, 169, 170.
Matthews, James, 172.
Maud, Margery, 37.
Mellows, Oliver, 255.
Mendenhall, Benjamin, 51, 244.
    John, 77.

Mercer, Thomas, 88.
Merriman, Nathaniel, 211.
Merritt, Thomas, 135.
Michener, John, 86, 196.
Miers, John, 37.
Mifflin, John, 88, 120.
Milan, Hans, 117.
Millard, Thomas, 227.
Millet, Thomas, 205.
Milnor, Joseph, 144, 145.
Miner, Thomas, 211.
Minor, Thomas, 87.
Mitchell, Experience, 33, 50, 151.
    Matthew, 167.
Monroe, Andrew, 93.
Montague, Peter, 158.
Moody, William, 50.
Moore, Benjamin, 179.
    John, (Mass.), 51, 173, 255.
    John, (South Carolina), 202.
    Richard, 164.
Moores, Matthew, 187, 188.
Morgan, Joshua, 180.
Morris, Anthony, 181.
    Evan, 136.
    Lewis, 115.
    Mary, 74.
Morse, Samuel, 255.
Morton, George, 236.
Moss, John, 46.
Mullins, William, 46, 50, 242.

Nash, Thomas, 167.
Nayle, Henry, 51.
Naylor, Robert, 196.
Newberry, Walter, 175, 177.
Newbold, Michael, 166, 206.
Newcomb, Andrew, 255.
    Francis, 50.
Newhall, Thomas, 182.
Newland, Mary, 175, 177.
Newlin, Nicholas, 51, 155, 156, 186.
Newton, John, 64.
Noble, Thomas, 256.
North, William, 114.
Noyes, Nicholas, 205.

Oborn, Henry, 159, 160.
Odell, William, 167.
Ogden, David, 159, 160, 185.
Oldham, John, 64.
    Thomas, 42.
Ong, Sarah, 217.
Op den Graef, Abraham, 69.
    Abraham Isaac, 47.
Orme, Richard, 194.
Osgood, Christopher, 205.

Pabodie, John, 46, 50.
Paddock, Robert, 58.
Painter, Samuel, 51.
Palmer, George, 86.
    John, 186.
    Walter, 210.
    William, (Mass.), 210.
    William, (Plymouth Colony) 255.
Pancoast, John, 159, 160, 186, 249, 250, 251, 252.
Pannebecker, Hendrick, 74, 118.
Parker, Edward, 211.
    Richard, 174, 175, 176, (2) 177.
    Robert, 187, 188.
Parrot, Francis, 205.
Parsons, Benjamin, 206.
Partridge, George, 211.
    William, 255.
Paschall, Thomas, 159, 160.
Patterson, Edward, 114.
Patteshall, Edmund, 50.
Pawlin, Henry, 144, 145.
Paxson, William, 196.
Pearce, George, 51.
Pearson, John, 51.
    Thomas, 189.
Peart, Bryan, 88.
Peck, William, 211.
Pell, William, 50.
Pennell, Robert, 51, 88, 244.
Penquite, John, 136.
Penrose, Bartholomew, 190.
Perkins, Isaac, 116.
Perrin, John, 151.
Perry, Anthony, 190.

Peterson, Olaf (William), 74.
Pettit, Thomas, 256.
Peyton, Henry, 93.
Phelps, William, 236.
Philbrick, Thomas, 116.
Philips, Elizabeth, 74.
Phillips, Rev. George, 148, 149.
Phipps, Joseph, 217.
Piat, (Le Fleur), Rene, 212.
Pierpoint, Robert, 206.
Pierson, Thomas, 77.
Pieterse, Louwrens, 144, 145.
Platt, Richard, 31.
Plumer, Francis, 50.
Poat, William, 51.
Poore, Samuel, 50.
Pope, Thomas, 50.
Potter, Thomas, 114.
Potts, David, 74.
    Mary, 196.
    Thomas, 95, 202.
Powell, Walter, 93.
    William, 113.
Powers, Walter, 151.
Pratt, William, 211.
Preston, William, 42.
Price, Edward, 139.
    Robert, 93.
Pritchard, Roger, 46.
Pugh, David, 194.
Putnam, John, 192.
Pyle, Robert, 159, 160.

Quinby, William, 136.

Rambo, Peter Gunnarsson, 121, 193, 207.
Randall, Stephen, 211.
    William, 51.
Rapalje, Joris, Jansen, 235.
Redfin, William, 109, 110.
Redington, John, 211.
Rees, (see Price).
Reynolds, Catherine, 74.
Rhoads, John, 62.
Rice, Edmund, 151.
Richards, Joseph, 51.

Richardson, Samuel, (Mass.), 151.
   Samuel, (Penna.), 32, 65, 67, 68, 140, 169.
Richmond, John, 50.
Ridgway, Richard, 85, 116, 217.
Riggs, Thomas, 46, 206.
Ring, Richard, 50.
Ringe, Daniel, 205.
Rittenhouse, William, 53, 128, 129.
Roberts, John, (Gwynedd, Penna.), 196.
   John, (Merion, Penna.), 246.
   Owen, 51.
   William, 108, 118, 212.
Robinson, Abraham, 205.
Rodman, John, 229.
Roe, Hugh, 211.
Rogers, John, 59.
   Thomas, 50.
Rolfe, John, 50.
Rowley, Henry, 255.
Rush, John, 88.
Rutter, Thomas, 57, 98, 99, 202, 235.

Sabin, William, 132, 255.
Sackett, John, 210.
Sanders, John, 205.
Sanford, John, 242.
   Thomas, 167.
Sargent, William, Sr., 46.
   William, 2nd, 204.
Sawyer, William, 206.
Scales, William, 50.
Scattergood, Thomas, 206.
Schumacher, (Shoemaker), Peter, 225, 226.
Scott, Benjamin, 115.
Searl, Joanna, 255.
Seeley, Robert, 167.
Selden, Thomas, 210, 211.
Sellen, Hendrick, 74.
Sellers, Samuel, 88, 113, 122, 159, 160.
Severance, John, 58.
Shapleigh, Nicholas, 51.
Sharp, William, 128, 129.
Sharples, John, 34, 51.

Shattuck, William, 211.
Sheffield, Edward, 51.
Sheild, Robert, 208.
Shepard, Ralph, 151.
Shepherd, David, 213 (2).
Sheppard, David, 249, 251.
   Dickinson, 249, 251.
   John, 249, 251.
Sheriff, Thomas, 228.
Sherman, John, 211.
   Philip, 155.
Sherron, James, 214.
Shinn, John, 142, 217.
Shipley, John, 151.
Shippen, Edward, 82.
Shoemaker, George, 115, 215, 216.
   Sarah, 215, 216.
Short, Ann, 51.
Shotwell, Abraham, 114.
Shute, Thomas, 113.
Sille, (see de Sille).
Simmons, Moses, 46, 242.
Simpson, Alexander, 51.
Sipple, Garrett, 175, 177.
Skelling, (Skilling), Thomas, 205.
Skerry, Henry, 51.
Skute, Sven, 227.
Slecht, Cornelis Barentsen, 255.
Slocombe, Giles, 93, 94.
Smith, Christopher, 58.
   Giles, 167.
   John, 175, 177.
   Mary, 255.
   Ralph, 175, 177.
   Samuel, 46.
   Thomas, 51.
   William, 115, 133.
Smoot, William, 77.
Sotcher, John, 136.
Soule, George, 46.
Southery, Robert, 186.
Spence, Patrick, 93.
Spencer, Samuel, 136.
   Thomas, 211.
   William, 236.
Sperry, Richard, 211.
Sprague, Ralph, 51.

269

Walton, Daniel, 237, 238 (2), 239 (2).
William, 196.
Wanshaer, Jan Janszen, (van Tubingen), 256.
Ward, William, 33.
Warner, William, 118, 206, 212, 246.
Warren, Arthur, 255.
Richard, 33, 74, 242.
Warriner, William, 255.
Washburn, John, 151.
Washington, John, 105, 106, 107, 108.
Waterhouse, Jacob, 46.
Watkins, Thomas, 242.
Watson, Luke, 183.
Weaver, Clement, 136.
Webb, Richard, 187, 188.
West, Francis, 211.
John, 76.
Matthew, 136.
Wetherill, Christopher, 245.
Wheatley, John, 51.
Wheeler, Andrew, 172.
Thomas, 51, 167.
Wheelock, Ralph, 151, 255.
Wheelwright, John, 201.
Wheldon, (Whilldin), Gabriel, 172.
Whipple, John, 50, 205.
White, Robert, 114.
Thomas, 39.
Whitney, John, 34.
Whitton, Robert, 136.
Wickenden, Rev. William, 59.

Wight, Thomas, 35, 255.
Wilkinson, Lawrence, 59.
Rev. William, 123.
Williams, John, 253.
Williamson, Daniel, 88.
Willits, Richard, 53.
Wills, Daniel, 249, 250, 251, 252.
Willson, John, 115.
Wilson, Stephen, 115.
Winship, Edward, 211.
Wolcott, Henry, 205.
Wood, Richard, 253.
William, 206.
Woodin, William, 211.
Woods, John, 151.
Woodson, John, 93.
Woodward, Henry, 165.
Richard, 51.
Woody, Richard, 51.
Woolston, John, 116.
Worcester, Rev. William, 205.
Worrall, John, 159, 160.
Worth, Lionel, 51.
William, 59.
Wright, Peter, 128, 129, 217.
Wyllys, George, 241.
Wynkoop, Cornelius, 256.
Wynne, Thomas, 174, 203, 206, 246, 247, 256, 257 (2).

Yarnall, Philip, 51, 88.
Youell, Thomas, 93.
Youngs, Rev. John, 209.

www.ingramcontent.com/pod-product-compliance
Lightning Source LLC
Chambersburg PA
CBHW071849270326
41929CB00013B/2153